Economic Analysis of Ins
Change in Ancient Greec

This book presents an economic analysis of the causes and consequences of institutional change in ancient Athens. Focusing on the period 800–300 BCE, it looks in particular at the development of political institutions and taxation, including a new look at the activities of individuals like Solon, Kleisthenes and Perikles and on the changes in political rules and taxation after the Peloponnesian War.

The process of institutional change in ancient Athens is analysed with the methods and concepts of New Institutional Economics. This brings a fresh perspective to the understanding of the development of Athens. Using an economic theory-based approach allows different questions to be asked and different aspects of the ancient society come to the fore. This approach differentiates this book from previously published works on Ancient Athens.

This economic paradigm provides a consistent framework that allows us to apply its conclusions to the modern world. Relevant lessons include the ubiquity of unforeseen consequences, the fact that motivation for change usually comes from people trying to prevent something unpleasant from happening rather than trying to achieve some positive and specified goal, and repercussions from trying to divide the population into groups with different privileges. It is valuable reading for all economists, economic historians and classical scholars who believe that a modern theoretical approach can better help us understand the lessons of the past.

Carl Hampus Lyttkens is a Professor in the Department of Economics, Lund School of Economics and Management, Lund University, Sweden.

Routledge explorations in economic history
Edited by Lars Magnusson
Uppsala University, Sweden

Economic Analysis of Institutional Change in Ancient Greece

Politics, taxation and rational behaviour

Carl Hampus Lyttkens

LONDON AND NEW YORK

First published 2013
by Routledge
2 Park Square, Milton Park, Abingdon, Oxfordshire OX14 4RN

Simultaneously published in the USA and Canada
by Routledge
711 Third Avenue, New York, NY 10017

First issued in paperback 2014

Routledge is an imprint of the Taylor and Francis Group, an informa business

British Library Cataloguing in Publication Data
A catalogue record for this book is available from the British Library

Library of Congress Cataloging in Publication Data
Hampus Lyttkens, Carl.
Economic analysis of institutional change in ancient Greece/by Carl
Hampus Lyttkens.
   p. cm.
   1. Greece–Economic conditions–To 146 B.C. 2. Finance, Public–
   Greece–History. 3. Greece–Politics and government–To 146 B.C.
   I. Title.
   HC37.H36 2012
   330.938–dc23   2012023113

ISBN 978-0-415-63016-0 (hbk)
ISBN 978-1-138-90231-2 (pbk)
ISBN 978-0-203-07763-4 (ebk)

Typeset in Times New Roman
by Wearset Ltd, Boldon, Tyne and Wear

Contents

Preface

"There is nothing new under the sun", said the ancient Romans. This certainly has some bearing when we compare our society today with the ancient world. Ancient Greece and Rome gave birth to so very many of the ideas and concepts for human interaction that are still with us today. The people we meet, for example, in the speeches held in the Athenian courts in the fourth century BC seem very much like the people you read about in your daily newspaper or on the Web. In their speeches, they complain that other people try to avoid taxation, they find their spouse in bed with somebody else, they quarrel about their inheritances and so on. Judging by newspaper reports, one of the reasons for the current problematic situation in Greece is that paying your taxes is not something you do unless you actually want to, you do not pay taxes just because the law says that you should.

The premise of this book is that we can learn a lot about the ancient economies by applying modern economics to their situation, but also that we can use the ancient experience as a historical laboratory to gain insights of a general nature that are applicable to contemporary society.

In particular, we can use the ancient societies to study the mechanism involved in institutional change. Institutions, as Douglass North has suggested (1990, p. 3), are the rules of the game in society, the humanely devised constraints that shape human interaction. Institutions can be formal, such as legislation, or they can be informal, such as social norms. They shape the incentive of the actors in the economy and determine what kind of behaviour will appear to be in the individual's best interest. Thereby the institutional structure determines how well the economy functions, the level of affluence, the development over time and the distribution of income. To explore the processes involved in institutional change is therefore of paramount importance if we want to explain what makes some societies successful and others not.

Perhaps it is because I have lived in Sweden so long that I find one institutional feature particularly fascinating. This is the rules of taxation. When I began studying economics in the late 1970s, the marginal rate of taxation on personal income was above 90 per cent in Sweden, and that was without taking the payroll tax into account (in a true Orwellian tradition this tax is labelled "employer fees", but in reality, of course – Sweden being a small open economy

– the tax burden is mostly shifted to the employees). If nothing else, this provided great teaching material: for example, one could show that the taxation of income from capital actually *reduced* overall tax revenue.

To the modern mind, the most salient fact about ancient Greece is arguably that they developed a set of political rules that entailed direct democracy (for men). How and why this came about is also a central theme in this book. But the Athenians produced many other almost equally fascinating institutions, and this helps us explain the mechanism of institutional change. I am also happy to note that putting this manuscript together has left me with as many new questions for future research as answers to old ones.

Since my first studies of the ancient societies, the world around me has changed. It is no longer the case that Finley's position – that economics is disqualified in the study of ancient societies – dominates the field (Finley 1973, 1999). A number of classical scholars and economists are now increasingly arguing in favour of using economic analysis to explain what went on in ancient Greece and Rome. This pertains in particular to New Institutional Economics, which I use here.

My ambition has been to write a book that is accessible to a wide audience. The economic analyses are not presented in the form of mathematical models (which would put some people off). For those who are relatively unfamiliar with the ancient world, the historical background is briefly sketched in Chapter 2, the nature of the evidence is discussed in section 1.6, and a Glossary is provided on pp. 143–145 that explains ancient Greek terms (as well as a few economic ones). This I hope will enable fellow economists, classical scholars, and anybody who shares my interest in the ancient societies, institutional change or taxation, to read this book.

For the format of ancient names (and terms) I mainly follow the lead of the great Danish scholar Mogens Herman Hansen in his 1999 book on the ancient Greek democracy. Consequently I mostly use the equivalent of Greek name forms, but with some exceptions because some names seem so very well-known in a Latinised or Anglicised version (i.e. the form in which they are found in an English dictionary). So you will find in the text, for example, Kleisthenes rather than Cleisthenes, but Aristotle (not Aristoteles).

To have the opportunity to study the ancient world is a great privilege. It is a different world, but at the same time very familiar. My interest in ancient history goes back a long time. I cannot date it with certainty, but two books that I received as a gift when I was 14 years old definitely established a lifelong interest. The author was Alf Henriksson, a learned man, who also happened to be a highly productive creator of short poems about Life, the Universe and Everything (yes, *The hitchhiker's guide to the galaxy* is another favourite). In two volumes, he tells the history of the ancient world, but with a special emphasis on the tall stories, the yarns, the juicy gossip etc., which so many ancient authors were happy to convey to us. It is through him that I have learnt such useful things as the fact that Diogenes lived in a barrel, Demosthenes used to train his speech with pebble-stones in his mouth, and the Roman emperor Maxminius

Thrax's favourite pastime was to knock out the teeth of horses with his bare hands.

When I began my university studies, I had the opportunity to study the things that interested me; consequently I started off with parallel studies in Art History and Mathematics, and gradually drifted into studies of the ancient world. So when I came to economics[1] I had already made friends at the Department of Classical Studies in Lund where I had studied for one-and-a-half years, including a three-month course at the Swedish Institute of Archaeology in Athens. A few years after my Ph.D. in economics, I decided to try and mix my new and my old fields of interest. Since then I have refused to let go of my interest in antiquity, though I have only had the time to tackle the ancient societies in my research at irregular intervals.

With the publication of this book a long-term ambition of mine has been fulfilled. Over the years I have published a number of articles on the ancient economy and society, with a view towards the long-term goal of writing a monograph on institutional change in ancient Greece in the archaic and classical periods.

This preface gives me a welcome opportunity to express my great gratitude towards all colleagues from different disciplines (economics, economic history, political science, ancient history, archaeology, philology, etc.) that have showed an interest in my work and provided friendly and constructive criticism at seminars, conferences, dinners etc. This includes a long list of friends: Lee and Alexandra Benham, and John Nye in St Louis, Margaret Levi, Yoram Barzel and Carol Thomas in Seattle, Peter Fibiger Bang and Vincent Gabrielsen in Copenhagen, George Tridimas in the UK, Ian Morris, Josiah Ober and Walter Scheidel in Stanford and many others. My continuing contacts with the people in classical studies in Lund has been vital for me, a far from exhaustive list includes Carol Gillis, Paavo Roos, Arne Jönsson, Eva Rystedt, Örjan and Charlotte Wikander and Anne-Marie Leander Touati. I should add that the ancient Greek that I know is due entirely to Staffan Fogelmark. The list obviously becomes even longer when we turn to my own faculty and the Departments of Economics and Economic History, so I limit myself to noting that Lennart Jörberg and Ingemar Ståhl supported me when I first began my ancient studies, and I sincerely hope that all the rest of you feel included in my gratitude.

Foremost among those that I am indebted to is without question Douglass North. He and his work on institutions and institutional change has been my most important inspiration over the years in my studies of the ancient economies. In addition to this, since our first meeting in 1989, Douglass and his wife Elisabeth Case have become my very good friends, and their hospitality has been endless. There has been many a nice morning walk with Douglass and his dog – from Clio to Kore and then Lizzie.

The final stimulus was a series of visits in the fall of 2011: I spent two weeks at the Saxo institute in Copenhagen, made a visit to St Louis and one to Stanford, and I am very grateful for the generous hospitality at all three places. A special word of gratitude goes to Vincent Gabrielsen for very helpful comments on my chapter on taxation, and to three anonymous referees for substantially improving the manuscript. Anna Welander provided diligent administrative assistance in the final stages of the work. Obviously I am the only person responsible for any errors in the final version.

Financial support for this book project has come from several sources. A grant from the *Gyllenstiernska Krapperup Foundation* was instrumental by giving me time to put together the first version of the manuscript, and the same foundation generously provided additional means for the final preparation of the text. The visit to the USA in the fall of 2011 was financed by a grant from *The Foundation Rektor Nils Stjernquists forskningsfond*. The time for preparing the penultimate version of the manuscript materialized when I was granted sabbatical leave in the fall of 2011, for which I am very grateful to the Department of Economics and the School of Economics and Business Management at Lund University.

Finally, my eternal gratitude goes to my wife Kerstin – without her this book would never have come into existence. Though not an economist by profession, she understands not only theoretical economic principles but also how to apply them to everyday life. At timely intervals she has pointed out to me the opportunity cost of spending my time and research efforts on projects other than the completion of this book ("Do you want to write this book or don't you?"). She is also the perfect companion when you are trying to find some archaeological remains lost in the wilderness, because she is a radiologist and her whole professional life centres around spotting the detail that marks a deviation from the usual. The same gift she has generously applied to scrutinizing my manuscript for errors of reasoning, spelling or anything that really should not be there.

Carl Hampus Lyttkens
Lund, June 2012

1 Ancient Greece, institutional change and economic analysis

1.1 Why ancient Greece and why Athens?

In 487/6 BC the Athenians decided that the archon – the most important state official in Athens – was going to be appointed by drawing lots among the candidates. This was an extraordinary idea: think about running France, the United States or Iran by drawing lot among the candidates for president. In Athens, this innovative method of appointment was later extended to many other posts.

In this way the Athenians ensured that all candidates had an equal chance of being selected for office. In addition, they made sure that offices were rotated among the citizens: nearly all government officials were appointed for one year only, each individual was only allowed to hold a particular post once in a lifetime and to be a council member twice, and you were not allowed to hold different offices in consecutive years. Taken together, this is a recipe for extremely widespread participation in the running of the state. Hansen (1999, p. 313) estimates that every third male[1] Athenian citizen above 18 gained practical experience of how it was to be a state official.[2]

The municipality where I live in Sweden counted around 110,000 inhabitants in 2010, which is roughly the same number of inhabitants as the citizen population of Athens in the fourth century BC.[3] So running it on the same principles would mean that about 15,000 of the 44,000 male inhabitants above 18 years of age would at some point in time have been city councillor, or responsible for overseeing the serving of alcohol at the restaurants, or acting as a juror in the courts, etc. I think I can safely say that participation of so many inhabitants in the practical running of the municipality would have changed the nature of public administration in my home town dramatically.

The fact that the system of governance entailed such widespread participation was probably an important reason why the Athenians managed to run their state as a direct democracy for more than 100 years, in the face of serious challenges from other states and of opposition from elite groups within their own society, and to outdo their rivals in prosperity.[4]

The introduction of lottery in Athens was an institutional change, by which I mean a change in the rules of the game in society. These rules can be either formal (such as laws and regulations) or informal (such as social norms). It illustrates amply the general principle that institutional change is one of the most important factors for the future of a society. To explain what drives institutional change and to explore the consequences of institutional change are among the most important scientific challenges for the social sciences. This remains as true today as when Douglass North published his path-breaking book *Structure and change in economic history* in 1981.

For economic analysis, the ancient world is a largely untapped source of information about the mechanisms of different institutional set-ups and of institutional change. What we learn by studying those societies will help us explain the modern world. So, for example, an analysis of ancient Athens will increase our understanding of how a direct democracy works, and this can inform the current discussions about introducing more elements of direct democracy into modern constitutions, the referenda in the EU being a case in point.

The use of the term "democracy" for the political constitution that the Athenians gradually developed in the archaic and classical periods is not uncontroversial. It is of course well-known that it excluded women, non-citizens and slaves. The exclusion of women would certainly disqualify it as democracy in our time. The greatly reduced difference between men and women in terms of opportunities and outcomes in life is one of the most important social achievements of the modern era, together with freedom of speech and freedom of opinion (and a level of affluence that would have been unthinkable a century ago). Similarly, the presence of slaves would disqualify Athens as a successful society on moral grounds.

Nevertheless I use the word democracy, as do other scholars working in this area. It is also reasonable. In the words of Kurt Raaflaub (2007b, p. 12): "We are simply not in a position to deny that the Athenians had a democracy, even if we believe that it does not fit *our* concept of a democracy. After all they invented the word...". The word *demokratia* appears for the first time in the fifth century and was used frequently.

The level of democracy in ancient Athens is also astonishing. It is remarkable to find 2,450 years ago a society where all major political decisions were taken by majority vote in an assembly of all citizens, where every citizen had one vote and the right to speak and make policy proposals, where in practice all these citizens could hold even the most prestigious political positions, and where they were paid for doing so, which enabled more or less everybody to participate in the running of the state.

Different authors place the advent of democracy in Athens at different points in time, which is partly because they employ different definitions of democracy (Raaflaub, 2007b, pp. 14f.). I will not enter the definitions debate, but will certainly have something to say about the timing and significance of different democratizing measures. I will use the terms democratizing and democratic pragmatically, and will consider an institutional change to be democratic if it (a) extends political power in terms of participation in political decision making or (b) extends access to offices to a larger part of the population.

This book presents a story of institutional change – its causes and consequences. It is also a story about ancient Greece, in particular ancient Athens in the archaic and classical periods. Why should we bother about the past, about what happened in Attica between 600 and 300 BC? The past is past and bygones are bygones, say you. Because studying the past is an excellent way of understanding the present, say I. Also, it is great fun.

This is also a story about ancient Greece written by a professor in economics. As I hope to convince you, applying New Institutional Economics (NIE) to the ancient world is a good idea for three reasons: (1) it helps explain what went on in ancient times, (2) the lessons regarding institutional change are often applicable to the modern world, and (3) we learn more about the potentials and limitations of economic theory.

By focusing on ancient Athens we can look into the mechanisms that produced a remarkable male democracy, made it successful and kept it going for more than a century. We can contemplate the interaction between institutional change and economic development. We will see the value of an economic rational-actor framework that helps explain what might otherwise appear as a set of divergent developments.

The archaic and classical periods in ancient Greece are fascinating in that seldom in human history has the pace of change been so dramatic. The outcomes have wielded a long-lasting influence, in particular on Western society and how that society views itself. Ancient Greece is also a magnificent laboratory for those interested in economic and political institutions. However, as mentioned above, this source of knowledge has hardly been tapped, and I hope that this book will stimulate many colleagues to join me in the study of the ancient world. In fact, the number of contributions from economists to the study of ancient Greece and Rome seems to be increasing rapidly at the moment (and is not restricted to the NIE approach).[5]

In 600 BC, Athens was ruled by a birth aristocracy (henceforth all dates are BC unless otherwise indicated). Some 150 years later, the city-state of the Athenians was a direct democracy.[6] To understand the mechanisms that produced such fundamental institutional change is an intriguing subject in itself, and one which has naturally been the subject of much discussion.[7] As we shall see, a rational-actor perspective sheds additional light on this process and the individual incentives involved. While changes in a democratic direction in ancient Greece were not confined to Athens, the Athenian case is interesting because the institutional development in Athens is by far the most well-known. It also appears that Athens was probably the first Greek city-state to introduce such a far-reaching citizen democracy, and democracy was remarkably stable in Athens.[8] In other words, this book is focused on the Athenian experience, both because of its intrinsic interest and because this is where our sources allow us to follow events in most detail. We will often deal with trends that are common to many city-states, but Sparta – the great adversary of the Athenians – followed a different path and will only concern us here to the extent that the Spartans and their actions influenced the development of Athens.

By studying the Greek experience we learn why institutions change. Institutions can, as mentioned above, be defined as the rules of the game in human interaction. This is the most important building block in a theory of why some societies are successful while others are not. Institutions are the key to explaining the success and problems of transition economies – China, Russia and others – as well as the progress (or not) of the developing economies (North, 1990). They are also the key to explaining why some countries have reached the level we call "developed", and will determine whether these countries will stay ahead in the world race.

Until recently, economic analysis and the study of the ancient world would have seemed like surprising bedfellows. On the one hand, many who have read Sir Moses Finley's influential book *The Ancient Economy*, which first appeared in 1973, probably still believe that economic analysis is not applicable to the ancient societies.[9] On the other hand, while many fellow economists are interested in ancient history,[10] I suspect that it may nevertheless come as a surprise that modern economics can help us understand the ancient world, and also that we can increase our understanding of contemporary society by studying the ancient societies.

The premise of this book is precisely that by applying economic analysis in a sensible way ("sensible" will be specified below) to the ancient societies, we can increase our knowledge both of the ancient world and of contemporary society and, indeed, of the relative usefulness of economic analysis.

1.2　New institutional economics – the toolkit

The scientific approach in this study is one of New Institutional Economics (NIE), in particular as formulated by Douglass North (1981, 1990, 2005). The Northian tradition is to view institutions as the rules of the game in a society, the humanly devised constraints that shape human interaction.[11] As mentioned above, institutions comprise both formal rules (political constitution, legislation, etc.) and informal rules (social norms, conventions etc.). This approach distinguishes institutions from organisations, which are important players; for example, families, companies, labour unions, and religious organisations.

Institutions shape the incentives of different actors in the economy, and they largely determine transaction costs.[12] Hence they are central to the functioning of society. An invariably topical example is taxation, which will figure prominently in this account. The rules of taxation have a large impact on whether economic activities take place in the open or whether they are hidden – hidden, that is, from the tax collector. To place an activity in the hidden sector of the economy may be preferable because of the tax savings involved, even though the activities in themselves are often less efficient there.[13] The activities are relatively inefficient, for example, because transactions costs increase when a breach of contract cannot be resolved through the legal system; property rights are insecure which militates against long-run investments and so on. The nature of taxation in a society tells us (to be frank) a hell of a lot about that society, as I will argue in Chapter 6.

Individuals are assumed to act with intended rationality. They strive to further their own interest over their lifetime, within the constraints given by the relative prices, technology and transaction costs in the economy, as well as their information and cognitive abilities. Individuals will sometimes find it to be in their interest to endeavour to change the institutions, rather than just adapting their behaviour to the existing institutional structure. Some of the elements in NIE are now integrated into mainstream neoclassical economics, such as the importance of social norms and transaction costs. Others remain to be fully appreciated, such as the importance of how the individual's perceptions of the world influence their behaviour and how these beliefs are shaped by experience and external factors (North, 2005).

In the analyses to follow, individuals are assumed to strive for power, wealth and status.[14] While individuals try to be rational, they can only be so in a limited way, displaying bounded rationality, as suggested by Herbert Simon (1955, 1956). It is relatively common in NIE to observe that individuals base their decisions on limited information and on their expectations and beliefs, including their perception of how the world functions, and that they have limited reasoning capacity. The feedback they receive on their actions does not necessarily improve their mental images of how the world functions (North, 2005). Another aspect of individual decision making that is related to the issue of limited rationality is the importance of habits. In individual everyday decision making, calculated decisions where costs are weighed against benefits constitute the exception, while an unreflective following of habits is the rule (Hodgson, 1997; Lindbladh and Lyttkens, 2002).

However, in NIE, as in other branches of economics, individuals are still usually assumed to endeavour to *maximise* utility. In my view it is worth taking the ideas of Herbert Simon seriously, and assuming rather that individuals display satisficing behaviour (Selten, 2001). This means simply that individuals, in view of the cost of seeking information, of calculating consequences of different courses of action etc., stop searching for superior alternatives once they have found one that is sufficiently good, i.e. one that is "satisfying".[15] This is a much more plausible description of individual behaviour than the expected utility model; it has long been known that there are many systematic violations of the latter.[16]

Satisficing also seems to aptly describe behaviour in the ancient world, when we can follow it in more detail.[17] Compare the following statement of John K. Davies about political decision making in ancient Greece: "the world of Herodotos was not being driven by a conscious outreach towards any identifiable "democratic" goals or ideals; [...] the system which its inhabitants came to call *demokratia* was little more than a bodged-up set of responses to particular situations and crises; and [...] insofar as it had any unifying principle at all, that principle [was] the perceived need to *prevent* this or that unpleasant or undesirable development or practice from continuing or from gaining a foothold" (2003, pp. 320–323).

This conclusion appears to me entirely sensible and in line with my own interpretations of the events in question (cf. Chapters 4–5). In other words, neither of the two "fathers of democracy" – Solon and Kleisthenes – was trying to maximise utility (or indeed anything). Nor were they democrats. They were trying to prevent a revolution against aristocratic rule (Solon) and to prevent a competitor from gaining the upper hand in the struggle for power (Kleisthenes). And they were probably perfectly happy when they had found a solution that fitted the bill, irrespective of whether there might have existed even smarter things to do. If you are not an ancient history buff, please see the chronological chart and the historical outline in Chapter 2 for more information on these two characters, and of course Chapters 4–5.

1.3 Economic analysis and the ancient societies

Because of the importance of institutions, understanding institutional change is one of the greatest challenges for the social sciences, as noted above. This challenge encompasses changes in political rules as well as legislation and social norms. Ancient Greece provides a fruitful testing ground – a laboratory – for many of the issues concerning the causes and effects of institutional change.[18] Morris and Weingast (2004) single out the development of democracy in Athens (Chapters 4–5 below) as an interesting point of intersection between NIE and the study of the ancient world. The usefulness of a NIE approach to the ancient world has been emphasised repeatedly the last decade, for example in the *Cambridge economic history of the Greco-Roman world* (Scheidel *et al.*, 2007) and in *L'économie de la Grèce des cités* by Alain Bresson (2007, Chapter 1).

Applying NIE to the ancient world serves as a useful corrigenda to the tendency within the humanities to produce "economic history without economics" (Morris and Manning, 2005, p. 3). Improving our knowledge of historical societies is interesting in its own right, and this is true in particular for ancient society because of the role played by the heritage from antiquity in many domains – it affects how we perceive our own society. Furthermore, however, the conclusions regarding institutional change and effects of institutions that we can draw in our historical laboratory can have direct relevance for contemporary society. This is relatively obvious for developing countries and transition economies, but the applications extend to the high-income countries as well. In other words, using the tools of NIE to explore phenomena in the ancient world can enhance our understanding both of the ancient societies and of our own time.[19]

Morris and Weingast (2004) point out that the social sciences are noteworthy by their relative absence in the study of the ancient world, despite the fact that the archaeological and textual record provides an astonishing degree of information about these societies. There is definitely no lack of material. Hansen summarises:

> the Greek *poleis* in general were characterised by the abundance of their political institutions, and democratic Athens was notoriously in the lead; in

fact, never before or since has such an elaborate network of institutions been created and developed in order to run a quite small and fairly simple society.

(1999, p. 319)

Hence we have sufficient information to make the analysis interesting: at the same time, the ancient Greek societies were comparatively simple which makes it easier to pinpoint important factors.

As indicated in the beginning of this chapter, the use of an economic, rational-actor perspective in a study of the ancient world is not uncontroversial. In my view it is reasonable, however, given that proper account is taken of how self-interest is likely to have been conceptualised in Greek society in this period. Economic analysis has been criticised primarily on the grounds that economic life was "embedded" so that market forces played no independent part. This so-called substantivist position is above all, I would say, associated with Finley (1973, 1999).[20] Finley's work is being continuously re-evaluated. Although many ancient historians would now consider him mistaken on a number of specific points, the importance of his work is shown by the continuing need to take a stand with respect to his arguments.

The issue of embededness, however, is arguably a matter of degrees. On the one hand, much economic behaviour in the modern world is also "embedded", so the ancient world is not that different (Bang, 2009).[21] The importance of embededness is for example often a major issue in development economics. Upon reflection one realises that much of everyday "economic behaviour" in the industrialised world is governed by religious, moral and social concerns. Hence it becomes a matter of good judgement to what extent such "non-economic" factors need to be included in economic analyses.

On the other hand, embededness still leaves considerable scope for analyses based on NIE with its emphasis on social norms, on the interaction between economic and social domains, and people's beliefs.[22] Development economics, for example, has shown that formal models can make sense of economies in which markets are shallow and fragmented, contradicting Finley's presumption (Morris and Manning, 2005, p. 30).

Among the facts mentioned to substantiate that the ancient world was different are the existence of loans to friends without payment of interest, and the fact that loans were not taken for productive purposes but to pay taxes, to finance lavish consumption, etc. A tiny dose of introspection suffices to show that the ancient world may have been quantitatively different but that it was not necessarily qualitatively different. In my view, the substantivist position is based on an implicit assumption that the modern world is a very economically rational society. This seems to assume too much rationality in our society, which becomes obvious if we study the real world today in some detail (the misunderstanding may of course be due to the tendency within mainstream economics to make the same assumption). For example, individuals still sometimes lend money to friends and relatives without interest. Similarly I have several colleagues who have bought apartments for their children; the children do not pay rent on the implicit loan. People sometimes sell things to friends and relatives below market price (not only to avoid capital gains taxation), etc. Similarly, the ancient world was of course to a large extent one of subsistence farming, but that is also the situation in many developing countries today.

In the Classical Greece volume of the *Short Oxford history of Europe*, Paul Millet (2000b, pp. 23–26) illustrates from a substantivist position the embeddedness, and hence supposed "otherness", of the ancient Greek economy with the case of an Athenian citizen who was accused of having uprooted an olive tree, which was sacred to Athena and hence uprooting it was illegal. His speech in the Athenian law court, which has been preserved for us because he choose to engage one of the leading orators of his time (Lysias 7), shows that "the minor economic act of uprooting an olive tree turned out to have religious implications, legal repercussions, and possibly political ramifications" (political because the speaker tries to distance himself from the recent regime of the 30 tyrants).

Consider the following hypothetical case for comparison: the chairman of the board of a Swedish municipality is a farmer, and by mistake (or so he says) he messes up an archaeological site when ploughing. This is illegal in Sweden – hence in Sweden immaterial values are protected by law just as in ancient Athens. Furthermore our friend may have to pay a fine, and the whole affair can be embarrassing for him in the coming elections. In sum, I fail to see that the case of uprooting the olive stump marks the ancient world as qualitatively different from our time. Or, to put it another way, the assumptions and methods of economics are neither better nor worse when used to analyse the ancient world than they are in standard analyses of contemporary society.

It seems fair to say that Finley's arguments have been taken to imply that market relationships were not very important in the ancient world, including classical Greece. Finley was completely aware, however, that there were markets and market forces at play in classical Greece. He notes, for example, that Aristotle "knew perfectly well that prices sometimes responded to variations in supply and demand" (1970, pp. 13–14).

Hence the issue is rather how we should judge the importance of these markets and their independence from other social domains. Among classical scholars, the tide seems increasingly to be turning against Finley's position. As we shall see, it is now increasingly argued that classical Athens was characterised to a large extent by market relationships, at least in the fourth century, and that individual actors in Athens displayed economically rational behaviour (sections 1.4 and 7.2). For example, Bresson (2003) argues against the Finleyan tradition that merchants in classical Greece: (a) were not illiterate and (b) not poor, they were (c) not insignificant, were (d) happy to take risk to increase their profits, were (e) also happy to spread risks, and (f) they included in their ranks both foreigners and citizens. Using the NIE framework allows us to focus on the actual economic practices in ancient society and to avoid the not so fruitful substantivist–formalist dichotomy.

To readers only vaguely familiar with economics and its paradigm, a word about the scope of economic analysis might be appropriate: economics in general (and NIE in particular) deals with many things besides price-making markets and profit-maximising behaviour. Notably, the existence of actors in the economy that do not attempt to maximise profits does not invalidate economic analysis. To take an example from ancient Greece, Chankowski (2005, 2007) has shown in several penetrating studies how sanctuaries in ancient Greece (most notably in Athens and on Delos) had complex financial structures and sometimes performed banking functions, occasionally to earn a profit, but often manifestly *not to maximise* profits. To the modern economist, however, it is far from surprising to find a government enterprise focusing on other aspects than profits or economic efficiency.[23]

1.4 Market relationships in ancient Greece 800–300 BC[24]

Trade expanded from at least the eighth century with concomitant specialisation.[25] In the late seventh century, "a handful of Greeks were aggressively pursuing gain all across the Mediterranean and doing very well out of it" (Morris, 2002, p. 32). By the sixth century, there were true cities with resident artisan and traders. Probably by 500, major Greek cities such as Athens were permanently reliant on imported grain, and olive oil and wine were exported by a number of Aegean states (Davies, 2007; Hansen, 2006). In other words, specialisation and division of labour was increasing rapidly in the Aegean (Bresson, 2007, p. 115). Harris (2002) has documented extensive horizontal specialisation in the form of diversified occupations in classical Athens.

The expansion of trade was facilitated by the introduction of coinage. Kim (2002) has shown that small denominations, conducive to monetising everyday transactions, had already appeared in connection with the beginnings of silver coinage in the sixth century. "The Greek micro-states all became monetised fiscal systems in the fifth century" (Davies, 2007, p. 358).

As a result of grain imports and specialisation, Athens ceased to be a community of self-sufficient farmers. In the classical period, the Greek city-states formed a network of trading partners with extensive international division of labour (Bresson, 2008, p. 176).

Reliance on the market was not restricted to the rich. "In bad years most and in normal years many Athenians had to buy their cereals. Aristophanes tells us about a peasant who carries his wine to the market to sell it and buy flour instead" (Hansen, 1987, p. 12). "Extensive specialization of labour made it inevitable that the average Athenian [...] would have dealings with those outside the restricted circle of family, neighbours, and friends. When he bought and sold, he thus had to enter the world of market relations" (Harris, 2002, p. 76).

According to a story told by Herodotos (I. 152–153), and hence implicitly credible by the mid-fifth century, the Persian ruler Cyrus (*c*.557–530 BC) replied to a Spartan embassy:

I never yet feared men who have a place set apart in the midst of their city where they perjure themselves and deceive each other.

(Herodotos, 1. 152–153)

Cyrus is referring, Herodotos explains, to the Greek marketplaces (agora). Davies (2007) notes that the growing importance of the market is illustrated by an innovation in language; the word agora originally signified public meeting place, but by the middle of the fifth century a new verb, agorazo, "I buy" had appeared (p. 335).

At least by the late fifth century, it is evident that market forces are at play and that people are aware of this. Several remarks in the comedies of Aristophanes make it clear that prices fluctuate with supply. Land was being bought as an investment to improve and resell (Xenophon *Oeconomicus* 20. 22–26), and deliberate investment for profit becomes visible in the form of urban rental property (Davies, 2007, p. 357). The fact that the Athenians tried to stabilise grain prices also shows that price fluctuations was something people were aware of. Loomis (1998, p. 254) argues that "economic forces of supply and demand are a [...] likely explanation for differences in wage rates across occupations and over time in Athens in the fifth and fourth centuries". By the fourth century, there were private banks in Athens that took deposits and lent to private entrepreneurs.[26] The famous orator Demosthenes (16.11) states: "the bank is a business yielding a hazardous revenue from money which belongs to others".

Both the Athenians and other city-states took measures to ensure that the agora was a legal space where transaction costs were minimised: officials checked weights and measures, the coins used and the quantity and quality of goods exchanged. Furthermore, cheating in the agora was outlawed.[27]

We have now reached the point where we find scholars (economists it is true) taking the position that Athens became "a vibrant market economy" (Bitros and Karayiannis, 2008) and that this development was encouraged both by a value system conducive to entrepreneurship and by measures that facilitated private contracting. Similarly, Amemiya (2007, p. xi) argues that "fifth and fourth century Athens had an extensive monetary and market system".[28]

Hence we have increasing trade and specialisation, and a movement towards a monetised market economy. The pace and scope of this development are open to debate, but the direction seems clear. It should be envisaged as a gradual process, beginning no later than the seventh century and possibly accelerating after the Peloponnesian War. It was accompanied by significant economic growth; per capita incomes increased by some 50–100 per cent from the beginning of the eighth to the end of the fourth centuries (Morris, 2004).

1.5 A different paradigm

The use of economic methodology to study the ancient world entails something of a shift of paradigm in more ways than one.[29] An economic approach is distinguished not only by its assumptions about individual behaviour, but also by its scientific methodology. That different styles are involved is immediately clear when you realise that economics is deductive, individualistic, inevitably with a firm theoretical basis, and aims at generalisations, while ancient history is empiricist, positivist, inductive, and particularistic (Morris and Manning, 2005, p. 3).

Before exploring these differences is worth noting that the use of a theoretical framework in itself is not a difference between economics and the humanities, even though some may believe it is; a theoretical framework is inevitably involved when someone tries to understand a historical process, even if it is not made explicit (Ober, 1996, Chapter 2), and the relative lack of empirical evidence for the study of ancient societies makes a theoretical framework all the more necessary as a guide to our interpretations (Finley, 1985, p. 18). As eloquently formulated by Alain Bresson (2007, p. 8): to deal with the economy of ancient Greece without theoretical reflections is like walking on a mountain path at night without any light – the result is only too predictable. To apply other paradigms than the usual one to study ancient Greece seems like a good idea in general, because, as Murray (1990) observes when writing about the *polis*, the application of different styles of approach is commendable in view of the relativity of scientific methodology.

Murray (1990) tells a lovely story from Bertrand Russell, which I try to disseminate to new audiences whenever I have the opportunity. The message is about the relativity of scientific knowledge and how much we are influenced by our preconceptions. It is a story about the ability of apes to solve problems. An experiment gave completely different results when conducted by either German or American scientists. When studied by the Germans, apes sat quietly and often found a solution to the problem of how to get the bananas that constituted the reward for solving the problem. When the experiment was conducted by the Americans, the apes ran about in their cage and hit at everything at random, finally after much effort accidentally hitting upon the solution.

The reason was the following. The German researchers believed that apes were stupid and could not solve problems; hence they were given extremely simple problems, which they could easily solve, gained confidence in their ability to do so, and approached the problems calmly. The Germans concluded that they themselves had been wrong – the apes could indeed solve problems. The fact that the researchers were proven wrong increased their confidence in their conclusion, as any bias from their preconceptions ought to have resulted in proofs that the apes were stupid. The American researchers, on the other hand, believed that apes were smart; hence they gave them very complex problems to solve – problems that would have baffled even the Einstein of apes. The apes consequently gave up trying and concluded that running around and smashing wildly at everything in sight was the only way to get any bananas. The researchers concluded that they themselves had been wrong – apes were stupid. The fact that they had been proven wrong increased the researchers' confidence in this conclusion, as any bias from their preconceptions ought to have resulted in proofs that the apes were smart.

Here we see that our preconceptions can influence our results by influencing how we structure a problem (and it would not matter if the story is true, the point is that it could have been true). I agree wholeheartedly with Murray that it provides a very good reason to approach a problem from several scientific perspectives.

To use the NIE framework means that the theoretical framework is made explicit, which is a Good Thing.[30] The present endeavour is encouraged by the admonitions of Morris and Manning (2005), that ancient historians need to be more explicit about processes of model building, and the observation of Manning that major advances have taken place when ancient historians have reversed their usual style of analysis and begun – rather than ended – with model building.

When economics is criticised by outsiders it is commonly (and not surprisingly) the assumptions about individual behaviour that end up in the line of fire. However, when we think about the potential contributions of economic analyses, the more important aspect (to me at least) seems to be the way research is being conducted; how economists actually go about things in their everyday research practices. The most important characteristics of the economic approach are that it is deductive and individualistic. While economic research often starts with an empirical observation, it then typically takes a step back to ponder how the theoretical model should be constructed, which would allow us to analyse phenomena of this kind. Then the model is analysed, conclusions drawn about, for example, the effects of various external changes, and finally this is confronted with empirical data.[31] Economics is also individualistic: an analysis of anything that takes place in society should ideally be based on a model of individual (instrumental, cf. below) behaviour. Almost by definition, nothing exists purely as group-level phenomena.

These characteristics mean that economists focus very much on individual incentives, and that the economist asks rather different questions compared to the historian or archaeologist when confronted with evidence from the ancient world.[32] This I have found repeatedly. For example, Solon reformed the political constitution in Athens in 594, by substituting wealth for birth as a qualification for office – he divided the citizens into four property classes, and only the top one (or two) classes could henceforth be archons (the most important officials in Athens).[33] The obvious question to ask – if you are an economist – is how this affected behaviour, what kind of incentives it created. As far as I am aware it took an economist (yours truly) to ask that question and to analyse the consequences (Lyttkens, 1997, Chapter 5 below). Similarly, it is well known that the rich tried to evade taxation in fourth century Athens, but it took an economist to see that there were indeed very strong incentives to hide one's wealth for certain groups in society (Lyttkens, 1992, and Chapter 6).

When talking about theories, it is worth pointing out that the presence of "unrealistic assumptions" does not disqualify a theory. On the contrary, all theories are unrealistic – the purpose of a theory is to provide a simplifying and clarifying structure that allows us to focus on certain aspects of a problem. The important issue is whether the assumptions help us focus on the things we are interested in, whether they help us explain what we are trying to explain (Mäki, 1994).

1.6 The sources

Whatever approach we are taking to analyse the ancient world, we are inevitably constrained by the availability of sources, be they archaeological, epigraphical, literary etc. For the early period up to *c.*700 BC we have to rely almost exclusively on archaeology. While this material is rich in many ways, it tells us relatively little about human relationships, and any description of the evolution of society and its institutions is by necessity largely speculative. Our interpretation of the period is much influenced by how we read the Homeric poems, which have reached us in the form they had taken somewhere around 700. Most scholars now seem to accept the Homeric poems as evidence of an actual historic society, which should probably be dated some time before the completion of the poems.

From around 700, our first contemporary written sources kick in and the availability of such material slowly increases over time. First there is Hesiod, writing *c.*700, and then poets such as Alkaios, Tyrtaios and Sappho appear. While the presence of contemporary sources is extremely welcome, one should not be too optimistic about how helpful they are. Think about writing the history of Sweden in the twentieth century with archaeological remains plus some of the songs of ABBA and the poetry of Tomas Tranströmer.[34] Or the history of England in the fifteenth and sixteenth centuries with only Shakespeare as a written source.

Of particular importance in the context of this book are the actions of the Athenian aristocrat Solon. He was the architect behind a set of important institutional reforms, traditionally dated to 594. There is quite a lot of material preserved from later Athenian writers about Solon (including what purport to be quotes from him). Unfortunately (or perhaps fortunately for Solon's memory) it is impossible to tell with certainty which measures were actually introduced by Solon.[35] Apart from his own poetry (which is open to many interpretations[36]) and two relatively brief passages in Herodotos,[37] our material on Solon comes from fourth-century sources (or later), and belongs to the political debate of that century. By then it was common practice to describe any law (including some that were definitely passed in the fourth century) as "Solonian law", and his constitutional reforms are no less elusive. Some scholars go so far as to argue that Solon is a fictitious character and that all texts attributed to him are fourth-century productions (Lardinois, 2000; Stehle, 2006). Even the testimony of Aristotle is problematic, at least in parts.[38] "By Aristotle's time, more than 250 years after the events, and probably much earlier, people had no clear understanding anymore of how different archaic Athens had been from the community they knew [...] Much of what later authors [...] tell us about Athenian history thus needs to be [...] used with caution. This unfortunately applies to Plutarch..." (Raaflaub, 2007b, pp. 7–8).[39] Plutarch died after AD 120 and his work is relatively frequently referred to for issues dating back to the classical and archaic periods.

When we turn to the fifth century we are more fortunate. There is the work of famous historians like Herodotos and Thukydides,[40] playwrights like Aischylos, Sophokles, Euripides and Aristophanes,[41] as well as an increasing number of inscriptions. From this time and onwards, ancient writers often had at their disposal written material, now lost to us. And there was always the oral tradition.

Nevertheless, it is only when we come to the fourth century that we have significant contemporary sources that deal directly with the issues that are the focus of our enquiry. For example, Aristotle and his school described the constitutions of 158 *poleis* (consulting the material then available) and we are fortunate that the invaluable *Athenaion Politeia – The Athenian Constitution* – was discovered and published in 1891 and so is now available to us. Then there is Xenophon, who wrote not only the *Anabasis* but also about matters economic.

From the fourth century, we have a wealth of forensic speeches preserved from famous orators, with Demosthenes being the most famous one (yes, the guy with stones in his mouth). Additionally, there are now numerous inscriptions, recording, for example, the decisions of the Assembly. Our sources for the fourth century are thus much richer than for the fifth. In fact, much of what is being told today about the institutional details of the fifth century rests on the assumption that we can infer the situation in the fifth century from what it was like in the fourth. This is problematic, not least because what we are told in the fourth century about older times is manifestly a function of the political debate current in that period and so not necessarily reliable, especially not for the situation 100 years before.

We have, for example, numerous quotes that indicate that rich Athenians in the fourth century tried in various ways to avoid the obligation to pay taxes. We have no such evidence from the fifth century before the Peloponnesian War. But we do not know whether this is because we do not have the same kind of sources for that century (i.e. published speeches held in courts) or is it because there was more tax compliance in the fifth century? This issue will be discussed in section 6.3.

There is also the general problem of determining the meaning of a specific term or expression *at the time when it was written* (if we still use the same word today, this may be more confusing than helpful). The word "democracy" is a good case in point (Hansen, 1999, Chapter 4). Similarly it is not necessarily obvious what a term like "the people" (*demos*, as in democracy) means in a particular context. In the fourth century, for example, it could mean the whole population, the poor masses, or the "more moderate" party (Robinson, 1997, p. 80, n. 59).[42]

Even for the fourth century there is no end to the things that we do not know for sure, such as the number of citizens, the number of slaves, the incomes of ordinary people, the proportion of consumption of an ordinary citizen that went through the market, etc. In several cases we do have a good idea about the likely order of magnitude of these factors, thanks to the diligent and extensive efforts of classical scholars over the centuries.[43] Nevertheless we usually at best have to be content with scattered occasional figures on important economics facts. Bresson (2008, p. 67) points out that until the publication in 1985 of a Roman maritime contract, we had precisely *one* complete private business contract from all of antiquity. Or take the case of Athenian government revenue. We can surmise that it amounted to 400 talents in 431 at the beginning of the Peloponnesian War. This is based on the fact that the total revenue, i.e. the external tribute from the Empire plus the ordinary internal revenue, according to Xenophon was 1,000 talents (*Anabasis* 7.1.27), and the tribute by itself amounted to 600 talents annually according to Thukydides (2.13.3).[44] Around 90 years later, Demosthenes in one of his speeches tells his audience that:

> There was a time not long ago when the revenue of your state did not exceed a hundred and thirty talents [...] since then fortune has smiled on us and increased our revenues, and the exchequer now receives four hundred instead of one hundred talents.
>
> (Demosthenes 10.37–38)

Finally, under Lykourgos leadership after 338 revenues soared to 1,200 talents (Burke, 1985). Thus we have three figures for roughly a period of 100 years which is fine as far as it goes (and much better than many other areas and other cities) but we cannot check these figures, and the numbers provided obviously leaves us ignorant about revenue in the intervening years.

As if this was not enough, our sources sometimes conflict with each other. For example, Herodotos and Thukydides paint substantially different pictures of the motives of Kleisthenes (section 5.3 below). Furthermore Herodotos saw Kleisthenes as the founder of the Athenian democracy, for Aristotle it was Solon. Even worse, Aristotle in *The Athenian Constitution* (8.1) contradicts Aristotle (*sic!*) in *Politics* (1273b35–41) with respect to the introduction of lottery as a way to select magistrates (section 5.4 below).

The archaeological evidence has its own problems. What has been found cannot be a random sample of what once existed, because the fact that we have found it means that it has survived several selection processes – it has been preserved, it has been excavated, it has been published, etc. Coins and ceramics are among the finds that indicate trade, but how great a volume and between whom is another matter. Amphorae, for example, could be reused, and it is no easy task to infer from a pile of sherds how many vessels one has actually found the traces of. Similar considerations apply to inscriptions — there is a reason why they came into existence and a reason why they have been preserved.

Our information about the institutional structure in Athens and its changes over time is however relatively good, as noted above. Nevertheless there are often important gaps in our information. For example, we know (subject to the caveats above) that Solon divided the Athenians into four property classes, as already mentioned. This is a comparatively commonly accepted fact (but that does not mean that it is uncontested).[45] We know that in 457, the third property class (the *zeugithai*) was admitted to the archonship. It is presumed that the first property class was admitted from the inception of the system in 594. But when was the second class admitted? Most scholars seem to guess that it occurred from the very start. But we do not know this – we only know that 457 presumably is last possible date for this extension of political rights to the second class.

Given these problems with our sources, a viable reaction is that in order to be able to say anything you need to specialise on a limited problem, so that you can at least make sense of that and the meagre evidence that is at hand. This is a perfectly respectable position. However, it is also possible to argue that precisely this lack of relevant information means that it is very useful to work with a structural approach, because that will help us fill in the gaps of our knowledge and help us make sense of the relationship between different actions and activities. The next section is about this.

1.7 Structure and individual

This study falls into the social-scientific tradition and so it will (for the most part) necessarily and happily ignore a wealth of seemingly important details in order to focus on the general structure of the process of institutional change. As noted by Morris and Manning (2005), the social sciences focus on *explaining* the world, in contrast to humanistic thought, which aims at *understanding* the world, implying that, in the latter approach, God is in the details, while the former aims at finding underlying structures and principles.[46] The main reason economists focus on structural factors is of course that the discipline is very much concerned with prediction.

In terms of explaining what happened in the ancient world, the view proposed here is that a structural approach is useful, identifying the factors that tend to drive the development in certain directions (e.g. changes in relative prices or other exogenous factors). This sets the limits for the possible and makes certain developments more likely to ensue than others. The economic approach provides a consistent framework that explains what might otherwise appear as a set of diverse developments. We also need to be aware, however, that particular actions at critical junctures, by individual actors, can be instrumental in pushing society in a particular direction *within* the bounds given by the structural factors. Or, in the words of Raaflaub (2007b, p. 16), "historical processes advance by incremental change and by sudden ruptures". Once again, a rational-actor framework can help explain the actions of individual actors, and provides a better understanding of some of the crucial moments in Athenian history.

When we focus on structural factors, this inevitably means less attention will be given to details; as so often is the case, we face a trade-off. The more details we bring into the picture, the more difficult it becomes to discern the general pattern. If you are in a place that is dense with trees, you cannot see if you are in a huge forest or in a small coppice. But if you cut away a number of trees you begin to see longer. The trick, of course, is to know which of the trees you should take away, i.e. which simplifications that are most useful, given your line of enquiry, and which details it is comparatively safe to ignore (cf. Mäki, 1994).

An analogy might be useful. If you take a birds eye's (or, even better, a Concorde's view) of France you can easily see that in southern France much of the water that flows in rivers and streams end up in the Rhone valley, and the overall tendency for this water is to flow in a southerly direction towards the Mediterranean. To the west of the watershed of the Cevennes, on the other hand, water flows north-west. If we move closer, and focus on the area east of Lyon, we can no longer be so certain that the main flow of Rhone and its tributaries is to the south. The Rhone, for example, seems magnificently undecided whether to go north or south. If we move even closer, to the area just north of Aix-les-Bains, you could easily happen to be in an area where you would conclude from what you see that water flows mainly north, even if some smaller rivers has a southerly direction.

So to get a correct overall picture you need to take a step back and ignore many minor rivers, i.e. focus on structure. At the same time, however, we must recognise that for people who lived to the north of Aix-les-Bains in, for example, antiquity, the fact that the Rhone flows north in that area and the presence of all the small tributaries might well have been be precisely what was important for your daily life.

A structural approach allows us to see beyond individual heterogeneity. If, for example, technological change makes it cheaper to produce tinned tomato soup, then prices for this product will tend to fall, and people in general will increase their consumption. However, some might reduce their consumption instead, for example, because they interpret a price reduction as a reduction in the quality of the product or because they can no longer impress their neighbours by eating expensive tomato soup. To understand a *specific* individual we may need to know their preferences in detail and about their life situation, while for the overall development of the consumption of tomato soup we need a structural approach. However, the lattter does not claim to explain all individual behaviour.

There is also what Peter Bang (2008, p. 9) calls "the dangers of trespassing". He notes that working – as he does – with comparative history, there is no way he can be as expert on every society as those who specialise in just one of them. For the economist working on the ancient world, this argument applies with a vengeance – you are often less expert regarding details than the historian working on a specific set of issues. I do not apologise for this as it seems to me inevitable, but would ask the reader to kindly keep it in mind. The problem is amplified when you work not only on a long period but also with things both economic and political. It sometimes seems to me that there is not a single uncontested fact in the study of the ancient world.[47] As an illustration of the magnitude of this issue, I refer you to the survey by Sitta von Reden (2002) of research about money in the ancient economy. The bibliography of that article covers six pages (single space) and contains 231 references, of which more than 30 per cent are books. This is just one of the many relevant issues for this work;

admittedly it has been one of the more popular issues, but it still is only one theme. It is my conviction, however, that despite these disadvantages, a structural economic approach can provide new insights and stimulate important debates about the ancient world.

The lack of specific data outlined above means that we cannot (as we can for the modern world) evaluate the structural model by statistical methods. Whether we believe in the economic structural explanations depends to a large extent on the credibility of the story that enfolds.

Like Acemoglu and Robinson (2006), I see no fundamental analytical divide between structural factors and strategic choices by individual actors – they are all natural ingredients in an economic approach. In other words, we will be dealing both with what historians call event history and with what happens in social or structural time, the time of economic cycles and institutional changes.[48] While events is an important category of analysis, "they only really make sense when set into grander flows of conjuntural and structural time" (Morris, 2000, p. 17). On the other hand, I will not discuss factors of "*la longue durèe*" – the limits set by geographical and other extremely slow-moving factors.

From a NIE perspective, Williamson (2000) suggests a time-structure where changes at the level of embeddedness (social norms, customs, traditions, religion) occur with a frequency of 100–1,000 years and formal institutions change within 10–100 years. Together these factors set the stage for standard economic analysis which focuses on economic transactions while holding the institutional structure as (implicitly) given. This means that the standard analyses are limited to dealing with relatively short-run phenomena.

A structural approach may seem particularly useful when dealing with an issue such as trying to explain the ancient world. A structural account will fill in the gaps when our sources are silent, and it will help us decide between different competing and conflicting interpretations. It allows us to present a more comprehensive picture of the development of society. However, this advantage to a structural approach may seem like unwarranted and unfounded guesswork to someone focused on the detail.

The fact that economists focus on structure while historians focus on providing all relevant details carries over to the actual style of writing, or so it seems to me. As an illustration, I submit the following observations. About a year ago, I listened to the specialist brought in to teach our doctoral students in economics how to get published. She began by stating that the most important advice was to delete everything from the paper that did not point straight at the upcoming conclusion. (In fact, this is precisely what you spend a lot of time doing as a researcher in economics – streamlining your text.) Second, in economic journals footnotes are actively frowned upon and often expressly prohibited. Third, in a random pick among my historical references there were on average 3.5 footnotes per page. Having read a paper by a historian, many economists will (I guess) at the end of a paper find themself not knowing what the purpose of the study was and not knowing what the conclusions were. So if you are an economist dealing with historical material you face a trade-off which is particularly acute if you hope that both tribes will read your text. What I end up doing is a sort of compromise, which I guess means that historians will find that much too much important material has been delegated to footnotes, while fellow economists will be annoyed by the fact that there is some important action in the footnotes (and, incidentally, there are 1.7 footnotes per page).

1.8 Individual rationality and unintended consequences

The approach to individual behaviour employed here is that it was self-interested, instrumental and rational. By rationality I mean essentially that individuals are assumed to have reasonably well-defined preferences with regard to the outcomes or consequences of their actions, which may be seen as the core of rationality in an economic approach (Acemoglu and Robinson, 2006).[49] This rationality assumption is of course an important simplification. In reality, the formation of preferences is a major issue (Lichtenstein and Slovic, 2006), as is the question of whether experiences guide us in the right direction. The rationality concept used here also means that utility is a characteristic of outcomes and not of the nature of the decision process. In this sense of well-defined preferences over consequences, rationality was a trait of the ancient Greeks early on. For example, Murray (1990, 1996) argues that institutional change in ancient Greece, including the archaic period, displays a high level of rationality, based on recognition of the reasons for change and the consequences of institutional reform. Similarly, Bresson (2007, p. 30) argues that the ancient Greeks were not irrational but they sometimes acted under a different set of constraints.

However, from the rational-actor framework it does not follow that all consequences of an action are necessarily intended by the actor, in particular in view of the bounded rationality of human action. Unintended consequences of an action are a ubiquitous phenomenon and they may occur for a variety of reasons.[50] "Unintended consequences" will be used here as a label for consequences that are neither foreseen nor desirable for the actor, i.e. unwanted and unexpected.[51] This does not preclude the possibility that the decision maker could have envisaged the outcome as, for example, remotely possible. The relevant point I wish to make is straightforward – quite often something other than what we believed would happen happens. Ordinary people do not think in terms of probability distributions. Occasionally, an individual might hope that the unlikely will happen. Unintended and surprising consequences may follow from an action because of faulty reasoning or erroneous beliefs (Weesie and Wippler, 1986). Both are likely important – individuals often have difficulties in reasoning correctly from the evidence at hand (Evans, 1989), and many individuals have substantially incorrect models of the world. In addition there is bad luck (and Murphy's law).[52]

In the Athenian case, unintended consequences are often due to the cumulative effects of interaction between agents making strategic choices over time. To foresee consequences is particularly difficult when it involves predicting how other people will change their behaviour, as is often the case. That an individual dislikes the final outcome of his action does not mean that he is irrational, only that he was wrong. Or, for example, that he was myopic at the time of the decision. His rate of time preference may have been high and what *we* tend to think of as the "final outcome" may have been so far in the future as to in practice carry very little weight. The decision-relevant outcome may have been much closer in time; for politicians, staying in power would be a good example of this. Anything that secured continued rule in the short run may qualify as a satisfactory solution, and put an end to further attempts to find more attractive alternatives.

1.9 Individual beliefs

If it seems that an individual chose an action that in retrospect hardly served her best interest, it could be thus due to bad luck, or perhaps we misjudge the rate of time preference. However, the explanation can also be that they hold erroneous beliefs about how the world functions.

An important ingredient in the behaviour model of NIE is the emphasis on the beliefs of individual actors. Among the different determinants of individual behaviour, this is probably the most fundamental and important, and at the same time the least incorporated in economic analysis. How individuals define their self-interest is determined by their beliefs and perceptions about the world and their society (North, 1990, 2005). To take a relevant example, the reforms of Solon are sometimes portrayed as the first step towards democracy in Athens. This could have been correct[53] in the sense of leading the development in that direction, but this obviously does not mean that Solon himself had any idea that this would be the case. There is a danger of anachronism here, as Foxhall notes:

> modern scholars have often been tempted to fix on Solon as the "father of Athenian democracy" [...]. Although Solon may have triggered off processes which eventually led to the emergence of Athenian democracy, it seems to me ludicrous that Solon had any inkling of this – it is just that we know the end of the story.
>
> (1997, p. 114)

Let us return to the already mentioned comment by Davies (2003, pp. 320–323) regarding the rationale behind the actions that led the Athenians towards democracy. He notes that his comments follow from a "deep and long-standing unease about current ways of approaching the phenomenon of the emergence, consolidation and spread of Greek democracy". He notes that (almost) all "approaches share the basic assumption that [...] ideas, ideals and theories [of antiquity] played a major part in the processes of social, political, and institutional change". However, "without any substantial body of comparative evidence, without any general theory of politics [...] it must have been impossible, except in the crudest way, either to produce a detailed analysis of existing society or to create in the imagination an ideal towards which existing society might be directed."

Davies argues that almost all the approaches in the modern literature "seem extraordinarily remote from the actual business of managing a polity on the ground, or from the sorts of preoccupation and language which one can see in the public documentation [...] from the end of the sixth century onwards". He suggests instead that (here it comes again) "the world of Herodotos was not being driven by a conscious outreach towards any identifiable "democratic" goals or ideals; that the system which its inhabitants came to call *demokratia* was little more than a bodged-up set of responses to particular situations and crises; and that insofar as it had any unifying principle at all, that principle [was] the perceived need to *prevent* this or that unpleasant or undesirable development or practice from continuing or from gaining a foothold" (Davies 2003, pp. 320–323).

This of course does not mean that the Greeks were incapable of rational decision making on political and institutional issues in the archaic or classical periods. However, it does mean that with a rational-actor model, we should think carefully about what the actors are likely to have seen as being in their best interest, which should be based on what they can reasonably be assumed to have known and to have been able to imagine, and also what kind of measure would have seemed to fulfil a satisficing criterion.

An important aspect of rationality is learning over time, as hinted above. Many economic models of individual behaviour are based on the presumption that individuals learn from their mistakes; that if their actions do not lead to the expected outcome, they revise their perception of the way the world works so that a more correct mental image emerges. This in general increases the probability of equilibrium solutions. However, in many situations it appears highly doubtful that the individual is able to draw the right inference from their experience so that a more correct image of the world is formed.[54]

Another aspect of learning is that since individuals learn, the effects of an institutional change is likely to vary over time. Suppose, for example, that income tax rates are raised, and then, at some point in the future, lowered again to their original level. People will be learning new things during the period with high tax rates. The increase in tax rates makes it more profitable to learn about different means of legal and illegal tax evasion; hence people will invest more time and other resources in this. In the modern world, you find magazines full of helpful advice of how to reduce your taxes, and tax consultants make a good living. In ancient Athens we find, for example, people selling their landed property because cash is easier to conceal (Chapter 6). All these tax-planning activities are of course a social waste (we may think of them as part of the transaction costs in the economy), but that is not the point here. It is instead the long-run consequences of these incentives to learn about tax evasion. When we come to the time when the tax rates are reduced to their original level, individual behaviour will not be the same as before the original tax increase. Suppose, for example, that the high tax rates have been in place for 20 years. This means that citizens have spent 20 years learning about tax evasion. This knowledge will be intact after the tax reductions and it will influence behaviour, which will be different compared to a situation where tax rates had remained low during the whole period.

There are two important lessons in the previous paragraph. One is that the effects of institutions change over time, as individuals adapt to them. The other is that the institutional set-up has consequences that linger long after an institutional change, because it has affected the stock of human capital. This is one of the reasons why institutional change exhibits path dependency. The incentive to change institution depends not only on the current situation but also on the path we have travelled to get here.[55]

1.10 The state and credible commitments

Because individuals are assumed to be self-interested, the analysis of the government will be based on the predatory model of the state as an agency of a group or class with the function of extracting income from the rest of the constituents (North, 1981, 2005).[56] Furthermore, "A state is an organisation with a comparative advantage in violence, extending over a geographical area whose boundaries are determined by its power to tax constituents" (North, 1981, p. 21). In general, rulers will use any means at their disposal to maximise their own utility. Depending on the circumstances, they may try to change political institutions, property rights, terms of trade, etc., or simply try to maximise tax revenue (North, 1981, 1990).

There are two relatively common fallacies regarding institutions and efficiency. On the one hand, it is often assumed that if a particular institutional set-up would be efficient, then it will come into existence. In reality, it will only come about if the individual incentives for the relevant decision makers are sufficiently strong. The other fallacy is to assume that if an institution exists, then it must be efficient.[57] In general, institutional change requires that some individual(s) have incentives to spend resources in order to affect the change, and this need not be the case even if the potential institution is efficient from a societal point of view.

Two fundamental problems impede the establishment of institutions that foster economic growth. First, the ruler may refrain from introducing efficient institutions because it may not be in his personal best interest to do so; it depends, for example, on the cost of extracting resources from the economic agents (North, 1981). Second, even if potentially efficient institutions are in place, they do not necessarily lead to efficient economic activity. The reason is that "a state strong enough to protect property rights is also strong enough to abuse them" (Greif, 2005, p. 747).

Hence since North and Weingast (1989), the potential to make credible commitments has increasingly been emphasised in the literature on institutional change and economic development. Unless the state can credibly commit not to tax (or confiscate) any increase in income, individual citizens will have very small incentives to make investments to increase the future productivity of their assets. In the same vein, Greif (2005) argues that both private and public contract-enforcing (market-enhancing) institutions tend to reveal the property of those who utilise them. Therefore for such institutions to have beneficial effects on trade and growth, it is necessary for the state to credibly commit not to use the information revealed in order to confiscate the property. In other words, "there must be institutions that limit the government from preying on the market" (North, 2005, p. 85). For these reasons, the ruler may choose to shift some political power to the taxpayers (Barzel, 2000). A consequence is that "coercion-constraining institutions conducive to the growth of the market also likely lead to the endogenous emergence of political institutions associated with liberal societies" (Greif, 2005, p. 728).

Rational behaviour is much influenced by the time preferences and associated discount rates of the individual decision maker. The attitude towards the future determines the extent to which future consequences of one's actions are taken into account in current decision making. The importance of this becomes particularly apparent when we study the behaviour of those in power. For example, discount rates will sometimes be very high, as when the ruler is threatened by a rival, by a revolution from below etc. All that matters then is to find a short-term solution that allows the ruler to stay in power. Satisficing behaviour implies that the decision maker will stop looking for alternatives once an alternative which satisfies that condition is identified. The long-term consequences will be heavily discounted and hardly affect the current decisions.

1.11 Outline of the rest of the book

This book is written with a mixed audience in mind and in the hope that it will be of interest to economists and economic historians, classical scholars (historians, archaeologists, etc.), as well as members of the general public with some knowledge of economics. The economic analysis in this work is not complex, and it does not use mathematical models. It should be accessible to anybody who, for example, reads the economy reports in the daily newspaper, on the Web etc.

However, the ancient world is not necessarily well-known outside the Classics departments. Hence for the benefit of colleagues in economics, and other non-classicists, a brief chronological outline of ancient Greece from around 1200 BC and up to 322 is provided in Chapter 2, together with a table with some important dates in Athenian history. Much relevant additional historical detail will be provided in connection with the analyses in the coming chapters.

It is with some hesitation that I write the following paragraphs, because I wholeheartedly agree with McCloskey (1985) that the kind of paragraph that he calls "a roadmap" is unnecessary in scientific papers in economics. I strongly suspect that very few people read these paragraphs, which usually begin with "the rest of this article/paper/essay is organised as follows". Furthermore, the structure of the text should appear self-explanatory to the reader (the roadmap should be unnecessary). In the present case, however, we are first of all dealing with a book, not an article, and second with a book of a somewhat unusual kind, and I think a roadmap, which also includes an *amuse bouche* in the sense of highlighting some of the features of the landscape that we will be travelling through, may be useful.

The rest of the book is organised around several closely connected and inter-related themes. Institutional change is the common denominator, both the reasons for institutional change and the effects thereof. Within that overall per-spective, frequent themes are individually rational action, unintended con-sequences, credible commitment, competition within the elite, transaction costs, taxation, and the emergence of market relationships.

After the fall of the Mycenaean palace societies after 1200 BC, Greek society was greatly reduced in scale and by 1000 BC it consisted of small isolated settle-ments. From this situation, the city-state (*polis*) emerged in Greece in the course of four centuries as a political, geographical and judicial unit, with political insti-tutions and written laws.[58] Chapter 3 sets the institutional stage by looking at this early development of the *polis* and its institutions. It has been argued that what sets ancient Greece apart from surrounding areas was the absence of heavy taxation on the common people, and I suggest a likely explanation for this in terms of a historical coincidence. In the subsequent development, two issues stand out. One is the formation of property rights that eventually must have followed the formation of territorial boundaries. The gradual consolidation of boundaries arguably contributed to population growth, inter-state conflicts, colonisation and competition for power. Competition within the elite is the engine of institutional change, including some attempts by the elite to self-regulate their own behaviour. Such an attempt to ensure that those in office cred-ibly committed not to abuse their power was probably an important factor behind the earliest written laws. Variations over time in the conditions for competition explain both the introduction of formal political institutions and their overthrow by tyrants.

We then turn to look at the emergence, development and tenacity of Athenian democracy. Chapter 4 argues that the most important structural determinant of the constitutional changes on the road to democracy was the issue of credible commitments. In some situations, only by transferring some political power could those in the position to rule over the Athenians credibly commit to protect those being ruled from economic exploitation. This explains several of the con-stitutional changes, both the early move away from the rule of a birth aristocracy and 200 years later the move away from a "radical" democracy to one where the elite regained some political influence. This analysis is inspired by the theoret-ical framework of Acemoglu and Robinson (2006), which emphasises the impor-tance of credible commitments from the ruling group in society not to exploit the other inhabitants. This may give the rulers an incentive to shift some political power to the others, including partial control over the tax system, as a long-term guarantee against economic exploitation. Another important aspect is once again competition within the elite, which in the fifth century drove them to propose democratising measures in order to gain the support of the common people. Con-tributing structural factors are changes in ideology and in warfare (development of the hoplite and of naval warfare, both of which entailed more expenses and shifted the military roles in the population).

Chapter 5 deals with the same developments as Chapter 4, but now we explicitly focus on decisions by individuals. We will take a further look at the three pivotal changes in the political rules of the game, only this time at the micro level. I argue that the actions of both Solon and Kleisthenes – the two candidates for the title "father of democracy" – are readily understandable as self-interested behaviour, that their actions had important unintended consequences, which may be the result of faulty reasoning, bounded rationality (satisficing), or simply that they perforce acted with very short time horizons. Neither of them had democratic intentions. The third change concerns one of the most striking features of the Athenian democracy, namely the introduction of lottery as a principle to appoint magistrates. This provides another example of the usefulness of a rational-actor perspective, and of unintended consequences.

Few things tells us as much about a society as the nature of its taxation. Taxation as social phenomenon appeared in Chapter 3, as it may have played a role in the formation of city-states. Furthermore it was instrumental in the analysis in Chapter 4 where the focus is on credible commitments from the rulers to the taxpayers. Hence taxation interacts with other institutions. In Chapter 6, we take a comprehensive look at taxation in Athens. First, the structure of Athenian taxation suggests that the Athenians – true to our predatory theory of the state and our rational-actor perspective – taxed wherever, whatever and whoever they could, but also that they were very conscious of the importance of transactions costs which they consistently shifted to private parties. Despite these characteristics taxation, somewhat unexpectedly, may have been beneficial to economic performance, for example by pushing the rich into the market sector. The development of taxation over time shows the balance between the rich and the poor in society.

In Chapter 7 we turn to the two-sided relationship between institutional development and economic life. The Athenian economy thrived during much of our period, and notably also in the fourth century when the Athenian Empire had long ceased to exist. Over the years, the Athenians introduced several institutions that promoted efficient economic activities, such as protection of property rights and rules facilitating the adjudication of commercial disputes. Similarly, standardised weights and measures and sound money reduced transaction costs. The existence of the tax system encouraged trade, thereby contributing to Athenian prosperity. The development of market relationships, at the same time, probably did much to change the outlook of the rich and the ordinary Athenians both. Market relationships typically entail a measure of trust in persons outside your close group of relatives and friends, and this experience probably contributed to the survival of Athenian democracy. It seems likely that the tenacity of the democratic rules of the game were helped by widespread political participation and a growing tendency to view each other realistically as economically rational agents. The link between the functioning of the economy and institutional development is relatively less explored in the literature, compared to the effects of institutions on the economic sector. Nevertheless it is in principle equally obvious (North, 1990, p. 48).

The book ends in Chapter 8 with some reflections on what we have learnt not only about Ancient Greece, but also about institutional change. The Athenian case is highly interesting in its own right in view of the renown of the Athenian democracy, but a study of Athenian history and experiences of institutional changes also provides lessons for today. We found that a New Institutional framework is very useful for understanding institutional change in ancient Greece. Individual decision making at the time seem to reflect boundedly rational, satisficing behaviour. Rationality of course does not rule out unintended consequences of purposeful actions. Such consequences indeed seem ubiquitous in the modern world, and characterise important parts of the Athenian experience as well.

Several important aspects of institutional change are illustrated by our Athenian laboratory. Competition for power emerges unsurprisingly as a major engine of change. An interesting fact is that when individuals engage themselves in non-marginal institutional changes, the reason in ancient Greece is usually not that a marginally superior alternative to the present situation has appeared. Instead the reason is usually to prevent something unpleasant from continuing or materialising (often in a great hurry, because one has waited until the last moment). The recent developments as regards public finance in, for example, Portugal and Greece, are modern cases in point. In other words, reactions are provoked to prevent loss, not to achieve gain. Athens is an example of a society that for a long period was able to make both marginal and non-marginal institutional changes that worked well. Contemporary Sweden is another. Among the instrumental societal aspects that are conducive to such relative successes are probably political systems that rely on widespread information gathering, so that many view points are represented, rely also on opportunities to reach a consensus on how the world works.

2 Historical background

Ancient Greece from the demise of the
Mycenaean society to the death of
Alexander the Great

This chapter, and particularly the accompanying tables, is provided with those in
mind who, in their younger years, found themselves in a schooling system
similar to the Swedish one that I grew up with. If you attended school in the late
1960s and early 1970s in Sweden (yes, around 1968 in other words), you very
likely found yourself in a situation where, it seems fair to say, a classical education was not exactly top priority.[1] For these and others similarly unfortunate, this
chapter provides a brief outline of the political history of the period covered in
this book, with a certain emphasis on relationships between the *poleis*. Table 2.1
gives us an overview of the traditional periodisation, while Table 2.2 provides
some important dates (again as traditionally given). All dates in the study are BC
unless otherwise stated.

The overview below focuses on the political and military history in broad
outline.[2] Details are presented in the different chapters as they become of interest. Similarly, the changes in economic life will be dealt with in the analytical
chapters. The story presented is the traditional one. The overview will – I hope –
fulfill the same comforting function for many readers as the text reputedly
written on the outside cover of the famous *Hitchhikers' guide to the galaxy*:
"Don't panic!"[3]

2.1 Demographic and economic changes

The size of the population in ancient Greece and in Attica is a thorny issue,
closely connected to the size and timing of grain imports. There seems to have
been population growth from the ninth century and until the fourth or third centuries (Scheidel, 2003). Concomitantly there was economic growth – Morris

Table 2.1 Standard periodisation of ancient Greek history (years BC)

Mycenaean (Late Bronze Age)	c.1600–1200
Dark Age (Early Iron Age)	c.1200–750
Archaic period	c.750–480
Classical period	480–323

Table 2.2 Chronology for Greek and Athenian history (BC)*

Kylon attempts to establish a tyranny in Athens	*c.*630
Drakon's law code in Athens	621/0
Reforms of Solon in Athens	**594**
Tyranny of Peisistratos and his sons in Athens	(561)546–510
Reforms of Kleisthenes in Athens	**508/7**
Battle of Marathon	490
First use of ostracism in Athens	487
Archons selected by lot in Athens	**487**
Battle of Salamis	480
Battle of Himera in Sicily (Greeks vs. Carthagians)	480
Formation of the Delian league	478/7
The **Areopagos deprived of most of its powers** in Athens	**462**
Building of the Parthenon on the Acropolis in Athens	447–438
The Peloponnesian War	431–404
Death of Perikles in Athens	429
The 30 tyrants in Athens	404
Restoration of democracy in Athens	**403**
Corinthian War	395–386
Second Athenian Confederacy	378
Battle of Leuktra, Thebes (briefly) top nation	371
Philip II ascends to the throne in Macedon	360
The Social War (end of second Athenian Conf.)	357–335
First speech of Demosthenes in Athens against Philip II	351
Battle of Chaironeia, Macedon rules Greece	338
Death of Alexander the Great	323
Democracy suppressed in Athens	**322**

Note
* Traditional dates. Events of special interest for the purposes of this book are given in **bold**.

(2004) has estimated that per capita incomes grew by 50–100 per cent over the period 800–300 and an increasing part of the economy was characterised by market relationships and market forces (see Chapter 7).

According to Hansen (1999) there were 50,000–60,000 Athenian (male) citizens before the Peloponnesian War, and most likely considerably less in the fourth century. For the later period he suggests 30,000 male citisens and 20,000 metics (resident foreigners) resident in Attica. For ancient Greece in general, Hansen (2006) shows that the population could considerably exceed the carrying capacity of the land (the number of people that could be fed). He argues that the best measure of the carrying capacity of Attica is 100,000 persons (p. 90), while the actual population comes to 250,000 plus children in the fourth century (and more in the fifth). This means that grain for more than two-thirds of the population had to be imported and consequently belonged to the market part of the economy. Bresson (2008, Chapter 5) provides a detailed illustration of a population exceeding the carrying capacity for the city of Hermione in the Argolid.

With respect to the number of slaves, not much is known in reliable detail. Modern guesstimates vary wildly. I appreciate the salutary comment of Hansen (1999, p. 93), that the Athenians themselves did not know the number of slaves, only that there were more slaves than free in Attica. This gives at least a lower limit for the number of slaves as *c*.100,000 while a more probable figure is 150,000. Andreau and Descat (2011), for example, argue for a slave population of 200,000 to 250,000 towards the end of the fourth century.

2.2 Recovery after the fall of the Mycenaean society and the emergence of the *polis*

Towards the end of the Bronze Age, Greece was dominated by the Mycenaean palace society.[4] When Michael Ventris deciphered the language of the Linear B tablets (AD 1957), he showed that the Mycenaeans were Greek. Theirs was a hierarchical society, organised around the palaces in Mycenae, Tiryns, Pylos, Athens, etc. Around 1200 BC, this society collapsed, with signs of conflagrations at many sites. Literacy was lost and regained in the ninth century, building on the Phoenician alphabet.

Ancient Greece then entered the so-called Dark Age. By the early tenth century, the ensuing result was a fragmented society much reduced in scale, where life was lived in small, often short-lived and relatively isolated settlements. Population had declined significantly. From these humble beginnings, the city-state (*polis*) gradually emerged as the dominant social organisation.

2.3 The archaic period

By the end of the seventh century, the basic institutional framework of the *polis* is in place. These institutions include magistrates with a limited and short time in office, a council, and an Assembly. The now rightly famous Copenhagen inventory of the ancient Greek *polis* lists 1,035 communities known as *polis* (Hansen and Nielsen, 2004). The Greek city-states were typically small; the median *polis* in the inventory falls in the category $25–100 \, km^2$. In other words, it would have been perfectly possible to walk from one end to the other and back again during a day (Hansen, 2004b), enabling, for example, a farmer to take part in an Assembly meeting.

Most city-states are ruled by aristocratic oligarchies. This is also the case in Athens, but in *c*.630 a member of the elite and former Olympic victor named Kylon attempted to seize power alone – to become what the Greeks called a tyrant. This term signified a sole aristocrat who had seized power unconstitutionally, and this new phenomenon first appeared in Greece in the seventh century. Kylon failed, however, and was killed with his followers. Another new phenomenon in the seventh century was the introduction of (some) written law. This occurred in Athens in 621/0,[5] when a certain Drakon introduced a written law code.

The sixth century witnessed many instances of continued political turmoil all over Greece (Robinson, 1997).[6] The material is often very scanty (and we sometimes have to rely on Hellenistic or later traditions), but it appears that new tyrants appeared, usually by overthrowing the rule of aristocratic oligarchies, and sometimes tyrants were expelled. In some instances it is reported that this ended with the *demos* taking control,[7] but it is difficult to know precisely what this means, as the details regularly escape us, and it remains a possibility that this was under aristocratic leadership. Similarly, sometimes rule by the *demos* was overthrown by aristocratic groups.[8]

Political turmoil was in other words relatively common in Greece in the archaic period, and in 594 the people rose against the elite in Athens. The aristocrat Solon was appointed mediator and he reformed the constitution and the laws of Athens. In particular, he co-opted the rich non-aristocrats into the ruling elite by changing the rules of eligibility – instead of belonging to the right families you now needed to be rich enough. Things did not quiet down however, and in 561 the aristocrat Peisistratos made his first attempt to establish a tyranny in Athens. He was soon kicked out both this time and the next, but in 546 he succeeded, and he and his sons then ruled Athens until 510.

By this time, the external relations of the Greeks were undergoing important changes. Already in the Mycenaean age, Greeks had settled on the coast of Asia Minor, and these settlements represented an important part of the Greek world in the archaic and classical periods. From *c*.750 the Greeks began a substantial colonisation movement, founding many new city-states in Sicily and southern Italy (together known as *Magna Graecia*) and around the coast of the Black Sea. Through their presence in Asia Minor, the Greeks came into contact with the expanding Persian Empire. The Persians under Cyrus the Great conquered Lydia in 546, which brought the Persians into direct contact with the Greeks in Asia Minor, who now exchanged the Persian Emperor for the Lydians as overlords. The Persians followed this up with taking Babylon in 539 (Cyrus), Egypt in 526/5 (Kambyses), and Thrace in 512 (Darius).

2.4 The classical period part 1 – fifth century

In 499, the Greek cities on the coast of Asia Minor revolted against the Persians, and Athens among others sent them support. Arguably not an extremely wise move, as the revolt failed. The Persians decided that teaching the Athenians a lesson would be a good idea (who do they think they are, anyway?), and perhaps the Persian emperor saw it as his obligation – ordained by God – to provide peaceful conditions to surrounding peoples by incorporating them into the Persian empire.

The Persians launched a punitive expedition in 490. The rest is history, as we say. The Persians were beaten at Marathon in 490, returned a few years later with a fleet, were beaten at Salamis in 480 (the fleet) and at Plataiai in 479 (the army). For the Greek success at Salamis, an important ingredient was the fact that a few years previously Themistokles had persuaded the Athenians to use the proceeds from new silver mines to expand their fleet.

An incidental effect of the Persian intervention in Greece is that we have such a lot of nice sculpture to look at from the archaic and classical periods. Some of the sculpture was dumped as filling when the Athenians started restoring the Acropolis buildings after the Persian sack in 480. The Parthenon was built upon the site of a temple destroyed by the Persians, and the money to build the Parthenon probably came from the war chest intended for fighting the Persians.

The Greeks who fought at Marathon did so as hoplites – heavy infantry – who arranged themselves in tight formations (the phalanx). This military technology dominated in Greece from the archaic age and at least until the Peloponnesian War. The equipment of a hoplite was fully developed by *c*.650 and the bulk of the hoplites are assumed to have been well-to-do farmers who could afford the equipment, but who did not belong to the aristocratic elite. The latter provided the cavalry.

While Athens is by far the most well-known Greek *polis*, and also the one we know most about, she was not alone. On the contrary, the Greek landscape was dotted with *poleis*, with more than 1,000 being known to us (cf. above). The average *polis* was small – but some were more powerful than others, like Athens, Sparta, Thebes and (in Sicily) Syracuse.

The events in Athens had parallels in other city states. Tyrants, for example, ruled in Samos (Polykrates), in Sikyon (Kleisthenes[9]) and in Corinth (Kypselos and others). Written law was introduced in several *poleis* in the seventh and sixth centuries. The Greek states in general kept in close contact with each other and borrowed institutions and other ideas freely from each other (Snodgrass, 1986). Contacts were also the result of pan-Hellenic sanctuaries and festivals, such as the sanctuary to Apollo in Delphi with the famous oracle and the games in Olympia, which the Greeks in the classical period believed had begun in 776.

Sparta of course was a special case in terms of institutional set-up. Already in the seventh century they had reformed their state in order to be able to suppress the other inhabitants in the area and to maintain a large force of well-trained hoplites. Those suppressed were first the helots, an indigenous population enslaved collectively, who cultivated the land of the Spartiates so that the latter could focus on their military services. Second there were the *perioikoi* – living in subjected neighbouring communities. For a long time the hoplites of Sparta formed the most efficient army among the Greek city states and the 5,000 Spartiates present were instrumental in the Greek victory over the Persians in 479.[10] The Spartan state was governed by the executive offers of the Assembly (the five ephors), by two hereditary kings and by the council of elders (*gerousia*).

Athens went another way, and during the first half of the fifth century a number of democratising changes were made. Why and how this occurred is something we will return to in Chapters 4 and 5.

After the victories at Salamis and Plataiai, many Greek states joined Athens in a confederation aimed at defence against the Persians in 478/7. The treasury of the organisation was placed at Delos (another pan-Hellenic sanctuary), hence the name the Delian league. Sparta did not join and Athens took the lead. Gradually it became clear that membership was no longer voluntary – Athens forced those who wished to leave the league (and to stop paying tribute) to remain with the organisation. Athens benefited from its position in the league, the treasury was moved to Athens in 454/3, and Athenians served as sailors in ships paid for by the tribute of the members of the league. Over time, conflicts sometimes led to conquest of territory and Athenians settled abroad. Consequently the league turned into what is usually called the (first) Athenian Empire, though this term may be misleading (Morris, 2009).

At the same time relations between Athens and Sparta were deteriorating. In 510, the Spartans had helped the Athenians in their revolt against the Peisistratids.[11] In 508/7 the Spartans backed the loser in the struggle for power in Athens, and a group of Spartans capitulated when they were unexpectedly besieged on the Acropolis. Then the two states collaborated against the Persians, as we have seen. In 462 the Spartans asked the Athenians for help against a domestic revolt, but sent the Athenians home again when they arrived to help. This gave the anti-Spartan faction the upper hand in Athens, and from this time it became increasingly clear that there would be a military conflict between the two.[12] The Peloponnesian War began in 431 with Athens and Sparta as the main adversaries. Joining Sparta were her allies in the Peloponnesian league and Thebes.

The Athenians lost the war, partly by their own doing, such as the decision to send a military expedition to Sicily against Syracuse in 415. However, the war dragged on until the Athenians capitulated in 404. Sparta was now the undisputed leader among the Greek mainland city-states, but Athens was soon back in form.[13] In 404, the Spartans imposed an oligarchic regime on the Athenians ("The Thirty Tyrants"). In less than a year the oligarchy was violently overthrown and democracy was restored in 403, and reformed (cf. Chapter 4).

2.5 The classical period part 2 – fourth century

The fact that Sparta emerged so powerful also meant, however, that the other Greek states were nervous about Spartan intentions, a suspicion that soon proved to be well-founded.[14] As a consequence, several *poleis* were more than willing to try and cut Sparta down to size, should the opportunity arise and someone (else) take the lead. Consequently in 395 Thebes, Athens and Corinth joined against Sparta in the Corinthian war which dragged on for 10 years, and only ended because of the threat of another Persian invasion.

Despite the peace treaty, aggression continued between Sparta and other *poleis*, and in 371 the Thebans under Epaminondas beat the Spartans in a set battle, which left 400 of 700 participating Spartiates dead. This was a disastrous loss, representing perhaps as much as 40 per cent of their maximum manpower at the time (the number of Spartiates probably declined gradually from 490). Thus, Spartan supremacy "was forever ended" (Robinson, 1967, p. 303).

The following decade was one of continuing conflict within and between *poleis*. With the death of Epaminondas at Mantinea in 362, the heyday of Thebes was over. The Athenians tried to achieve hegemony, but lost the Social War in 357–355. In fact, peace was a relatively rare event in fourth-century Athens: "from the end of the fifth century to the middle of the fourth, Athens was a society at war, relieved by occasional short periods of peace" (Hansen, 1999, p. 116).

Meanwhile, the role played by the Persians as the main external threat to the independence of the Greek *poleis* was taken over by Macedon. Philip II succeeded to the throne in 360, and within five years he beat back external aggressors and united the country internally. He reformed and expanded the army and the cavalry (making the latter an effective weapon). In 352 he took control over Thessaly, and when he brought pressure on the Chalcidice (Olynthos etc.), Demosthenes urged the Athenians to take action against him before it was too late. Eventually several *poleis* joined Athens against Philip, but the coalition was thoroughly beaten at Chaironeia in 338. For the Macedonian kings southern Greece was, however, a sideshow, as their main attention was directed east.

In 336 the first Macedon forces crossed into Asia, and the interest in eastward expansion continued uninterrupted when Philip died in 336 and was succeeded by his son Alexander. He in turn conquered Persia and only stopped at the Indus River because his troops refused to move further east. When he returned to the Mediterranean he issued the Exiles' Decree, ordering that all Greek exiles should be allowed to return to their home city, have their possessions returned etc. Not surprisingly Athens and others revolted but were defeated in this so called Lamian War. The independence of the Greek city-state was now effectively dead, and Athens was given a new and oligarchic constitution. And they all lived happily ever after (not quite).

3 The emergence of the *polis* and its institutions

In the archaic and classical periods, the *polis* (city-state) is the archetypical social organisation in Greece.[1] The institutional set-up that characterises the *polis* emerged gradually in the centuries that followed upon the collapse of the Mycenaean societies. This decline produced a society much reduced in size, so that around 1000 BC, Greek society consisted of small isolated settlements with almost no social stratification. In the course of the following four centuries, the *polis* emerged in Greece as a community of citizens, as a political, geographical, religious and judicial unit, with an assembly, council, elected magistrates and written laws.

Greek society in this period is characterised by a comparatively modest rate of taxation of the common population. Ordinary farmers control a substantial part of the agricultural surplus, and this is the feature that according to Bresson (2007) sets ancient Greece on a path of trade, specialisation and growth.

Three facts point to the second half of the eighth century for the emergence of the early *polis*. First, to this period belong the earliest communal wars and wars for the control of land ("true wars") of which there was any memory (Raaflaub and Wallace, 2007, p. 27; Hanson, 1999). Second, the "Greek colonisation" of Sicily and the south of Italy began around 750 or slightly later. Both these developments are usually taken to imply that the participants belonged to a relatively well-defined political system. Third, there is evidence of the *polis* in the writings of Hesiod from *c*.700 (Raaflaub, 1993).

In the process leading to the *polis*, the formation of territorial boundaries suggests itself as a fundamental institutional change with far-reaching consequences. It arguably contributed to population growth, inter-state conflicts, colonisation and competition for power. Furthermore, elite competition is an important factor in the process of institutional change. Variations over time in the conditions for this competition explain both the introduction of formal political institutions and their overthrow by tyrants. Several of the mechanisms that are important in the analysis of these institutional changes (below) will reappear in later chapters.

3.1 The rule of the *basileis* – informal power relations[2]

The decline of Mycenaean society was part of a broader eastern Mediterranean and western Asian collapse, but with Greece as an extreme case. The subsequent growth phase was a Mediterranean-wide pattern, probably helped by improving climatic conditions from around 850.[3] As we shall see, however, the regeneration followed different paths in different societies.

By the early ninth century, the recovery from the post-Mycenaean decline was under way in Greece. Settlements were stable and there is now evidence of social stratification, increasing wealth, communication and substantial population centres. The population had increased from the tenth century and continued to do so into the fourth century.[4] During the following centuries, life centred on the households of local chieftains – the *basileis*[5] – who would seek to gain domination over other communities and *basileis*.

Having relatively little coercive power, the *basileus* based his position on the resources of his household and on his ability to attract followers (*hetairoi*, warrior companions) to increase his military power. The followers were rewarded with feasts, gifts and a share in plunder. Raids on sea and land were important sources of wealth. The *basileus* formed ties of marriage and guest-friendship with other *basileis* (a practice which continued in the archaic period). Below the *hetairoi* we find the farmers, the slaves etc. It is assumed that the common people made contributions to the *basileus'* wealth in return for protection and administration of justice.

Gradually separate communities began to identify land with people, both signified by the term *demos*. The word *demos* could signify a single village, but more typically the demos contained a central village and some lesser settlements. A settlement was often known as a *polis* but was much smaller than the towns and cities later known as *poleis*. Eventually different settlements came to regard themselves as belonging to the same *demos*, and finally the crucial notion of a single land-people emerged. Within a *demos* there would be competition among different *basileus*.

An important source of knowledge for these early Greek societies is the Homeric poems. It is nowadays predominantly argued that the Homeric writings reflect an actual historical society, possibly somewhat older than the poems themselves, and in any case, fragments of different periods are present in the texts (Raaflaub and Wallace, 2007). The majority view among classical scholars seem to be that the Homeric poems probably reached the form in which we know them in the late eighth or early seventh century.

In the Homeric poems we find an early *polis*. There is a political community where the crucial identification of land with people has emerged, and the land is conceived of as a bounded territory with several settlements, one of which is identified as the central one. One of the *basileis* is recognised as the paramount chief and both the idea and reality of central government existed. The institutions of assembly, council and law court appear in a comparatively informal version. There are examples of freestanding monumental temples in Homer, which corresponds to the archaeological record, where the emergence of these edifices belongs to the eighth century. On the other hand, there is a discrepancy between Homer and the archaeological remains in that cities with walls appear in the former, whereas archaeology so far suggests that such features belong rather to the seventh century or later.

Donlan (1994) makes the important observation that the *basileus* had a relatively weak position – his authority could be challenged by another leader, or he could face opposition from the *hetairoi* acting in unison. Donlan shows, for example, that the Odyssey provides a vivid picture of the tensions between leaders and between leaders and the *hetairoi*.[6] For what is coming, it is important to note that Donlan describes the relationship between the leaders and the warriors, not the population as a whole.

3.2 The origin of Greek egalitarianism and market orientation

In beginning of the dark ages, ancient Greece saw comparatively little social differentiation, but already in the early ninth century this is changing, as noted earlier. However, there is no indication that anything resembling the Mycenaean palace societies was in the offing. On the contrary, what is conspicuously absent in the process of state formation during the centuries of recovery after the Mycenaean system collapse is any sign of a centralised and hierarchical structure of the kind that dominated not only Mycenaean Greece but also contemporary Egypt and Mesopotamia; both the latter saw the revival of old centralised kingdoms but often with new levels of militarism. The Western Mediterranean at this time saw its first really powerful chiefs and cities (Morris, 2006).

Bresson (2007, Chapter 4) emphasises that a distinctive and unique feature of the Greek society that emerges from the dark ages is that we find ordinary farmers being able to control a large part of their agricultural surplus above subsistence. This is in sharp contrast to the Mycenaean palace society and the other centralised societies where the ruler or ruling elite appropriated a large part of the peasants' agricultural production, leaving the ordinary farmers with little above subsistence. Bresson argues that the fact that the ordinary farmer controlled a large part of his surplus production was the main factor behind the expansion of trade in ancient Greece, and with trade followed specialisation and economic growth. Already in the archaic period, ancient Greece was thus set on a path of self-sustained growth, based on the institutional fact that the market functioned as the means to transfer agricultural surplus among the actors. As a consequence, Greece was quickly moving towards a monetised market economy already in the archaic period (Bresson, 2007, p. 115).

Since taxation is an important theme in this book, it is worth pointing out that this means that it was the *absence* of taxation (of elite exploitation) of the ordinary farmers that was the key factor behind the economic development of ancient Greece. From an economic perspective, it is of course obvious that if the state lays its hands on all production above subsistence, then there is no incentive for farmers to specialise, invest in technological improvements, work hard, or indeed do anything that increases a surplus that will only be taxed away anyway.[7]

The fact that taxation of the commoners was less heavy in Greece suggests that Greek society was comparatively egalitarian – power was more evenly distributed than in other societies of the time. This is consistent with the picture we receive in Homer as described above. The poems display a society where the leaders are in a comparatively weak situation and hardly could exert heavy taxation on their followers (Donlan, 1994; Morris 2006). Agamemnon, Odysseus and the other leaders in the Trojan expeditions had a very different relationship to their followers than, for example, Sargon II of Assyria.

The essentially egalitarian structure seems to have survived the institutional changes in the early archaic period (councils, magistrates, legislation) which increased the relative power of the rich elite (see section 3.6). At the same time, egalitarianism was supported by the development of hoplite equipment. Such an egalitarian trait can (and did) have important implications not only for the economic development but also for the political development.

This is fine, but it still leaves the most intriguing and important question unanswered: Why did the ancient Greeks end up in this situation with an egalitarian power structure? What kept the rulers in their society from exploiting the farmers to the same extent as their predecessors and contemporary competitors?

It seems to me that there is one very good candidate to explain why the ordinary farmers in ancient Greece largely escaped heavy exploitation by the elite. My guess is that the peculiar Greek development was due to the confluence of two important but mutually independent factors.

On the one hand, the drop in population after the fall of Mycenaean society arguably must have made the ordinary people better off, just as the common people (who survived) benefited from the Black Death in fourteenth-century Europe. Land was abundant; irritating leaders could easily be avoided by voting with one's feet and moving to another place (especially to the extent that pastoralism replaced agriculture).

On the other hand, there was an important technological change. After the fall of Mycenaean society, iron made its way into Greek society, party replacing the more expensive bronze. Of the weapons found from Athens between 1050 and 900, all eight swords, all four knives, all three axes and both daggers are made of iron (Osborne, 1996a, p. 27). This meant that metal implements in general and weaponry in particular in all likelihood became considerably cheaper. The production of bronze implements relied on the import of tin, probably from the British Isles, and copper, whereas iron could be found more locally. In Bresson (2008, p. 47), the price of bronze is recorded as five times higher than that of iron in the classical period, which gives an indication of the relative prices involved, even though the exact figures obviously cannot be transposed several centuries. This technological change meant that a ruler's monopoly on violence would have been impossible to uphold, as possession of weapons became an economic possibility for a much larger part of the population.[8]

So we have two more or less simultaneous trends. On the one hand, the prosperity among the ordinary famers would have been on the increase as soon as things became more settled after the Mycenaean collapse, when trade revived and land was abundant. On the other hand, the introduction of iron reduced the price of weaponry. This coincidence – that the introduction of iron came precisely in the period when there was essentially no central government that could control what was going on – probably provided the unique circumstances that allowed a comparatively large part of the population to acquire some degree of military power and establish themselves as one of the players when and if violence broke out. From this position it would be difficult to budge them during the centuries to come; in fact their position was strengthened to the extent that they came to be among those who could afford the developed hoplite equipment that was in existence by 650. The presence of a relatively large group who could afford to arm themselves was arguably also a prerequisite for the development of hoplite warfare and tactics. Violence potential was found in a considerably larger group than the former warrior companions of the *basileus*. I hasten to add that this does not mean that their position remained unchanged, so the effects of the egalitarian development did not automatically include the development of democracy (this is obvious since democracy was only to be found in a limited set of *polies*).

The reason that this occurred specifically in Greece and not, for example, in the western Mediterranean may potentially be explained by the fact that Greece was an extreme case in terms of systems collapse.[9] This will have given the common people a stronger position than elsewhere at the time when weapon technology was changing.

3.3 The establishment of a territory: a spontaneous and efficient solution?

The fall of Mycenaean society led to the very unusual situation where

> the idea that any part of the inhabited space must belong either to one community or to its neighbour must [...] have arisen freshly.
>
> (Snodgrass, 1993, p. 37)

An analysis of the emergence of boundaries from a situation where there probably were none, is necessarily highly speculative. Nevertheless, it seems worthwhile because once you have taken in the idea of such a unique situation it becomes clear that the establishment of community boundaries may have played an important role in the development of the *polis* institutions (Lyttkens, 2006). In general, the widely diverging size of *poleis* in classical times, sometimes defined by "natural" boundaries and sometimes not, suggests that we should seek an explanation in the sociopolitical sphere for the delineation of the *poleis*. Note that the formation of boundaries must be envisaged as a gradual process.[10]

The formation of boundaries implies a statement of property rights – a certain area belongs to one group of people and not to another. Hence a natural explanation for boundary formation lies in scarcity of land. Raaflaub argues that "boundaries of the community and secure ownership of land emerge as central social concerns only when land becomes scarce" (1993, p. 78) and "as the *polis* territories were filled up, land became precious, resulting in conflicts both within each *polis* and with neighbouring *poleis*. There emerged the notions of 'territoriality' and fixed boundaries" (1997, p. 52). Consequently Raaflaub places the establishment of boundaries in the late eighth century, following upon the accelerated population growth that is often argued to have taken place during that century.[11] From an economic perspective, scarcity of land is a relative concept, so we may take Raaflaub's position to imply that scarcity, and hence incentives, would not have been pronounced enough until the second half of the eighth century.

Such an account implies that the creation of boundaries occurred as a spontaneous solution to social problems. This view has its obvious merits. With population growth from the tenth century onwards, land becomes scarce, and the value of the rights over a piece of land increased. This change in relative prices is likely to lead to a change in land use, from pastoralism to less land-intensive farming, a tendency that seems to be suggested by the evidence (just as pastoralism is a rational response to the depopulation following the fall of the Mycenaean society). Furthermore, as the value of an asset increases, it becomes more interesting to exercise and delineate rights over it, and this is what seems to have happened with land. In a functioning society, the creation and abandonment of rights is an ongoing process (Barzel, 1989; Demsetz, 1967).

However, as emphasised in Chapter 1, efficient institutions do not appear just because they are efficient, and we see here a potential collective action problem. We should consider the *incentives for individual agents* to devote resources to the establishment of boundaries. We should not just accept that this occurred because it was beneficial to the society as a whole. To delineate property rights by establishing a boundary is costly, including some expected opposition from neighbouring communities. Hence incentives must be of a certain magnitude to make the effort worthwhile.

The common people faced the free-rider problem of collective action (Olson, 1971): everybody would benefit from stronger property rights, but everyone would benefit irrespective of whether they personally took any part in the action. Snodgrass (1993) surmises that conquest and allotment of land occurred as a part of the process of boundary formation, and that private ownership of land followed naturally with this. However, the initial definition of community territory did not necessarily make individual property rights – the primary concern of the farmer – much stronger. We know that eventually non-citizens were excluded from owning land, but this was not necessarily the case from the beginning. On balance, however, it seems likely that the formation of boundaries by analogy gradually spilled over to individual property rights.

Because of the free-rider problem, the ruler   here the *basileus* – is often a more promising candidate as an active agent in institutional change (North, 1981, p. 32). He may have seen establishment of boundaries as part of the informal exchange with his followers and as a fulfilment of his implicit obligation to provide protection. To the extent that Snodgrass was right and acquisition of land was involved in the process, the *basileus* most likely was the main beneficiary. However, as far as the land-value argument goes, the *basileus*' personal incentives to engage in such an enterprise does not appear strong. Furthermore, it is sometimes argued that scarcity of land was not a prominent factor even in the eighth century. Foxhall (1997, p. 127), for example, argues that survey evidence "hardly suggests overpopulation or a landscape approaching its carrying capacity in the Archaic period" and that "such extensification seems to start no earlier than the late sixth century".

Donlan (1989) in fact suggests that boundary formation may have taken place earlier. He argues that the community as a comprehensive unit with known boundaries had emerged already by the late ninth century, i.e. long before the acceleration in population growth in the eighth century. He suggests (pp. 22, 24) that the coalescence of the separate small communities of the early Dark Age was a reflection of "the universal tendency [in all Greek societies] of local chiefs to seek precedence over other local chiefs" where "ambitious *basileis* enlarged their spheres of influence by recruiting non-local supporters [...] thus building up regional pyramids". This coalescence was a process fuelled by population growth and increasing contacts between communities, and it implies some economics of scale in violence (protection and plunder). The problem remains that the process of boundary formation probably is not cost-free. We turn, therefore, to the competition between rulers.

3.4 Territoriality as an instrument in aristocratic competition

So far we have assumed that the efficiency argument for border formation will eventually have made incentives strong enough, despite the collective action problem. However, a more individualistic interpretation seems possible. Territoriality could have been used as an instrument in the competition among leaders. In his institutional theory of the state, North (1981, pp. 27–28) emphasises that the presence of rival rulers is an important determinant of ruler behaviour (a competitive constraint). The *basileis* had a strong incentive to engage themselves in the issue of territorial boundaries, because the idea that a certain territory and a certain group of people naturally belonged together would, by definition, effectively *exclude* from the local competition for influence such rival rulers as came from other territories (from "outside").

It is not difficult to envisage situations where a ruler would find it advantageous to actively propagandise for the land-people identity with territorial boundaries, for example, when his authority is severely challenged by rival rulers so that his rate of discount is high. A ruler is always in a potentially unstable situation, and this was manifestly so in the present case, where the *basileus* lacked a formal apparatus of government, and it seems probable that any one area could contain adherents of different *basileis*.[12] In order to influence the belief system of his potential followers and of the common people, the *basileus* could promote the ideology of the *demos* as a single land-people. This would have been a relatively cheap way of strengthening his position and of legitimising his rule.[13]

In other words, the effects on the competition for power provide a substantive reason for rulers to invest resources in the issue of territoriality, and specifically for some of them to actively promote the idea of a land-people identity. The probability of this occurring seems likely to have increased over time, *ceteris paribus*, as population and contacts between communities increased from the tenth century onwards, i.e. as the conditions for elite competition changed.

Another possible incentive for rulers to strive to define their territories comes from the expansion of trade, which is pronounced in the eighth century but which had begun at least by the ninth century (Osborne, 1996a, Chapter 2; Thomas and Conant, 1999, Chapter 4). According to the predatory theory of the state, rulers will normally attempt to maximise revenues within the constraints they face (Levi, 1988; North, 1981). Taxation of trade is a universal phenomenon; it is attested for archaic Greece and appears in an informal form in Homer, namely as "gifts" from visiting traders to local rulers.[14] Hence it is conceivable (I would say likely) that, as trade expanded, the *basileis* realised that taxation of trade was a new way to gain wealth. Taxation of trade implies authority over a territory rather than over people, and a concern over boundaries may have followed long before scarcity of land became a major issue.

Common cult was one of the important characteristics of the *polis*. Religion and cult helped to define territories and territorial belonging.[15] Again, it is conceivable that religion partly served this purpose because it was consciously used by the *basileus* to strengthen his own position, just as, for example, the Peisistratids in sixth-century Athens promoted public cults in order to weaken the influence of the aristocracy – qua local leaders of cult – over the population.

The conditions for aristocratic competition will have varied considerably across ancient Greece, and this could conceivably help explain why the *polis* structure evolved in some areas but not in others.[16] In particular, it suggests the hypothesis that later *polis* areas would be characterised by a relatively high degree of competition among *basileis* (possibly associated with short distances between settlements). An indication along these lines is Raaflaub's (1993) observation that settlements in areas of later *poleis* seem to indicate the co-existence of several leaders that probably balanced each other.

If the process of boundary formation began early, it helps explain the growth in population and in real incomes per capita that occurred in ancient Greece, an increase of 50–100 per cent over the period 800–300 (Morris, 2004), cf. Chapter 7. To the extent that boundary formation served to increase individual property rights, we would expect it to enhance agricultural production and nutrition.[17] Other factors that could have given the first impetus to population growth include the return of more peaceful conditions, the switch to farming (Snodgrass, 1980, pp. 35ff.), or perhaps it simply represented a normal swing in population, the fall of the Mycenaean society having reduced population size to very low levels. From an economic perspective, the switch to farming implies an incentive to raise larger families, because the marginal productivity of labour would be greater than under pastoralism.

If the consolidation of boundaries were perceived as a strengthening of individual property rights, the leaders in territories where this occurred would likely become relatively more prosperous than their peers. At first sight it might seem that such an effect would be of a too long-term nature to affect behaviour. However, the experiences of, for example, the early Soviet Union show that agricultural production can change quickly in response to variations in the security of ownership over land and produce (Hedlund *et al.*, 1989). Consequently measures that strengthened property rights may well have been copied from other successful rulers.

3.5 The establishment of a territory: consequences downstream

Whatever the reason for the new phenomenon, the gradual acceptance of the fact that a certain territory belonged to a particular incipient *polis* is likely to have had far-reaching consequences. We have already discussed the effect of more secure property rights on economic development and population growth.

The emergence of boundaries likely provided a new focus for armed conflicts – the acquisition of land. "By the classical era the boundaries of the *poleis* seem so firmly set that one may forget how much the wars of the eighth and seventh centuries changed the map of Greece" (Starr, 1986, p. 39). In other words, instead of conflicts over land leading to the definition of boundaries (as suggested in the literature), the causation may have been running in the opposite direction.

Perhaps most importantly, the gradual establishment of community boundaries substantially changed the opportunity costs of both the common people and the proto-aristocracy. For the ordinary farmers, the possibility of exit was reduced. Previously, dissatisfaction with the local *basileus* could be alleviated by moving to surplus land in an area dominated by another *basileus*. As the idea and reality of "national" boundaries took form, exit would, however, gradually become a less attractive option, even if land remained plentiful. Property rights to land were now gradually associated with one's own *demos* and territory, and ownership would be correspondingly less secure when moving to the area of another *demos*. This is reflected in the later Greek practice of formally allowing only citizens to own landed property. With well-defined boundaries it became less easy for an individual farmer to escape exploitation by the local *basileus* (and therefore such exploitation became, *ipso facto*, more likely).

Such a secular deterioration in the relative position of the ordinary people may help explain the extensive colonisation movement briefly mentioned above. During the last third of the eighth century a new town was founded in southern Italy or Sicily about every other year. Such a development, i.e. for "whole groups to move [...] into areas not previously settled by Greeks, demanded peculiar conditions", as noted by Osborne (1996a, p. 125).

Osborne argues that the reason for the colonisation was not that there was no land available at home. Instead, the colonists were people who jumped (rather than being pushed) because they saw a better future elsewhere (better climate, desirable minerals, trading opportunities, etc.). This is consistent with the view (presented above) that the Dark Age-rulers were in a relatively weak position, and hence would have found it difficult to prevent tax payers from exiting this way. Osborne (1996a, p. 125) suggests that the colonisation "is not a measure of state power but a measure of the limits to the control rulers could exert".

Others include push factors in their explanation of the colonisation. Thomas and Conant (1999, pp. 125–134) suggest that the proto-aristocracy increased their land holdings and, as land grew scarce, increasingly turned to exploiting the ordinary farmers. The possibilities of exploitation may have increased as the leading families increased their economic power by expanding their estates and turning to trade (Donlan, 1997; Thomas and Conant, 1999, pp. 130–133). Furthermore the elite controlled the government and the interpretation of the unwritten law. Around 700, Hesiod (*Works and Days* 30–39) complained that the aristocracy gave crooked sentences and violated justice for the lure of gain.

The formation of boundaries also changed the conditions for competition within the elite. It has been argued that the upper class in Greece had become more fiercely competitive in the eighth century, including an intensified search for wealth (Starr, 1977, 1982). Around 600, Solon of Athens noted that the rich had twice the eagerness of others in their search for wealth (Solon, fr. 13). Similarly, Theognis of Megara complains that bad men harm the people for the sake of personal wealth.[18] As the scope and volume of economic activity grew, new avenues to acquire wealth were opened, and concomitantly new competitive uses for disposable wealth appeared, such as conspicuous consumption of luxury imports. This provided new opportunities to invest in status and could easily have fuelled an inflationary spiral in such expenditures.

Additionally, however, the delineation of boundaries may suggest a reason for an increased competitiveness among the proto-aristocracy. First, both the population and per capita income increased and an increase in wealth in society would make it more interesting to invest resources in the competition for power, since being a ruler means being in a position to tap into this wealth (Levi, 1988; North 1981). Second, for the *basileis*, the quest for power became more of a zero-sum game: with well-defined community territory competition took place within a closed set of actors, whereas previously power relations would have been less precise. With risk-averse individuals, this seems likely to produce a tendency for leaders to invest more efforts in the competition for power and eminence.[19]

In summary, the formation of boundaries may have contributed to prosperity, population growth, conflict over land and mass fighting, exploitation of the common people and colonisation and intra-elite competition. Furthermore, by fostering conflicts over land and by contributing to intensified elite competition, the formation of boundaries prepared the ground for further institutional changes. We now turn to the mechanisms of aristocratic competition under these new circumstances.

3.6 Self-regulation attempted and failed

Increasing tensions between the elite and the rest of the population

As we approach the end of the eighth century, we may think of the association between land, people and cult within recognised boundaries as an established fact of life. This organisation of society is firmly incorporated into the inhabitants' view of the world. Society is characterised by fierce competition for power and status among the members of the leading class. This competition could sometimes turn violent and lead to civil strife. In the course of the seventh century this aristocratic competition led to the rise of tyrants as a new political phenomenon – a single member of the elite seized power. It appears, however, that this was preceded roughly around 700 by the introduction of impersonal offices and collegial boards to run the incipient *poleis*. In the seventh century this is followed by written law. Impersonal offices and written laws thus emerge as the first formal institutions of the *polis*.

Both in the archaic and early classical periods, competition within the elite stands out as the engine of change. A fiercely competitive spirit vis-à-vis one's personal status was an outstanding characteristic of the Greek upper class.[20] Several factors may have contributed to an intense struggle for power within the elite in the archaic period, as noted in the previous section. At the individual level, exploitation of the common people may have been facilitated by an increase in economic power within the elite and also because exit became less of a viable option.

Competition within the elite intensified and concomitantly tension mounted between the elite and the rest of the population. One reaction to the growing tension was the colonisation mentioned above (section 3.5) which was such a prominent feature of the eighth and seventh centuries – large groups of people moved away to found city-states elsewhere. This was not the only reaction, however. The mounting tension occurred at the same time as military power in the incipient *poleis* gradually shifted from the elite to the ordinary well-to-do citizens with the emergence of hoplite technology and tactics.[21] Hence the aristocrats as a group would find it more and more difficult to oppose a would-be tyrant who acted with the explicit or implicit support of the rest of the population.

Morris (2000) proposes that the elite had to contend with a general trend in attitudes in Greek society towards egalitarianism and a conception of the state as a community of middling citizens (e.g. p. 156). Such an attitude could be a natural reflection of the egalitarian nature of post-Mycenaean society in Greece (section 3.2) and the subsequent change in military technology. With the survival of the state in the hand of the hoplites, a more egalitarian view of the world could be a natural consequence. Morris points out that the concomitant discontinuation of rich (private) burials and proliferation of elite (public) expenditure in connection with the emerging sanctuaries may reflect a trend to regard private ostentation as being in bad taste (p. 279). In other words, the elitist ideology was under pressure, and aristocratic competitive outlay had to take new and more socially acceptable forms.

Morris argues (2000, p. 156) that many scholars today take the pure elitist ideology too literally and consequently overemphasise relations in the polis as a zero-sum game of intra-elite feuding for power. From the eighth century onwards, Morris suggests, some members of the elite "assimilated themselves to the values of ordinary citizens" (p. 163) and gave voice to a "middling ideology" – a representation of the voice of the man in the street. This did not mean, however, that the aristocrats gave up their claim to constitute a ruling class (pp. 163, 169). But by adopting the middling ideology these aristocrats helped erode the basis for elitist rule and contributed to a structural trend that made the introduction of democratic institutions a real possibility (Chapter 4).

The elite faced something of a prisoner's dilemma. Individually they had incentives to try to eclipse their peers and to exploit the rest of the population. However, their internal conflicts could weaken the community in relations with hostile neighbours, which also jeopardised their position within the community. Constitutional change often occurred in connection with severe military setbacks (Robinson, 1997, Chapter 3). The pressure individual members of the elite exerted on the rest of the population could provide explicit or implicit support for tyrants. Some of the aristocratic voices for a middling ideology may in reality have been exhortations from aristocrats to their peers to avoid paving the way for tyranny by exploiting the population. For example, this could be the case when they argue (Morris, 2000, pp. 169–170) for restraint and moderation in behaviour and that an excessive focus on gain is disruptive to society.[22] Solon of Athens is a case in point.

The elite had a collective interest in preventing anyone from their own group from becoming tyrant, and also in preventing a situation where political turmoil could lead to the *demos* taking power. By the sixth century, both these outcomes would have seemed possible in the elite's perception of the world. An important aspect of both the introduction of magistracies and of the formalisation of laws – two sets of formal institutions – is therefore probably that the members of the elite were trying to regulate their own behaviour.

Political institutions

Around 700, the informal system of the *basileis* was replaced in many Greek communities by a formal system of power sharing (Donlan, 1989), suggesting that the leading *basileis* and their followers alternated in exercising executive power. The different functions and powers of the *basileis* were largely shared out among a set of magistrates, non-hereditary, with a limited and short term of office. For example, in Corinth the introduction of offices and a council is traditionally dated to 747 (Thomas and Conant, 1999, pp. 121–122). In Athens the most powerful magistrates were the nine archons, and the Athenians believed that the archonship went back to 683 (Hansen, 1999, p. 28). Eligibility was often restricted to a birth aristocracy. An assembly and a council probably existed before these changes, but it is likely that the council now became more formalised, and also possible that other collegial boards were created.

Raaflaub (1993, p. 81) argues that

> pressure exerted on the *polis* either from a hostile environment [...] or [...] by long wars [...] must have enhanced the unity and solidarity of the community and forced it to formalize its institutions, to adopt (written) laws and thus to eliminate as far as possible the causes of domestic discord.

Raaflaub (1997, p. 57) adds that "the decisive factor perhaps was danger from within the *polis*: in-fighting among elite families [...] posed existential threats to the *polis* as well". Thomas and Conant (1999, p. 132) notes that the reform fulfilled an administrative necessity – with increasing population size and more diversified activities in the community "the leadership of a single person was no longer effective or even sufficient". These underlying causes for the introduction of offices seem plausible, but lacks a connection with individual incentives.

Lyttkens (2006) suggests that the new rules of power sharing may have reduced the perceived probability of internal conflict and facilitated co-operation. Formal power-sharing facilitated co-operation by making it more difficult, and hence less attractive, to try to achieve a dominant position by violent means. As noted by Weingast, "a constitution serves as a coordinating device, helping citizens to coordinate their strategy choices so that they can react in concert and police state behaviour" (1995, p. 15).[23]

In particular, Weingast shows how a formal constitution facilitates agreement on *when* a transgression of rightful behaviour has occurred. In the emerging *poleis*, the introduction of rules for power sharing arguably co-ordinated opposition by signalling when and if someone was attempting to seize power.

A parallel case is presented in the penetrating analysis of medieval Genoa by Greif (1994, 1998) who shows how an increase in external threat AD 1154 changed the nature of a mutual-deterrence equilibrium between competing clans and enabled them to co-operate because the threat reduced the gain from being in control of the city. When the threat unexpectedly dissipated AD 1164, the old equilibrium was no longer viable, because the gain from controlling the city had increased during the period of co-operation, and civil strife ensued. When a severe external threat again materialised AD 1194, the Genoese altered the rules of their political game by introducing a self-enforcing organisation. This organisational innovation was an externally recruited, impartial and short-term administrator of the city, the so-called *podestà*. The possibilities for a clan to credibly commit itself to reward a *podestà* who colluded with them was limited. If he supported a clan so that they took control over the city then they could also decide not to reward him for his services. Therefore the *podestà* could be counted upon to uphold the balance of power in the city (that was the only way for him to get paid). With the *podestà* in place, it had become more expensive to try to gain control over the city.

It is a viable hypothesis that something similar happened in archaic Greece around 700. In the eighth century violence was probably endemic, both between and within communities. In Homer, the authority of the leader is especially connected to military leadership, and warfare appears as one of the traditional exploits of the aristocracy, where status could be gained (Adkins, 1972; Donlan, 1997; Finley, 1991). The late eighth century, however, witnessed wars that threatened the very independence or subsistence of the *poleis* (perhaps a natural consequence of the growing scarcity of land).[24] These conflicts probably posed a greater threat than the earlier Dark Age conflicts. A system of formal offices and collegial boards for the governing of the state might then seem attractive, because it represented a change in the rules of the game for political competition that facilitated co-operation. The external threats made it individually rational for members of the elite to agree to such a change in the rules of the game. The increased external threat made it less interesting to be in control of the *polis* and suggested that the value of co-operation increased.

It is not surprising that such an arrangement for power-sharing and co-operation had a tendency to spread across the *poleis*. Many *poleis* would have faced similar pressures and seen the benefits of a reduction in internal strife (Raaflaub, 1993, pp. 81–82).[25] In so far as the reform succeeded in fostering co-operation it probably also led to advantages in inter-state conflicts, which motivated imitation by other *poleis*. Such a competitive edge may be part of the explanation for the early ascendancy of Corinth, where impersonal offices were probably introduced already soon after 750, as noted above.[26]

Snodgrass (1993, p. 38) argues that local *basileis* need not have been opposed to their territory being incorporated into a larger *polis* because they exchanged an uncertain claim to local power for "the chance to share in power on a larger scale, through a mechanism which gave official sanction and apparent permanence". This implies that by instituting a formal system of power-sharing, the rulers of an expansionist community could defuse the opposition from neighbouring leaders.[27]

One important effect was probably that the introduction of formalised political institutions increased the power of the upper class vis-à-vis the common people; the formalisation of government increased the cost of non-compliance compared to what it had been under the relatively loose authority exercised by the early *basileus*, largely based on custom (Donlan, 1997). Furthermore, to the extent that the traditional assembly of warriors had any real influence in Homeric times, rather than just to ratify decisions already taken in elite circles, this influence in all probability was reduced by the introduction of magistrates and the formalisation of the council. In particular the latter would over time gain in influence, treating issues before they were taken to the assembly, etc.

It seems likely that power-sharing reduced the level of internal conflict for a while. In the course of the seventh century, however, wars between the *poleis* gradually came to have less dramatic consequences. "Phalanx fighting [...] was increasingly 'ritualized'" and war came to "determine the prestige rather than the existence of the [...] *polis*" (Raaflaub, 1997, p. 56).[28] The reason for this change is less than clear. The best explanation for the changing nature of these encounters is the fact that it increasingly relied on the well-off ordinary farmers, who could afford the cost of the hoplite panoply, which had been developed by about 650, and included greaves, shield, helmet, etc.[29]

The well-to-do group had the greatest incentive to reduce the level of inter-*polis* conflicts, and their increasing importance may have moved the conflicts in that direction.[30] If the independence of the *poleis* or the lives or livelihood of the citizens were at stake, the well-off farmers had less to gain in case of victory and more to lose in case of defeat than those who were less well-off. At the same time, they were probably not driven by the desire for status in the same way as the aristocrats. Hanson (1991, 1995, 1999) argues that many aspects of hoplite warfare suited the well-to-do farmers, e.g. short campaigns, no real danger to mutual agricultural prosperity, etc.

Whatever the underlying reasons, a reduction in the level of threat implied by inter-*polis* conflicts may have had repercussions for the internal affairs of different *poleis*. If an equilibrium with relatively few violent intra-*polis* conflicts had been supported by external threats, this equilibrium need no longer have been stable when the external threat subsided (as in Genoa after AD 1164). The picture of the seventh century that we get from the literary sources is one of violent quarrels within the elite, using whatever means at their disposal, and a concern over the effects of aristocratic competition. So we should not be surprised that the seventh century was the time of the new phenomenon – the rise of tyrants. While the emergence of tyranny is often associated with aristocratic competition (Osborne, 1996a), a reduction in external threats provides a more specific explanation for the timing of this new phenomenon.

Tyranny, as Osborne (1996a, p. 193) notes, could occur because of mutual distrust. It seems that there was no way for an aristocrat to credibly commit to abstain from attempting a violent takeover once the external threat was reduced. Consequently it was a question of trying to "do it to them before they do it to you". Expectations based on previous experiences generate path dependency by forming individual perceptions, in this case of what kind of behaviour you could expect from other members of the elite.

Written law

The other main institutional change in the seventh century was the emergence of the first written laws. Again the most natural interpretation is that these laws represented an attempt at elite self-regulation. The laws were largely about delineating the powers of magistrates.

> [T]he purpose of the regulation was not to control the powers of the élite with regard to the people, nor to restrict the arbitrariness of those with authority, but to control the distribution of powers within the élite. This is élite self-regulation...
>
> (Osborne 1996a, p. 187)

The laws served to restrain the aristocrats in their *internal* struggle and prevent the magistrates from abusing their position. Such behaviour could otherwise be expected to increase as the aristocrats learnt over time how to adapt their actions to the new institutional framework (the effects of an institutional change vary over time). In other words, laws that regulate the exercise of power are in a sense a natural corollary to the introduction of magistracies. It is an interesting parallel to the *podestà* in Genoa that – according to Greek tradition – many of the early lawgivers were outsiders to the community (Osborne, 1996a, p. 189). This use of an outsider makes sense if the aristocracy tried to regulate their own behaviour and find stable solutions.[31]

So the laws were not primarily designed to restrict aristocratic exploitation of other segments in society. In fact, just as with the political institutions, formalisation of laws would have made non-compliance more costly. While jurisdiction may have become less arbitrary, it was still in the hands of the elite. Hence the formalisation of the laws was not necessarily to the advantage of the common people.

Self-regulation failed

Subsequent developments showed that the attempts at self-regulation had done little to change the basic incentive structure in society, in particular regarding the relationship between the elite and the rest of the population. The rich aristocrats still had *individual* incentives to exploit the poor and they had ample opportunities to do so. There was violent competition in the acquisition of wealth.[32] Furthermore, the institutional changes introduced to mitigate within-elite conflicts (written laws, formal offices) may easily have amplified tensions between the elite and the rest of the population, because these formalisations of *polis* institutions probably facilitated exploitation by increasing the power of the upper class vis-à-vis the common people. In other words, not only did the individual incentives for aristocrats to exploit individual farmers increase, but their individual possibilities also increased. This occurred at the same time as military power in the incipient *poleis* gradually shifted from the elite to the ordinary well-to-do citizens.

A final source of tension in the community was that certain individuals outside the nobility also had been able to enrich themselves in the new social and economic environment.[33] By the latter part of the seventh century, they had become noticeable, but by definition they were excluded from political power and the interpretation of the law. We may well imagine that – over the generations – a new and wealthy family would occasionally be accepted as belonging to the elite, provided that they emulated the lifestyle of the aristocracy. In people's minds, great wealth was associated with being an aristocrat and with political power. Furthermore, marriage was a way for rich non-aristocrats to use their wealth to form alliances with noble families (Finley, 1991, p. 66; Murray, 1993, pp. 39–42). In the seventh (or sixth) century, Theognis of Megara (183–192), deplored that aristocratic men and women married the "lowly born" for their possessions. The process of being admitted to the elite is, however, likely to have been much to slow to satisfy the ambitions of the nouveau riche.

With such a precarious balance, it should come as no surprise that the continued rise of tyrants demonstrates that the attempts to regulate elite behaviour were often less than successful. From the seventh century and for centuries onwards, individual members of the elite sometimes found it to be to their advantage to step outside the traditional aristocratic competition. Neither should we be surprised that occasionally "the people" were called in to support the overthrow of tyrants, nor that these situations sometimes could end with the *demos* in control. Successful tyrants needed at least the passive acceptance of the hoplites. Sixth-century tyrants reputedly often relied on help from outside and on mercenaries, but the stories of early tyrants suggest that they rarely came to power with outside help (Osborne, 1996a, 271–272). Attempts at elite self-regulation (and its failure) is something that we will come across again.

3.7 Concluding remarks on the first institutions of the *polis*

In this exploratory account of the formative period in the development of the *polis* as a social organisation, we have encountered several features that we will come across repeatedly as we study institutional change in archaic and classical Athens. We have seen that competition within the elite can be an important driving force in institutional change, including variations in the conditions under which this competition took place, and that this competition is accompanied by attempts at elite self-regulation to prevent the consequences of the competition from reaching dangerous levels. Occasionally a self-enforcing solution was established, but more often the competition for power and status drives the members of the elite to actions that can be detrimental for the elite as a group in the longer run.

We have also seen that a rational-actor perspective can be a useful tool to organise our thinking on institutional change in early Greece. It was suggested that formalisation of territorial boundaries may partly have been a consciously driven process. This may have been one of those happy cases where a ruler finds it to be to his advantage to implicitly strengthen individual property rights, thereby contributing to the long-term economic growth in ancient Greece.

The gradual consolidation of the boundaries of the incipient *poleis* changed the incentives of the actors in the communities. Among the possible ensuing effects were population growth, inter-state conflicts, colonisation and a fierce competition for power. Variations over time in the conditions for this elite competition can help explain both the introduction of formal political institutions and the overthrow of these institutions by tyrants.

The power-sharing through appointed magistrates represented a change in the rules of the political game and was introduced by the upper class because of external threats (conflicts between the early *poleis*). It could serve as a self-enforcing equilibrium for a while, but as the external threat subsided in the seventh century, the equilibrium was no longer stable and tyrants occasionally seized power. The formalisation of laws entailed attempts at stabilising the situation, but since this did little to change the underlying incentive structure, it could only be moderately successful in preventing civil strife.

An incidental effect of the formalisation of the political game is that it may have been instrumental in establishing exactly who belonged to the elite (the aristocracy). With the introduction of magistracies, it became necessary to determine who was eligible.[34] No such delineation of eligibility had been required as long as power and government was rested in informal structures. This is the first of a series of reforms which changed the incentives within the *poleis* by establishing that membership of a certain group carried privileges.

4 The road to democracy part one

A structural approach

We will now focus on the development of democratising institutions in Athens.[1] As mentioned in Chapter 1, Morris and Weingast (2004, pp. 310–319) single out precisely the development of democracy in Athens as an interesting point of intersection between New Institutional Economics (NIE) and the study of the ancient world, and this view is endorsed by the editors of the *Cambridge economic history of the Greco-Roman world* (Scheidel, Morris and Saller, 2007). As we shall see, an economic framework helps explain what might appear as a set of separte institutional developments.

Around 600 BC, Athens was under aristocratic rule, as were most of the Greek city-states. The Athenians were ruled by a hereditary oligarchy consisting of noble-born families (the Eupatrids). Members of these families had monopoly on the offices of the state and administration of the law. Some 150 years later, the political institutions had been transformed into a radical (male) direct democracy.[2] All important decisions were taken in the Assembly where all citizens could attend, speak and vote. All important office-holders (except the generals) were appointed by lot, as were jurors. Citizens of all classes could serve as jurors and in office. Citizens were paid for serving as jurors, on the council and in other offices.

The democratic institutions showed remarkable tenacity, and survived the tensions of (losing) the Peloponnesian War, the financial low tide that followed with the dissolution of the Athenian Empire, as well as many large and small crises. It survived, however, by subtly changing the rules of the game (Lyttkens, 2010a). In this chapter, some of the most important structural factors in this process of institutional change are scrutinised. In particular, the analysis emphasises the importance of credible commitments from those in power to other groups in society.

Since we are now entering a period for which there are written sources, in addition to the archaeological finds, the reader is reminded that in focusing on the structural factors in the process of institutional change we will ignore a wealth of seemingly important details. Some of these details will be discussed in the next chapter.

4.1 Theoretical framework: credible commitment and political institutions

Ancient Greece witnessed frequent political transitions in the archaic and classical periods, from oligarchy to democracy or tyranny and back again. Such political transitions, as well as several other aspects of institutional change, are intrinsically linked to the issue of credible commitment (North and Weingast, 1989), and to the predatory model of the state as an agency of a group or class with the function to extract income from the rest of the constituents (North (1981, 2005). There is a close connection between economic and political institutions.

In their stimulating book on the economic origins of democracy, Acemoglu and Robinson (2006) argue that elites, when threatened by revolution from below, will sometimes choose to democratise, even though economic concessions may seem preferable. The reason is that promises of economic concessions are not credible into the future unless there is a shift of political power to the poor majority, because the revolutionary situation will eventually abate, and when it does, there is nothing to stop the elite from taking back any economic concessions if they retain the same political power as before. A revolutionary situation is intrinsically transitory – in some situations, revolutions are easier and less costly to carry out. This occurs typically in times of economic or military crises, which lead to short-term fluctuations in the violence potential of different groups. It is possible to prevent a revolution, because a revolution is costly and much of the wealth of a society may be destroyed (to everybody's loss). Therefore even if the revolutionaries seem to be winning they might prefer a compromise with less destruction.

Similarly, with a democratic constitution, where the poor majority rules, the majority may seek to reduce the threat of an elite coup by shifting some political power to the elite, as a guarantee (credible commitment) that exploitation of the rich through taxation, etc. will not become excessive. The presence of a middle class, finally, may act as a buffer. The middle class "will typically support policies much closer to those that the elite prefer [...] making democratisation more attractive for the elites than repression and changing policy enough that the citizens are content not to revolt" (Acemoglu and Robinson, 2006, p. 39).

The formal rules in a society may promote efficient economic behaviour, but that is by no means necessarily the case, as the ruler's best interest depends *both* on the cost of extracting resources from the economic agents *and* on the size of the extractable surplus (North, 1981; Olson, 2000). Additionally, even if potentially efficient institutions are in place, it does not automatically foster efficient economic activity in society, because as Greif (2005, p. 747) says "a state strong enough to protect property rights is also strong enough to abuse them". In other words, there have to be coercion-constraining institutions as well.

Greif (2005) argues that contract-enforcing institutions, i.e. market-enhancing institutions, have a tendency to reveal the property of those who utilise them. Therefore, for such institutions to have beneficial effects on trade and growth, it is necessary for the state to credibly commit to not using its powers and the information to confiscate the property so revealed. This problem can induce the ruler to shift some coercive power (e.g. political power) to the taxpayers. Greif also points out that

> a ruler's costs and benefits from abusing rights depends on administrative capacity and who controls the administration […] in particular, if the state's administration is controlled by the asset holders, abusing their rights can undermine, rather than foster a ruler's welfare.
>
> (2005, p. 748)

Hence the administrative control by asset holders may provide the expectation that a ruler will not abuse rights, and provide conditions favourable to the growth of the market.

In a paper dealing with ancient Greece, Fleck and Hanssen (2006) show that an elite may *voluntarily* introduce democracy as a way to credibly commit not to confiscate the increase in income that would be generated if ordinary farmers made long-term investments in their land. The elite benefits from democracy because the revenues from taxation of the farmers – now determined by the farmers themselves – could be higher than under aristocratic (oligarchic) rule. When the political power has been transferred to the *demos*, the elite cannot expropriate their production and the ordinary farmers have an incentive to make long term investments. Fleck and Hanssen (2006) show that the extent to which democracy emerged in different ancient Greek societies is consistent with their theoretical predictions.

However, this begs the following question: if the ordinary farmers are given the right to decide on taxation, *why should they tax themselves and not the aristocracy?* This must have been an issue in Athens at least by the first half of the fifth century, because in classical Athens the rich paid various taxes (cf. Chapter 6 on the structure of Athenian taxation). As will be argued below, a major issue for both the introduction and the stability of democracy must have been the ability of the poor majority to credibly commit not to tax the rich excessively. Second, neither of the first two sets of "democratic" reforms in Athens was voluntary. Third, we need to accommodate the fact that the development sometimes took a turn in a non-democratic direction in Athens. Such issues are incorporated in the extended theoretical framework of Acemoglu and Robinson, which therefore provides a better understanding of the emergence of democracy in Athens, the one case in ancient Greece where we can follow events more closely.[3]

4.2 The reforms of Solon

The previous chapter ended with a picture of increasing tensions in ancient Greek society in the early archaic period, and the city-states of ancient Greece witnessed many violent shifts of political regime in the seventh and sixth centuries. These shifts occurred in particular in connection with military crises, which of course easily turned into economic crises. Sometimes a single member of the elite took control over the state as a tyrant. The material is often very scant, but it appears that tyrants usually replaced aristocratic oligarchies. In the seventh century it appears that tyrants rarely were significantly assisted from outside the polis except for receiving advice (Osborne, 1996a, p. 272; Raaflaub and Wallace, 2007, p. 42). In contrast, the sixth-century tyrants often came to power with outside help. Arguably, however, also the latter ruled with at least the implicit consent of a large part of the population. From the middle of the seventh century and onwards, well-to-do farmers were of considerable military importance. They were the ones who fought in the hoplite phalanx, men who could afford the equipment of a hoplite (a heavy infantryman). It is often argued that the tyrants tried to please the common people, e.g. by spending on public works.

An important consequence of the appearance of tyrants and similar experiences is that it gradually became less self-evident for the population at large that the traditional form of rule by the aristocracy was inevitable; it made other constitutional arrangements "thinkable", eventually making democratising measures seem less strange.

The Athenian development prior to 600 fits nicely into this general picture and is best understood against the background of overall social development in Greece. In particular the introduction in Athens of magistracies and of a written law code in the seventh century is consistent with the picture of attempted elite self-regulation. In the seventh century, Athens was ruled by a birth aristocracy, and Aristocratic rule was formally exercised through two institutions. It was an aristocratic prerogative to hold the offices of the state. The most important and powerful magistrates were the nine elected archons. The Athenians believed that the archonship went back to 683 (Hansen, 1999, p. 28). The singular archon commonly designates the highest official (after whom the year was named, the eponymous archon); traditionally, he was effectively the head of state. Ex-archons took seat in the Council of the Areopagos (the Areopagos for short), a very important body in Athens until almost all of its powers were transferred to the Assembly and courts manned by ordinary citizens in 462. The original powers of this Council were probably great, but very little is known about the details. The Areopagos probably "had oversight of the laws, the magistrates, the politically active citizens, and the general conduct of all Athenians, and it could pronounce judgement, not excluding the death sentence, in political trials (Hansen 1999, p. 37)".[4] Membership in the Areopagos was for life.

Around 630, a young nobleman and former Olympic victor named Kylon made an unsuccessful attempt to establish himself as tyrant in Athens, an event that suggests that Athens had witnessed a significant increase in social tensions.[5] In 621/0, a written law code was introduced in Athens by one Drakon. Osborne (1996a, p. 188), notes that the homicide law of Drakon is not so much a homicide law as a law that sets limits for family vendettas, conforming to the picture of elite self-regulation.[6]

As in many other states, the attempts at self-regulation did not eliminate elite factional struggle in Athens. Furthermore, they did little to change the individual incentives of members of the elite to exploit the ordinary farmers. In fact, the formalisation of the hierarchical relationship may even have facilitated exploitation, as argued in Chapter 3. Hence it comes as no surprise when at the beginning of the sixth century, social tensions in Athens led to what is often described as a revolutionary situation.

> Such being the system in the constitution, and the many being enslaved to the few, the people rose against the notables. The party struggle being violent and the parties remaining arrayed in opposition to one another for a long time, they jointly chose Solon as arbitrator and Archon, and entrusted the government to him.
>
> (Aristotle *The Athenian Constitution* 5.1–2)

This turn of events would hardly have been a major surprise at the time. As a result, we learn from Aristotle, the Eupatrid Solon was appointed mediator, apparently with full powers to reform the institutions of the Athenians.[7]

The situation that faced Solon is a clear case of a revolutionary threat – an economic crisis – like the one envisaged in the Acemoglu and Robinson model.[8] Several factors may have contributed to increasing tensions between the rich elite and the rest of the population during the seventh century. As we saw in section 3.5, the possibilities for the individual rich citizens to increase the burden on the poor in the neighbourhood probably increased, as well as their incentive to do so, but at the aggregate level the ordinary but somewhat well-to-do farmers increased in military importance. The situation would have been particularly delicate if Morris' (2002) suggestion is correct that population growth had reduced the production per capita, making dependent farmers increasingly worse off.

The divide between rich and poor may also have been exceptionally large in Athens (Morris, 2000, pp. 288, 304f.). As mentioned above, from the early ninth century funerals reveal competitive behaviour in Greece, but around 700 elite burials became much simpler, and competitive outlays appear instead in connection with (public) sanctuaries, with dedications, stone altars, temples (some in stone) etc. Such structures proliferated from *c*.700. In contrast to the general trend, however, the Athenian elite continued to focus aristocratic displays of wealth on burials rather than redirecting it towards votives at temples, which Morris (2000, Chapter 7) interprets as a sign of a refusal to accept that the traditional aristocratic displays were increasingly considered in bad taste and inconsistent with the growing importance of the common people.

In addition, it is generally presumed (not least on the basis of the subsequent reforms) that there were individuals in Athens who were wealthy but who were excluded from political and judicial power, qua not belonging to the old aristocracy.

For the purpose of this chapter, a minimalist version of Solon's reforms is sufficient. I focus on those measures that seem to have the greatest backing in the literature. I should also point out that it does not matter, for example, for the present analysis exactly how Solon alleviated the economic situation of the common citizens, only that he did so.[9]

To prevent a revolution, Solon gave political rights to the rich non-aristocrats and improved the economic situation of the poor.[10] Ober (1989, p. 64) is very likely right that "Solon was attempting to establish a sociopolitical order in which the privileges of the elite would be secured by granting minimal rights to the poor." First, he co-opted the rich non-elite by substituting wealth for noble birth as a qualification for holding office. He divided the citizens into four property classes, and members of the top one or two classes were eligible to become archons.[11] Whether he enacted other constitutional changes is more contentious. The Assembly of all citizens probably existed before Solon, but he may have instituted a new council of 400, where issues had to be discussed before being taken up in the Assembly.[12]

Second, Solon enacted economic concessions to the population at large – cancellation of debts, abolition of slavery for debt, etc. It is debatable whether these economic concessions were seen as a credible commitment to ease the economic situation of the ordinary population in the long run,[13] but given the fact that the most likely leaders of a revolt were given some political power, so that the collective action problem of the ordinary farmers was exacerbated, these measures were apparently sufficient to defuse the situation in the short and medium term. "It may be sufficient for the elite to co-opt the middle class rather than concede a comprehensive democracy" (Acemoglu and Robinson, 2006, p. 39).

Note that political power was given to those who were *rich*, but outside the traditional birth aristocracy – obviously there was no threat that this small step towards a more democratic regime would lead to the poor majority taxing the rich. If a non-democratic elite can manipulate the institutions of democracy so as to guarantee that radical majoritarian policies will not be adopted, then democracy becomes less threatening (Acemoglu and Robinson, 2006, p. 34).

4.3 The tyranny of Peisistratos and his sons

In the middle of the sixth century Peisistratos established himself as a tyrant in Athens, after two unsuccessful attempts. This turn of events is not particularly surprising because, I would argue, the Solonian measures had not entailed any fundamental change in the economic situation of the poor. In the long run, they could be expected to once again fall into debt to the elite, who could also use their control over the political and judicial system to further their own interests. Furthermore, while the poor did not risk slavery for debt (of which we hear nothing more in Athens), they may have suffered economically due to their inability to use their own person as collateral (Ober, 1989, p. 62). Hence, over time, it is likely that discontent with elite rule once again became widespread: only this time it led to tyranny.

Like other tyrants of his age, Peisistratos spent on public goods. He adorned the city and fostered public cults. This decreased the power of the old nobility, because their members had a considerable hold over traditional religion. The public activities strengthened the tie between the state and the common citizens and increased the legitimacy of Peisistratos' rule. Furthermore, he organised loans to farmers, and a system of travelling judges. Both these measures reduced the dependence of the common people on the traditional aristocracy. It was credible that Peisistratos would continue his policy of supporting the common people against the aristocracy – the latter were surely against him and he could not afford to alienate also the hoplites if he hoped to stay in power.

An important consideration for the Peisistratids – as for any ruler (North, 1981) – was their ability to reward those who supported their regime, which depended both on their revenues and on their other expenditures. Under Peisistratos, tax revenues likely increased with the increase in trade and real incomes. Another important source of revenue was the personal assets of Peisistratos and his sons (Hippias and Hipparchos), which included property in the Mount Pangaeus region (in Thrace), well-known for its gold mines. Peisistratos died in 527 and Hipparchos was assassinated in 514, leaving the other son, Hippias, as single ruler of Athens.

As time passed, the need for military expenditures increased in Athens. Peisistratos himself largely ruled without external conflicts (Aristotle *The Athenian Constitution* 16.7), but his sons were engaged in wars (Thukydides 6.54.5). Andreades (1979) suggests that their expenditures were greater than their father's. Furthermore, the threat from the Persians increased after the fall of Lydia in 546. About this time, the trireme – an expensive and specialised warship – was increasingly adopted. This added considerably to the cost of war and implied state navies (Gabrielsen, 1994; Morris, 2009). The Persians built a fleet in the late 520s. As a result of Darius' campaign against the Scythians, the Persians took control of much of Thrace, probably in 512, making income from the Mount Pangaeus area a very uncertain source of revenue for Hippias at best (Lewis, 1988, p. 297). The Persian expansion would also have reduced any revenue from Sigeon,[14] which may have been seen as a family possession (Andrewes, 1982b, pp. 403–404).

Hence at the structural level we would expect that Hippias was increasingly unable to credibly commit to rewarding his followers to the same extent as before. The deteriorating balance between revenues and expenditures helps explain why Kleisthenes of the Alkmaionid family managed to form a coalition that ended Hippias' rule. The loss of the Thracian possessions may have been instrumental – it certainly coincides nicely in time (probably in 512) with the first attempt by Spartans to oust him (probably in 511) and their eventual success (in 510). This being said, we should also note that the decline of tyranny was a trend in the Aegean at this time (Morris, 2009).

There appeared an additional reason to kick out the Peisistratids, namely a boost of government revenue. Picard (2001) shows that the rich vein of silver in Laureion which was used to build the fleet that defeated the Persians at Salamis, was probably discovered long before Themistokles persuaded the Athenians to use the accumulated wealth this way in 483/2. The important and overlooked point, Picard argues, is that it simply must have taken a long time to develop the mines. When this is taken into consideration, a likely date for the original discovery of the rich deposit is sometime before 510, i.e. before the fall of the Peisistratids. Such a discovery would have been a mixed blessing for Hippias. The richness of the find would have been obvious early on. In the long run, Hippias could expect an increase in revenue that would be used to reward his followers. In the short and medium term, however, there would not have been great deal of silver available, and the main effect is likely to have been an increased propensity to revolt against Hippias' rule. An expected increase in state revenue also made it more attractive to be in a position to govern the state.[15]

4.4 A democratic shift in Athens, but not during the leadership of Kleisthenes

After the fall of the Peisistratids, it is a good guess that everybody expected a return to traditional elite competition for power. Tyranny was – after all – just an extreme outcome of the aristocratic rivalry (Osborne, 1996a, pp. 272–285). The Peisistratids had not changed the formal institutions. For the same reason, we would expect to see a new revolutionary situation build up, unless the Peisistratid measures protecting the common farmers from the elite (travelling judges, state loans, etc.) were retained. The outcome would probably have been a shift of political power of some sort to the poor majority, in particular as the military importance of the well-to-do farmers and the poor people continued to grow and was emphasised first at Marathon and later at Salamis.

However, in the ensuing political struggle, Kleisthenes inadvertently took a step that kick-started a long-term process of democratising developments – he turned to the common people for support in the aristocratic struggle. This was an unprecedented action (Ostwald, 1988, p. 305).

Kleisthenes' action and his success in the ensuing conflict temporarily put him in a position where he could reform the constitution. He divided Attica into 139 *demes*, distributed among ten new artificial tribes, and a new Council with 500 members replaced the Solonian council. We do not know if Kleisthenes made any changes in the criteria for eligibility, or any other significant changes with respect to the formal rules for the archonships, the Assembly or the Areopagos. Kleisthenes probably gave the Assembly the right to hear political trials – this was no longer the exclusive right of the Areopagos (Hansen 1999, p. 37). He probably introduced the well-known process of ostracism.

Many scholars argue that the *deme* reform was used to reduce the influence of the old nobility over the population (thus strengthening Kleisthenes' relative position), for example, by breaking the political influence of old cult centres (Salmon, 2003).[16] Furthermore, Ostwald (1988, pp. 310–319) and several other scholars suspect that Kleisthenes tried to manipulate the distribution of *demes* in order to increase the influence of his family, but we do not know if the irregularities were introduced after Kleisthenes.[17]

In the literature (including our ancient sources) Kleisthenes is depicted both as a self-interested manipulator and as a visionary democrat (Osborne, 1996a, pp. 299ff.).

Once again, Davies' (2003) sobering warning against the latter view applies. What is noteworthy, given the subsequent development, is, as Snodgrass (1980, p. 198) notes, the "absence of anything that was *necessarily* democratic about his administrative provisions". This is what one would expect, because there is no reason to believe that Kleisthenes was a democrat, and the structural forces discussed above would hardly have been strong as early as two years after the fall of the Peisistratids. We will return to Kleisthenes' motives and actions in the next chapter.

Despite these reforms, it seems likely that people expected that the running of the state would go on pretty much as before. The political institutions were the same, even if a new Council had replaced the Solonian Council of 400. The functions of the different bodies were also the same. "The elites could certainly hope to retain control of the state through elected magistracies, control of debate in the Council and Assembly, and the powers and moral authority of the Areopagus" (Ober, 1989, p. 73).

The most important of Kleisthenes' actions, however, was the fact that he violated the unwritten *informal rules* of the aristocratic struggle for power when he appealed to the common people – an important institutional change. The elite realised that they had a new tool to use against each other. As the aristocracy adapted to the new situation, they would become more and more prone to advocate measures that would benefit the common people. "Rich and well-born Athenians competed vigorously, sometimes savagely, with each other for political influence, and they used appeals to the masses as ploys in their ongoing political struggles" (Ober, 1989, p. 84).

Consequently, the changes that followed were an effect of the struggle for power within the elite. The crucial development ought to have been when the common people were used and allowed to choose between different courses of action and to choose which faction to support. Originally the common people had been only incidental to the aristocratic struggle for power, as dependants or followers of different noble families. The clash had not taken place in the Assembly, which was only used to ratify the decisions of the elite.

However, the rules of the game for aristocratic competition had now been changed. Kleisthenes had set a very important example when he appealed to the common people. It is possible that he took his issue to the Assembly.[18] Either way, it was apparently an unprecedented step to suggest that the people should directly take part in a decision, in opposition to the archon (Isagoras). Tridimas (2011) is likely correct when he sees the first real case of direct democracy – i.e. actual decisive voting by everyone in the Assembly – as a Kleisthenic innovation. The next logical step would be voting on issues in the Assembly after an open debate between different leaders and their policies.

Sometimes the society depicted in Homer is taken as an indication that the assembly had considerable power already before Kleisthenes turned to the *demos*. It seems to me that it is a mistake to make inferences from Homeric society with respect to Kleisthenes' relationship to the *demos* for two reasons. First, the Athenians had for several generations been living under the governance of magistrates and a council (probably the council of the Areopagos). So even if the assembly had some power at the time when Homer was composing the *Iliad* and the *Odyssey*, it would likely have been dissipated. The magistrates and the council had had more than 150 years to get a firm grip on the governance of the *polis*. Second, the situation in Homer when the elite have to contend with popular feelings is no general mass meeting – it is the army that they are facing, or the warrior companions of a *basileus*.

We learn from Herodotos (5.66.2) that Kleisthenes turned to the people (*demos*) and took them into his group of *hetairoi* (thus making precisely the distinction I am making here between the *hetairoi* and the common citizens)

At this point event history makes an inevitable appearance in this structural account. In the absence of Kleisthenes' particular action, Athens may well have remained an oligarchy with slightly more power to the common people than before Peisistratos (as the experiences of other Greek city-states show). Kleisthenes hit upon a solution to his short-term problems that had tremendous long-term consequences: since it changed the nature of aristocratic competition for power. It provides an example of how particular circumstances can set a society on a path that ends in democracy.

Gradually, as people became more aware of the issues at stake, and with new measures increasing the influence of the less affluent majority (cf. below), the process would become self-reinforcing. Those who tried to direct Athenian policy constituted a relatively small group and they were usually active in politics for a considerable time (Hansen, 1999, Chapter 11). They are traditionally labelled "politicians", although this term is somewhat misleading as, for example, there were no political parties or elections in the modern sense.[19] To be successful in the Assembly, a political leader would increasingly have had to advocate measures that benefited the poor majority, even though leaders themselves were initially of high birth. "Whatever authority they wielded was dependent upon the people's continuing approval [...] rhetores [politicians] were judged each time they stood up in the Assembly" (Ober, 1989, p. 121).

Once again, an important aspect of politics in ancient Greece is that there was abundant information about "how things might have been": information about other political constitutions and about the economic situation in socially and culturally similar neighbouring states. In history we often find ideas and institutions being borrowed across communities and Snodgrass (1986, p. 53) concludes that several examples "suggest that the Greek *poleis* kept an alert eye on the constitutional progress of their peers, and were ready to learn from them". Hence the belief system of the inhabitants in a *polis* encompassed the notion that other institutional structures were eminently feasible.

The Assembly was a forum for repeated transactions between politicians and the voting public. This made conditional co-operation possible. A politician could build up a stock of confidence, and the populace would vote for his proposals as long as he did not disappoint them. Political support depended upon the politician's reputation and the voters' confidence in him: that is, on his previous actions.[20] The politician who tried to shift his power base would reasonably be regarded with suspicion. The Athenians were also well aware that politics was an arena of conflicting interests.[21]

> Now, first of all, you should reflect that no human being is naturally either an oligarch or democrat: whatever constitution a man finds advantageous to himself, he is eager to see that one established.
>
> (Lysias 25.8)

When Perikles introduced public pay, allegedly to outdo Kimon in popular support (Aristotle *The Athenian Constitution* 27.3–4), he also became more dependent on the common people. If a successful politician was backed by the poor, he may have had little alternative but to try and maintain that support[22] (there was no body of government officials who could act as a power base for a ruler, which is in contrast to almost any other non-primitive society). Eventually all successful politicians had to conduct policies that were largely beneficial to the poor majority in the Assembly. This could help to explain the gradual introduction of public pay for jurors, council members and other magistrates. The pay to, for example, jurors, may also have been motivated by a need for an increased capacity to handle disputes that followed with the Empire and the increase in trade. The same applies, *mutatis mutandis*, to administrators.

The shift that occurred at the top of the political pyramid was mirrored in changing incentives for the individual citizen. Their material and psychological dependence on the local nobility disappeared gradually, but this would not automatically make them take part in the political process as free agents. Even a direct democracy faces the obvious free-rider problem: the cost of voting compared to the small probability that your own vote will count.[23]

However, with each new measure that favoured the common people their stake in the political process increased, and we can envisage an increasing awareness of what could be achieved through that process. They had more to lose and hence were more likely to attend the Assembly. Two additional factors favoured an intensified popular participation. First, the privilege of citizenship had become more important and therefore it was less attractive to emigrate (exit). This increased the likelihood that the inhabitants would take an active part in politics (voice). Second, for the ordinary people the incentives to take part in the political process increased, because trade and reliance on imports increased (cf. Chapter 6). Reliance on market relationships rather than self-sufficiency implies that one is more affected by public policy measures (price regulations, control of weights and measures, import and export policies etc.). Furthermore, the Athenian Empire meant that a significant portion of the Athenian population had a direct interest in foreign policy because it affected their livelihood.

Gradually the common people grew accustomed to taking part in the governing of the state. A series of victories – in particular those at Marathon (490) and Salamis (480) – emphasised that military power and the protection of the state depended on the population at large (Aristotle *Politics* 1304a17–24). Again their perception of the world arguably changed. In consequence they became more appreciative of democratic reforms and more hostile to those who tried to reduce their influence. For this development it was of considerable importance that many citizens served as councillors and magistrates (see below), and thereby were well-informed about the running of the state and the political process and mechanisms.

Taken together, these factors gradually led the Athenians through a number of democratising measures. From a beginning with competing leaders who sought their power base mainly among the aristocratic factions, the Athenians ended up in the situation where only those politicians who sought support from the poor majority would be successful in the long run. The irony, as Ober (1989, p. 85) has pointed out, is that "as the elites gained victories over their enemies by sponsoring democratic reforms, there were fewer and fewer institutions that they could control directly".

Between the year of Marathon and the outbreak of the Peloponnesian War (i.e. 490–431), the constitution of Kleisthenes was gradually transformed into what was for the male citizens a far-reaching direct democracy (women, non-citizens and slaves were excluded). When the transition was complete, archons, councillors and other magistrates were all chosen by lot for one year. Jurors were selected by lot for one day (from a panel of 6,000, drawn by lot for one year). The only elected magistrates of importance were the ten generals. Citizens of all classes could speak in the Assembly and serve as jurors in the popular courts. Theoretically, the lowest property class were still excluded from the council and offices, but this rule probably already ceased to function in the fifth century. Each man could only serve twice in his lifetime on the council (once in other offices). The Areopagos had lost almost all of its judicial powers. Citizens were paid for serving as jurors, on the council and in other offices.

Few of the changes can be dated with any certainty. Selection by lot for archons was introduced in 487. Several of the other reforms occurred around 460–450, and are associated with Ephialtes and Perikles. For example, payment to jurors and magistrates were probably introduced by Perikles in the middle of the fifth century, and made it possible for even the very poor to serve.

This development was not uncontroversial; for example, Ephialtes was murdered and Thukydides (1.107.4–5) mentions an abortive aristocratic coup in 458/7.[24] Thukydides, son of Melesias (i.e. not the historian in the previous sentence), tried to rally the elite opposition in the Assembly in the 440s (Ober, 1989, pp. 88–89). Nevertheless, the process continued largely without causing violent attempts by the elite to regain control of the Athenian state. Several factors help explain this. The necessary condition was that it remained credible that the poor majority would show restraint in using its political power to tax the rich.

First, the existence of a middle class of military importance, consisting of well-to-do farmers, made democracy more acceptable to the rich elite because it ensured that the poor would not conduct taxation policies that were too radical. Second, in 478/7 the Delian league, later to become the Athenian Empire,[25] was formed as a military coalition against the Persians. Over time, it increased the prosperity of Athenian citizens in several ways, despite the cost of keeping a fleet (Morris, 2009). The poor gained from employment in the fleet and (from the 440s) in the building projects on the Acropolis.[26] For the rich, the Empire brought overseas acquisitions, while the poor could move abroad as settlers in colonies (cleruchies). Trade increased, and the revenue from harbour dues increased as Athens benefited from its position. Hence the rich Athenians had a positive interest in not rocking the boat, and the situation of the poor could improve without increasing the tax burden on the rich. Finley (1983, pp. 106ff.) argues that the remarkable stability of the Athenian democratic institutions compared to other city-states were due to the Athenian Empire (but note that this can only refer to the fifth century experience, not the fourth century). Third, it has been argued that landholdings in Attica were relatively egalitarian by 500 (Morris, 2002, 2004). An egalitarian distribution of assets meant that there was less of a threat of excessive taxation of the rich (Acemoglu and Robinson, 2006, pp. 35ff.). While the distribution of non-landed wealth was probably much less equal, such wealth was also more difficult to tax, being less visible (Gabrielsen, 1986). Fourthly, there was the revenue from the silver mines in Laureion.

4.5 The tenacity of Athenian democracy

Then the Peloponnesian War (431–404) obviously changed the situation. The Athenians lost the war, and with the loss of the Empire, the poor could no longer credibly commit not to start taxing the rich at much higher rates than before. Military expenditures and other public expenditure would in the future have to be financed through internal revenues. The magnitude of the internally financed military expenditures had already increased during the war, and revenues from taxation of trade must have been at low ebb immediately after the war.

So it comes as no surprise that members of the elite staged a *coup d'état* in 411, in the aftermath of the disastrous military expedition to Sicily, and that they used the Spartans to set up an oligarchy in 403, after the end of the war. These attempts by the elite to take over failed, and there were lots of contingent reasons for these two oligarchic coups. Nevertheless, it seems obvious that something had to give if future attempts by the rich to put an end to democracy were to be avoided.

The solution was to reduce the power of the Assembly and to increase the influence of those institutions where the elite had more influence, in particular the Areopagos.[27] In 403–399, the Athenians codified and revised their laws, and Hansen (1999) argues that the Assembly was deprived of a number of its powers. For example, the right to pass laws (*nomoi*) was transferred to boards of *nomothetai*, appointed by lot for one day from the 6,000 jurors that were chosen by lot for one year.[28] The authority of the council of the Areopagos was gradually extended from 403 and through the fourth century (Hansen, 1999, p. 290). For example, in 403/2, the Assembly decreed that the Areopagos was to supervise the administration of the laws by the magistrates.[29] Around 355 the Assembly was deprived of its jurisdiction in major political trials (Hansen, 1999, p. 152).

With the restoration of democracy in 403/2, payment to jurors and councillors was reinstated. Payment to magistrates, however, was not reintroduced. Instead, Assembly pay was introduced and raised in the decade following the restoration of democracy (Hansen, 1999, pp. 188, 240–241, 254). It is probably significant that Assembly pay was introduced *after* the reduction of the powers of the Assembly, while payment to magistrates was discontinued, which meant that these positions would be in the hands of the relatively affluent in society. I would also argue that it is unlikely that the *working* poor could afford to sit as jurors. The expected pay for turning up would be around one obol – 1 in 3 chance of being picked, remuneration three obols (Hansen, 1999, Chapter 8) whereas the daily wage is usually thought to have been between one and two drachmas (1 drachma = 6 obols).

Hence the overall tendency of the reforms was to reduce the threat of excessively populist policy decisions. The elite was given more influence over what happened in the Athenian democracy, thus making it more acceptable to them. In retrospect (and arguably also as perceived at the time), this was necessary for the continued existence of democratic rule. It nicely illustrates Ober's (2008) argument that the Athenian democracy showed great capacity to adapt its institutions to changing circumstances. While many authors note that the Athenians wanted a "less radical" democracy, it is only with Lyttkens (2010a) that the changes have been connected to the issue of credible commitments with respect to treatment of the rich.

4.6 Ideology and belief system

Another structural argument is Morris's (1996, 2000) suggestion that the origins of Athenian democracy lie in a structural change in ideology. As noted in the previous chapter, he argues that from the eighth century onwards, there is a general trend towards egalitarianism and a conception of the state as a community of middling citizens. There is evidence in the material remains that the elitist ideology was under pressure, suggesting that private ostentation within the elite was considered in bad taste and that aristocratic competitive outlay had to take new and more socially acceptable forms. As also noted above, this trend was reversed in Athens around 700.

Following Morris, an increasing number of citizens in the archaic period came to believe in the "strong principle of equality", a belief that all members of society are sufficiently well qualified to take part in the collective decision making and none are so definitely better qualified that they should be entrusted with making the collective decisions. If one could point at a material explanation behind this ideology the importance of hoplite warfare is as good a candidate as any.

> [W]hen enough people hold views of this kind, it becomes possible – and perhaps logical – to respond to the collapse of an oligarchy [...] by developing new conceptions of majority rule, instead of simply finding a different group of guardians. This is what happened in Athens in 507.
>
> (Morris, 1996, p. 20)[30]

In support of this interpretation, there is some evidence for the emergence of "broadly egalitarian" political systems towards the end of the sixth century (Robinson, 1997). The problem however, as Robinson emphasises, is that even such a basic fact as what the ancient Greeks at that particular time meant by a term such as "the *demos*" is unclear and could vary considerably.[31]

A somewhat similar structural factor is the shifting military importance of different segments of the population. This has a practical side – the state is an organisation with a comparative advantage in violence (North, 1981, p. 21) – but also an ideological aspect. What kind of government is conceptually consistent with the distribution of military potential in the community? The importance of the hoplites has been noted several times,[32] but the military significance of the *thetes* has only been briefly mentioned. Raaflaub (2007a) argues compellingly that the growing importance of the members of the lowest property class in Athens, especially after Salamis and the formation of the Delian League – was an important factor behind the introduction of democratising measures from 462 onwards.[33] The importance of the navy (and the *thetes* with it) shaped the perception of the world of the Athenian citizens. It is conceivable that Kleisthenes contributed even less to the development than suggested above, but personally I believe his novel stratagem of appealing to the great majority was instrumental in bringing about democracy. We must remember that we know very little of what happened in the years 508–462, though we do know that lottery was introduced for the selection of archons in 487 (see section 5.3).

There is no need to choose between these structural factors and the structural account earlier in this chapter – on the contrary, they go very well together. It is certainly the case, for example, that a shift in ideological attitudes towards egalitarianism would have helped Kleisthenes in his appeal to the common people, and also possible that such a shift in attitudes made it successful (as a necessary or a sufficient condition). To my mind, however, the egalitarian ideology sits better as a complementary hypothesis than as *the* explanation. It cannot account for the slightly oligarchic changes after the Peloponnesian War, unless it is explained why and how the Athenians became less egalitarian in sprit.[34] Similarly, the poor became if anything more important in the military conflicts during the Peloponnesian War, with a greater use of lightly armed troops, so this does not help either with explaining the de-democratisation after the war.

If the ideological change is taken to be the explanation for the origin of democracy in Athens, it seems to imply that if Kleisthenes had not happened, somebody else would have, so Kleisthenes was incidental to the development of democracy. This is somewhat unsatisfactory, however, just as it is unsatisfactory to assume that efficient solutions will come about in society just because they are efficient. The same argument applies, *mutatis mutandis*, to the other structural discussions above. As I argued in the introduction, structural parameters set the limits of the possible, but for the actual course of events we should also look at the incentives of individual actors. This principle applies also, for example, to an event such as the popular uprising that followed upon the actions of Isagoras and the Spartans. So we will turn to look at individual incentives in the next chapter. First, however, property taxation in Athens also illustrates the importance of credible commitments.

4.7 Credible commitments and the changes in tax administration in the fourth century

The relationship between the power to tax and institutional change has already figured substantially in the account above. In this section we shall see that the risk of excessive taxation and the importance of credible commitments may help explain some specific institutional changes in the Athenian economy.

In the classical period, it was considered a duty and an honour for a rich Athenian citizen to perform a liturgy – to finance and manage certain functions for the common good. The trierarchy was a military liturgy; to commission and command a state-owned warship for one year. The other liturgies concerned the religious festivals. In the fourth century there were about 100 festival liturgies each year (Davies, 1967). The cost of a liturgy often exceeded the annual wage of a skilled workman. The major festival liturgy is first attested at Athens in 502/1 (Capps, 1943). The trierarchy is attested for Samos in 494 and for Athens and other states in 480.[35] Having been appointed to perform a liturgy, it was punishable to avoid it, and avoiding liturgical service could be used against you in court.

A few years into the Peloponnesian War (428/7) a direct tax on wealth is mentioned for what is perhaps the first time – the *eisphora* (Thukydides 3.19.1).[36] It was a tax on property, usually used in times of war. In the following century it was a normal feature of the economic and political life of the Athenians. In 378/7, the citizens liable for the *eisphora* were divided into 100 symmories and a general reassessment was made. This was probably also the time when the *proeisphora* was introduced; the 300 richest citizens (three for each symmory) could be called upon to advance the total amount of the *eisphora* to the state and thereafter to reimburse themselves from the other taxpayers. It also seems likely that in 358/7 the symmory system was introduced or extended to cover those liable to perform trierarchies.[37]

Volunteering liturgists were important throughout the classical period. Towards the end of the fifth century, however, and frequently during the fourth century, we hear of people being accused of evading their civic obligations, of not performing liturgies or not paying the *eisphora*, and of concealing their wealth (Cohen, 1992, Chapter 6; Gabrielsen, 1986; Lyttkens, 1994). It is difficult to tell if this was a new phenomenon, because we have few sources from before 430 that could be expected to bring up such issues. There are, however, several reasons to believe that tax evasion increased over time. First, the growing importance of non-landed wealth (in the increasingly monetised economy) made tax evasion easier. Second, the gradual emergence of economically rational behaviour in all likelihood reinforced the tendency of tax evasion.[38] Third, the expected average level of property taxation increased in the fourth century, when the tribute from the Empire was lost and the cost of running the democracy was higher (Hansen, 1999). Furthermore, the rich now had less to gain from the Athenian wars.

As tax evasion became an important topic in the forensic speeches, people's belief systems changed in the direction of expecting more economically rational behaviour from others (and less quasi-voluntary compliance), which would again increase the propensity to evade taxation.

On the face of it, the formalisation of the *eisphora* was to the disadvantage of the taxpayers. However, as noted in Lyttkens (1994), the introduction of the *proeisphora* meant that the rich elite had gained considerably in influence over the use of the tax. Arguably, it could only be used with the implicit approval of the rich elite. This change in the system of property taxation may then have been a necessary condition for the continued survival of Athenian democracy, in addition to the changes discussed in section 4.5. "A ruler's costs and benefits from abusing rights depend on administrative capacity and who controls the administration" (Greif, 2005, p. 748). When the rich control the tax administration, democracy becomes more acceptable.

It does not seem too far-fetched to suggest that the introduction of symmories for the trierarchies had a similar effect to the *proeisphora* system, namely that it increased the elite's administrative control over the use of the tax.

Finally, it is a common argument that a large part of the trade in Athens was in the hands of foreigners. This is often explained by the fact that the Athenians tended to take a disparaging view of commercial activities, and did not want to lower their own status by partaking in them (Finley, 1973, 1999; *contra* Bitros and Karayiannis, 2008). However, it has not been noted that there was a fundamental institutional reason for this "specialization". Foreigners were not allowed to own landed property in the Greek city-states. The Athenians developed some contract-enforcing institutions in the second half of the fourth century, which facilitated the use the legal system in commercial disputes (see section 7.3). The pertinent fact is that the use of these institutions inevitably entailed a disclosure of one's wealth. Therefore, these contract-enforcing institutions could be used efficiently only if the state could credibly commit not to transgress the property rights of those who used them. And this was possible precisely in the case of foreign merchants, who could easily move to another locality with their assets, assets which did not include landed property. Any attempt by the Athenian state to tax them at excessive rates would simply have led to exit. The Athenians themselves were in a very different position, often with a very substantial part of their wealth in landed property. Hence, the commercial activities of Athenian citizens were less likely to be favourably affected by this set of institutions.

4.8 Concluding remarks

In this chapter, I have argued that the development of political institutions interacted with the ability to extract revenue from different groups in society, and the concomitant ability to reward the supporters of the regime. It sheds additional light on the consequences of Solon's reforms, the fall of the Peisistratid dynasty, and, perhaps in particular, the deradicalisation of the democracy after the Peloponnesian War. An ideological shift towards egalitarianism and a shift in the military importance of the poor may also have contributed to these developments.

We have thus focused on the structural factors that lay behind the institutional changes in Athens. These structural considerations provide the overall parameters that delimit the potential paths for Athenian society. The rational-actor perspective, in particular the model of Acemoglu and Robinson, also provides useful insights into the specific decisions taken at important junctures. In the next chapter, we will look in detail into the decisions of Solon and Kleisthenes, and the decision to appoint archons by lot. The latter was arguably instrumental in dismantling the powerful position of the Areopagos.

Finally, we may note, as this account is based on the assumption of rational action, that this arguably becomes a better and better description of individual behaviour in ancient Athens as we move up in time. It seems likely that an increasing preponderance of market relationships changed peoples' view of the world, in particular regarding the behaviour they expected from others (namely rational-action, as time moved on). This would obviously feed back into the process of institutional change. This theme will be explored in Chapter 7.

5 The road to democracy part two

Institutional change as individually rational action

Rationality, self-interest and unintended consequences – three concepts that encapsulate the decision making on the Athenian road to democracy. In this chapter we will focus particularly on individual incentives. In the literature on Athenian history, it is usually implicitly assumed that the problem of collective action is somehow solved. For example, the "revolutionary situation" that prompted the appointment of Solon as mediator is taken on board without considering what kind of incentives could have motivated *individual* Athenians to take part in an uprising against the established elite rule. Similarly, the structural account in the previous chapters in some instances took for granted (or at least implied) that the emergence of structurally motivated changes needs no special explanation – they represent their own rationale. In contrast, the approach in this chapter is that usually nothing will change unless there are individuals with an incentive to act. In other words, the collective action problem comes to the fore.

The analysis will focus on three formative moments, where solutions to short-term problems put the Athenians on a path that eventually led them to a direct democracy. There are at least three reasons to look at these formative moments and the associated decision-making. The first is to show that the decisions taken at these junctures are entirely understandable as self-interested actions and that there is no need to attribute unselfish motive to these actors. The rational-actor perspective once again provides a consistent set of explanations for the institutional developments. In this sense it is a parallel to the analysis in Chapter 4. A lot more detail will be provided here, but this is not to say that all activities and decisions will be covered.[1]

Second, it will be argued that the rational-actor perspective adds to our understanding of the actions of key decision makers in Athens, and of the effects triggered by the institutional changes they enacted. Third, these effects in several instances demonstrate the importance of unintended consequences of purposeful actions. For example, Solon inadvertently paved the way for the tyranny of Peisistratos, and without the activities of Peisistratos and his sons it seems unlikely that Kleisthenes could have used an appeal to the people at large to get the better of his rival Isagoras.

The first two moments are intimately associated with the acts of two individuals – the reforms of Solon and Kleisthenes respectively. The third moment is the introduction of appointment by lottery. This is often associated with Themistokles – the architect behind the victory at Salamis. However, this association may be a spurious one of timing rather than Themistokles being the actual decision maker. These are three crucial moments in Athenian history: at each point things could have ended differently and the subsequent process of institutional change would have followed a different path.

As a preliminary, let us listen again (and this time more extensively) to what John Davies has to say about decision-making over formal institutions in this period. He expresses a deep and long-standing unease about current ways of approaching the phenomenon of the emergence, consolidation and spread of Greek democracy. He argues that (almost) all approaches:

> share the basic assumption that [...] ideas, ideals and theories [of antiquity] played a major part in the processes of social, political, and institutional change [...however...] without any substantial body of comparative evidence, without any general theory of politics [...] it must have been impossible, except in the crudest way, either to produce a detailed analysis of existing society or to create in the imagination an ideal towards which existing society might be directed.
>
> (2003, pp. 320–323)

Furthermore, nearly all the approaches in the modern literature seem very "remote from the actual business of managing a polity on the ground, or from the sorts of preoccupation and language which one can see in the public documentation [...] from the end of the sixth century onwards". He suggests instead that:

> the world of Herodotos was not being driven by a conscious outreach towards any identifiable "democratic" goals or ideals; that the system which its inhabitants came to call *demokratia* was little more than a bodged-up set of responses to particular situations and crises; and that insofar as it had any unifying principle at all, that principle [was] the perceived need to *prevent* this or that unpleasant or undesirable development or practice from continuing or from gaining a foothold.

I have quoted Davies extensively, because his comments represent a view which is very much like my own regarding the motivation behind the institutional changes that eventually produced the Athenian democracy. While his critique seems to fall primarily on those who see in Solon or Kleisthenes a democratic visionary, it also has implications for analyses based on the assumption of self-interested individuals. This is not tantamount to saying that the Greeks were incapable of rational decision making on political and institutional issues in the archaic or classical periods. However, it does mean that with a rational-actor model, we should think carefully about what the actors are likely to have seen as being in their best interest. This should be based on what they can reasonably be assumed to have known and to have been able to imagine.

As we shall see, the analysis of the specific reasons for institutional change is consistent with Davies' view of the motivation for the actors involved. So, for example, I will argue that Solon was trying to stop a revolution, to prevent the aristocracy from losing their dominant position and to prevent tyranny, while Kleisthenes was trying to prevent an aristocratic rival from taking the leading position in Athenian affairs (something which could have forced the Alkmaionids into exile again). We may note that the individuals' belief systems at the time would definitely have included revolutions and coups as realistic possibilities. That the loser in an aristocratic contest for power could suffer in status and influence would have been a very familiar situation at the time.

5.1 Solon and his reforms: wise decisions, hardly democratic, and with unintended consequences

To recapitulate from Chapter 4, the Athenian experience prior to 600 fits into the general social development in Greece. Intense rivalry within the elite, tensions between the traditional elite and other groups in society, attempts at elite self-regulation (magistracies, written law) and attempted violent takeovers by would-be tyrants.

As in many other states, the attempts at self-regulation did not eliminate elite factional struggle. Furthermore, they did little to change the individual incentives of members of the elite to exploit the ordinary farmers. Consequently, the "revolutionary situation" in 594 (section 4.2), with the people rising against the elite, is no surprise. It would hardly have been a major surprise at the time either. However, in a rational-actor perspective it would be gratifying to identify some incentive strong enough to motivate *individual* actors and to overcome the collective action problem. As we know, the outcome was that the aristocrat Solon was appointed mediator, apparently with full powers to reform the institutions of the Athenians.

We know very little about the details of the situation that produced Solon's reforms. The reforms themselves are better known, though much is also obscure. As mentioned in Chapter 1, it is impossible to tell with certainty which measures were actually introduced by Solon.[2] Almost all our material on Solon comes from fourth-century sources or later, and belongs to the political debate of that century. To describe any law (including manifestly new ones) as "Solonian law" meant that the law implicitly was a Good Thing (a current-day parallel would be when someone in a Swedish political debate claims that something "improves welfare"). Solon's constitutional reforms are even more elusive than his laws and probably did not form part of his formal law code. Even the testimony of Aristotle is sometimes problematic (Hansen, 1999, p. 50). The general problem, as Raaflaub (2007b, pp. 7–8) notes, is that people simply did not know much about what had taken place so long ago and they had no clear understanding of how different archaic Athens had been from the community they knew. Finally, the purpose of the reforms is a field open for speculation, because it has to be deduced largely from the reforms themselves.[3]

Hence the interpretation of Solon's measures depends on how one constructs the context of the reforms and the theoretical perspective employed. By combining the account of general social development in Greece with the rational-actor perspective, I suggest that we obtain a coherent and plausible account of Solon's reforms and the motives behind them. Furthermore, the literature generally seems to have failed to recognise that several details of the reforms are such that their effects plausibly coincide with Solon's self-interest.

Since Solon was of noble birth himself, the most straightforward assumption regarding his objectives is that his ambition was to secure continued aristocratic leadership. As noted in the previous chapter, Ober (1989, p. 64) argues that "Solon was attempting to establish a sociopolitical order in which the privileges of the elite would be secured by granting minimal rights to the poor."

Morris (2000, pp. 169–171) sees Solon as an exponent of the "middling ideology" that we encountered in Chapter 4, but Foxhall (1997, p. 121) argues that Solon's statements can just as easily be read as "a viewpoint from firmly inside the elite, but with some sympathy [...] for those outside the power-holding clique". When describing his reforms in retrospect, Solon says that he protected the rich against shameful treatment, and that they might deem him as a friend. To the poor, he says, he gave only as much as was fitting. He rebukes the *demos* for having demanded too much, but also announces that he has done more for them than they had ever dreamt of (Aristotle *The Athenian Constitution* 12). It is also noteworthy that Herodotos – the testimony that lies closest in time to Solon – knows him simply as a lawgiver, and attributes "democracy" to the actions of Kleisthenes. This seems to me clearly problematic for any attempt to attribute democratic visions to Solon.

In order to preserve the position of the traditional elite, Solon needed to reduce the dissatisfaction with aristocratic rule in general (among those who had "risen against the notables"), and to reduce the risk of tyranny. It would at this point in time have been obvious that tyranny was a realistic threat – a part of the perception of the world, both due to the experiences in other city-states and Kylon's unsuccessful coup in Athens a generation before.[4] The means chosen by Solon were economic and political reforms, but the outcome was one of continued economic problems and the measures contained the germs of a new conflict, eventually contributing to the rise of tyranny in Athens.

Economic reforms

Solon reputedly alleviated the economic problems of the ordinary people by cancellation of debts, by freeing a group known as the *hektemoroi* (sixth-partners) from their obligations and by abolishing slavery for debt. Solon claims that he brought back many who had been sold abroad. Modern scholars rightly question the practicality of this ambition. However, the existence of Athenians sold abroad is noteworthy. Dependent labour was not a new phenomenon in Solon's time, and it need therefore not in itself have led to civil strife. However, it is possible that the selling of Athenian farmers to slavery abroad was a new phenomenon. Even though we find slaves in Homer, chattel slavery was a product of the archaic age.[5] In Homer, slaves are obtained as booty in war, not by taking control of your neighbours. In fact, enslavement for default could have been a feature of Drakon's reputedly harsh law code in Athens in 621 (Andrewes, 1982a, p. 381). The risk of being sold abroad would naturally cause much alarm among the poor and middling farmers. This does indeed look like a stimulus that is strong enough to create a revolutionary situation and to outweigh the free-rider problem of organised opposition.

Unfortunately for Solon and his peers, it seems unlikely that Solon's economic reforms would have reduced the risk for civil strife in the long or medium term. As already noted in Chapter 4, it is unlikely that Solon's reforms eliminated economic grievances for very long among the poor and middling farmers.

First, a problem of debt presupposes that the farmers sometimes needed to borrow from their rich neighbours. It is occasionally noted in the literature that abolishment of debt on the security of a person was not necessarily only to the benefit of the common people (Ober, 1989, p. 62; Starr, 1977, p. 186). A crop failure tends to be a collective risk for small farmers. Nothing had been done to prevent them from falling into debt again. Before Solon, all borrowing was on the security of personal liberty (Aristotle *The Athenian Constitution* 2.2). After Solon's reforms, the farmer would presumably have to borrow on the security of his land, reasonably on less favourable terms than before, since personal liberty seems to have been the preferred collateral. Alternatively they would have to sell their land and become tenants of the local landlord. For many farmers, the financial troubles seem likely to have grown worse than before the reforms. Rhodes (1993, p. 127) notes: "Solon may even have made life harder for some of the poor in that they would probably find it more difficult to borrow after his reform."

Second, to the extent that the elite made financial losses thanks to Solon's reforms, it would have increased their marginal utility of wealth and so *increased* their propensity to exploit the ordinary farmers.

Third, *if* Solon enacted a cancellation of debts, this may also have served to undermine his aim to avoid social disorder and tyranny. We learn from Aristotle (*The Athenian Constitution* 13.5) that Solon's reforms had impoverished some of the elite and that these were sufficient in number to be mentioned among Peisistratos' early followers.

The situation was a prisoner's dilemma in the sense that everybody in the elite would have benefited if they all had shown some restraint vis-à-vis the common people, but every member of the elite also had individual incentives to maximise the revenue extracted from those without political power (such power, remember, had been extended but only to the rich non-aristocrats). In his poems, Solon blamed the revolutionary situation on the rich and their love of pride and goods (Aristotle *The Athenian Constitution* 5.3). As indicated above, I interpret this and Solon's emphasis on moderation primarily as appeals to fellow members of the elite to restrain their behaviour (in order not to jeopardise their dominant position as a group). One could say that Solon tried to provide a focal point for the individual members of the elite in their search for useful strategies.

Hence the overall conclusion is that despite – but also partly thanks to – Solon's economic reforms, we would expect that discontent would increase over time, and provide potential support for would-be tyrants.

It is also worth noting that Solon may have had a more direct private interest in his reforms:

> In these matters some people try to misrepresent him, for it happened that when Solon was intending to enact the Shaking-off of Burdens [cancellation of debts] he informed some of the notables beforehand, and [...] he was out-manoeuvred by his friends, but according to those who want to malign him he himself also took a share. For these persons borrowed money and bought up a quantity of land, and when not long afterwards the cancellation of debts took place they were rich men.
>
> (*The Athenian Constitution*, 6.1–4)

In our rational-actor framework, it is certainly conceivable that Solon took the opportunity to benefit himself and some close friends. Aristotle's grounds for rejecting the story seem rather thin, namely that by not availing himself of the opportunity to become tyrant, Solon showed that he was less interested in his own well-being than that of the state. However, it does not take a great deal of risk aversion to prefer the long-term benefit of landed property to the glamorous but insecure position as tyrant. After all, the followers of Kylon had been killed in 630.

Political reforms

On the political side, arguably Solon's most important reform was the substitution of wealth for birth as the eligibility criterion for office. By making income the prerequisite for office, the wealthy non-aristocrats were co-opted into the ruling elite, thereby, as noted by Ober (1989, p. 63), eliminating them as potential leaders of the population at large and at the same time strengthening the ruling elite. The old aristocracy probably counted on dominating in the foreseeable future both the archonships and the Areopagos, and also the new council of 400 instituted by Solon (if there was a new one).[6] We do not know the procedure for electing the archons or the members of the new council, but it seems to me that in particular the archons may well have been elected by the Areopagos.[7] In any case the aristocracy probably had a reasonably strong influence over the common people. One would expect these informal rules to diminish the initial effect of the formal change in the prerequisites for office.

Solon is often presented as the great arbitrator, an independent sage trying to strike a proper balance between the different groups in society and interested only in bringing order to the community. "Historians today describe him [Solon] (variously) as a founding father of democracy, a popular leader who broke the Eupatrid monopoly of power, a moderate but visionary politician who brought civic justice to his society" (Manville, 1997, p. 124). "[M]odern scholars

have often been tempted to fix on Solon as the 'father of Athenian democracy'"
(Foxhall, 1997, p. 114). Both Foxhall (1997) and Davies (2003) warn
against attributing, with hindsight, democratic visions to Solon. From a closer
look at his reforms, it appears indeed that we are justified in agreeing with Ober
(1989, p. 64) that Solon was attempting to retain the privileges of the elite as far
as possible.[8] He let, for example, the Areopagos retain its role as "guardian of
the laws" (Aristotle *The Athenian Constitution* 8.4). As mentioned above, it is
probably significant that Herodotos, who is closest in time to Solon of the
sources that describe his activities, does not mention any connection with democracy. In Herodotos account Solon is a lawgiver (Herodotos 1. 29–34, 86;
2. 177).[9]

In fact, it is arguable that Solon gave away even less than usually recognised
on the political side (Lyttkens, 2004). As mentioned above, Solon reputedly
created a new council with 400 members. It is usually presumed that his council
of 400 had a probouleutic role, which means that issues had to be taken up there
before being put before the Assembly. Ober (1989, p. 64) notes that since the
agenda of the Assembly would be prepared by the new council, this reform gave
the elite control over dealings in the Assembly. "In Greek thought a probouleutic
council is always a restraint on the sovereign assembly" (Andrewes, 1982a,
p. 387). In other words, by introducing a council with such a role, Solon in effect
reduced the power of the Assembly, which is where those outside the elite could
make their opinion known collectively.

The new council of 400 could also be a means for the old nobility to obstruct
undesirable policy suggestions from the non-Eupatrids. Solon opened entry to
the elite, thereby attempting to reduce the risk of uprising against aristocratic
rule and to reduce the risk of tyranny, but he seems to have endeavoured to
retain aristocratic influence as much as possible.

With respect to the position of the new members of the elite (the rich non-
Eupatrids), the first thing to note is that the Solonian property classes were
defined by income in kind, that is, by agricultural produce. This may imply that
theoretically land was the only kind of wealth that counted against the property
qualification (van Wees, 2006). Agricultural land must have been primarily in
the hands of the old aristocracy. They would have been large landowners traditionally, and even though land was probably alienable at this time,[10] there was
no proper land market, and it would have taken the nouveau riche considerable
time (probably several generations) before they could have become large landowners[11] – an important reason for the rise of a group of rich non-aristocrats was
precisely the emergence of *new* sources of wealth, such as commerce (Murray,
1993, pp. 220ff.).

This does not mean that in practice landed wealth was the only thing that mat-
tered, because in the absence of any formal inspection, the extent of a person's
property would have to be inferred from what was public knowledge and from
his behaviour, such as his spending habits (Lyttkens, 1997). However, the definition in terms of agriculture produce was still to the disadvantage of the rich non-
aristocrats. This implies that the traditional aristocracy would remain dominant

for a long time. Entry into the elite would have been even slower if the council of the Areopagos elected the archons.

Solon's other political measures also deserve some comments. He introduced the rule that it was possible to appeal against the decision of an archon. We do not know where the appeal was heard. Many commentators assume that it went to a new court – the *heliaia* – instituted by Solon, but it seems perhaps more likely that it was heard by the Areopagos. It is often assumed that the *heliaia* was the whole Assembly sitting as a court.

According to Aristotle (*The Athenian Constitution* 9.1), the right of appeal was the most democratic of Solon's reforms. This argument seems to have its merit for fourth-century Athens, but it is not necessarily true for Solon's time.[12] One suspects that the common people would have remained dependent on the local landlord in judicial matters. That Peisistratos 50 years later found it expedient to provide travelling judges suggests that the courts were dominated by the elite. It seems more likely that in Solon's time the right of appeal was an example of elite self-regulation, just as Osborne (1996a, p. 187) has argued for the early written laws. To put some restrictions on the archon's actions conforms nicely to the general picture of elite self-regulation at the time. The elite wanted to ensure that their peers did not abuse their position while in office.

Furthermore, I would suggest that the right to appeal against a decision of an archon might (also) have been conceived as a measure designed to protect the old Athenian nobility. For the first time, non-Eupatrids could now become archons. Perhaps the nobility did not trust their jurisdiction, and wanted the right to appeal to the *heliaia* (or the Areopagos), which they felt they could control through the traditional ties of clientship, religion and kinship.

Planting a seed of tyranny

Be what they may, the reasons for Solon's reform had an unintended consequence: his political reforms contained the germs of a new kind of conflict. It is often noted that the abolishment of slavery for debt also meant that Athenian citizenship was formalised as a by-product (only Athenians could not be enslaved in Attica).[13] It has not been observed, however, that who was and who was not a citizen simultaneously became a critical issue at the other end of the social scale, among the rich and powerful. Solon's institutional reform meant that anybody who was rich enough was eligible to become archon, *provided* (presumably) that he was regarded as an Athenian citizen. Previously such a distinction had been irrelevant for political power, because those who were eligible were those of the right families. Now individuals from outside this group were to take up office.

Hence one would expect the question of a rich man's citizenship to become a matter of political dispute for the first time, and also expect this issue to be used in the elite struggle for power. This effect is likely to have increased over time, as people became aware of the potential of this new political weapon. Hence for those aspiring to power it was realistic to fear an accusation of not being an

Athenian, at least for those who did not belong to the traditional nobility. Before Solon, it seems reasonable to envisage a relatively free movement into Attica and a gradual and informal assimilation into the citizen body. Hence the fear of being accused of impure descent may have been felt by many, in particular as there was in all probability no formal definition of citizenship, implying that the net of accusations could be cast wide. This threat would have been a concern not just for the rich non-Eupatrids. Individual members of the elite would have found it advantageous to claim that those indebted to them were not qualified to be citizens and hence could be enslaved.

This explains why Aristotle (*The Athenian Constitution* 13.5.) reports that among the early followers of Peisistratos were those who were not of pure descent and who joined him out of fear, a fact that is often neglected but which explains a lot. Since Aristotle connects these followers of Peisistratos with a revision of the citizen roll after the fall of the Peisistratids (see below), it is also conceivable (in fact likely) that some nobles actively advocated a purge of the citizen roll in the period after Solon's reforms.[14] It is likely that Peisistratos kept the support of those threatened by granting them citizenship. It is also probable that he encouraged immigration and gave the immigrants similar privileges, thereby binding them to him and extending his power base.[15]

Unintended consequences – as always

Hence, in several important ways Solon's reforms were doomed to fail in his purpose of retaining aristocratic rule by reducing tension between the elite and population at large and by removing support for potential tyrants. The economic reforms failed to remove the incentives and grounds for exploitation of the ordinary population. The individual members of the elite contributed unintentionally to the outcome by pursuing their own objectives, perhaps also acting by force of habit, unreflective behaviour being a source of unintended consequences (Merton, 1936). Two of the groups of followers of Peisistratos mentioned by Aristotle (*The Athenian Constitution* 13.3–5) – those impoverished by cancellation of debt and those who feared for their citizen status – had their origin directly in Solon's reforms. These groups would have included some who belonged to the group of recently co-opted rich members of the elite, but also some members of the traditional aristocracy.

These effects of Solon's reforms were arguably in important respects unintended, at least as far as they contributed to the rise of tyranny. First, tyranny was not Solon's intention. The assumption of power by Peisistratos is not consistent with Solon's objectives as presented above (nor is it with any other reconstruction of Solon's motives that I have seen).[16] Second, it is also reasonable to believe that the effects connected to citizenship were unforeseen. If Solon had realised what would happen, he ought to have regarded his reforms as temporary measures and envisaged the need to make further adjustments soon. On the contrary, tradition has it that after his reforms, Solon travelled abroad for ten years because he did not wish to alter his provisions, and he wished for his laws to remain unaltered for 100 years[17] (Aristotle *The Athenian Constitution* 7.2 and 11.1; Herodotos 1.29).

We see here unpredictability enhanced by complementary strategic actions in different domains in the vein suggested by Aoki (2001, pp. 267–270): the risk of tyranny increased as new conflicts in the political domain reinforced the effects of the failure to remove economic grievances. It seems very likely that Solon realised that those who lost much of their wealth would be dissatisfied. However, this group would probably have been relatively harmless unless they had been accompanied by all those who felt threatened on the citizenship issue.[18]

Arguably, given the revolutionary situation, Solon would have been satisfied with finding a solution that retained aristocratic and elite rule; opening the door in the long run to some rich non-aristocrats would have been an acceptable sacrifice and a satisfying solution.

Did Solon intentionally encourage public spending?[19]

We have seen that the issue of who was a citizen and who was not likely came to the fore soon after Solon's reform. Above we noted how the issue of citizenship could have become a weapon in the elite political infighting. In addition, the division of the citizen body into four property classes and the decision to tie eligibility to these classes contains a similar issue. How you could demonstrate which property class you belonged to was now an issue. The need to show that you were one of those wealthy enough to be eligible to become archon etc. may have provided the impetus to spend for the common good, the practice so common in later Athenian history, and this may in fact have been Solon's intention.

In section 4.7 we encountered the liturgy system as a way to finance expenditure for the common good. In the classical period, it was considered a duty and an honour for a rich Athenian citizen to perform a liturgy – to finance and manage certain functions for the common good. The two most well-known liturgies were the trierarchy – to commission and command a state-owned warship for a year, and the *choregia* – to stage a dramatic production at a religious festival. The cost of a liturgy often exceeded the annual wage of a skilled workman.[20] The *choregia* is first attested at Athens in 502/1 (Capps, 1943; Davies 1967, 1992) and the trierarchy in 480. By that time it appears that the trierarchy was a common solution to the financing of naval warfare among the *poleis*.[21]

Lyttkens (1997) argues that the original impetus for spending of a liturgical nature may have come from Solon's reform of the eligibility criterion. These reforms gave the rich Athenians a direct incentive to spend in an ostentatious way, in order to show that they were wealthy and eligible for office – a signalling device. The reform transformed the conditions for belonging to the ruling elite. Before the reform there was an informal definition; everybody knew who could claim to be a Eupatrid. After the reform, there was a formal rule for eligibility, based on a property qualification. For the first time in Athenian history, there was a need to know with some precision the extent of a person's wealth,

but no such information was available except what was already public knowledge. Information is costly, and the liturgy system was never based on any
public investigation into a person's wealth. Even for landed property, there was
no register of who owned what (Finley, 1952, pp. 14–15).

The most efficient way of signalling great wealth is to give things away for
free. This implies a low marginal utility of consumption and wealth, and thus
that one possesses great wealth.[22] The perceptions regarding a person's wealth
may be formed not only by his total spending but also the kind of spending he is
undertaking.

The rich non-aristocrats could now trade wealth for political power. One possibility was spending on their own consumption. However, *liturgical spending*
could also be an attractive way of fulfilling the eligibility criterion. Liturgical
spending was by its very nature more publicly visible than traditional aristocratic
spending. In other words, Solon's reform may have provided the original
impetus which produced public spending by wealthy Athenians for the benefit of
the population in general – the liturgical attitude had been born.

This shows how self-interested behaviour can produce what seems like cooperative behaviour: voluntary contributions to the production of goods that are
public (warships) or at least exhibit non-rivalry in consumption (e.g. dramatic
productions). It is not my intention to argue that liturgies in a more formal sense
existed in Solon's time. Rather, I see the development of liturgical spending as a
long process with a concomitant gradual change in attitudes. The formalisation
of liturgies may well belong to the last years of the sixth century.

It may seem like an obvious alternative to invite the inspection of one's
wealth. However, any inspecting officials would likely have belonged to the old
aristocracy and oppose the eligibility of the nouveau riche. Formal objections
with respect to the property qualification would probably come from the archon
in office. Decision by an archon could be appealed, as noted above, and plausibly this included whether someone was sufficiently wealthy to be eligible. Proof
of wealth would have to be produced orally, without written documentation. One
can imagine that a candidate for office would have pleaded his wealth on the
basis of his commonly observed public expenditure, just as contestants in the
courts of the fourth century would use their public expenditure as arguments for
their cases. As long as there was no formal inspection of wealth, the extent of a
man's property would have to be inferred from what was public knowledge and
from his behaviour, such as his spending habits.[23]

Initially, the eligibility of the old aristocracy was not in question, as there had
been an informal rule that they belonged to the elite. Informal rules can dominate formal ones for quite a while (North, 1990). In this case, however, the
process of change must have been reinforced by the rich non-aristocrats who
altered their behaviour, and made claims of eligibility on the basis of the formal
rule. This would gradually change people's view of the world so that it was no
longer automatically accepted that an aristocrat was eligible. It seems like a
natural reaction if many aristocrats now found it expedient to signal their wealth
by increasing their spending – on friends, themselves, or on the general public.

We may conclude that incentive-wise, it would not be surprising if rich Athenians began spending on public projects after Solon's reform. This is an enticing thought in view of three facts. One is that in the period following Solon's reform we find public projects under way that would need financing. The second fact is that Solon himself showed an interest in several of these areas. The third fact is that two of these areas nicely coincide with the ones where we find the fully developed liturgy system in the next century (warships, religion). Taken together, these facts imply that it may well have been Solon's intention to provoke public spending by rich Athenians (a tantalising thought for a rational-actor enthusiast). We will now look in more detail on the areas of spending.

Davies (1981) finds that political ostentatious spending first appeared in the first third of the sixth century, that is, precisely in the period immediately following upon Solon's reforms. The objective was to participate in the chariot races at the pan-Hellenic festivals, which brought glory to the contestant but also to his city. The first attested example appears in 592,[24] two years after Solon's reforms.

Soon several other areas of public spending emerged, areas that would have benefited substantially from "proto-liturgies": sacrifices, temples, other public buildings, water supply and war finance. Several new cults which were explicitly public and practised "at public expense" appear from 570–560 and onwards. Indeed the first step in this process may have been taken by Solon himself (Davies, 1988, p. 379; Jacoby, 1944). It is an open question how these cults were financed. Temples were becoming very costly, being erected in stone, a cult usually entailed costs for sacrificial animals, etc.[25] Several of our earliest known examples of temples in Athens belong to the first half of the sixth century (Wycherley, 1978, pp. 144–145, 155, 183, 194). It is tempting to speculate that the financing of these new cults relied partly upon contributions of a liturgical nature.[26]

Similarly, the earliest public buildings in the public square (the agora) in Athens also belong to the early sixth century. It has been suggested that one of these might have been connected to Solon's council of 400. Furthermore the area for the agora may have been cleared in Solon's time (Wycherley, 1978, pp. 27–28). Growing urbanisation was accompanied by a need for a reliable water supply. By Solon's time this had prompted building activities by the tyrants in nearby Corinth and Megara (Hammond, 1982, p. 349). Solon himself encouraged the citizens of Athens to dig wells.[27]

Finally, we come to the financing of the Athenian navy. The sixth century witnessed the emergence of state navies, from a beginning where naval power depended on private ships owned by the aristocracy (Gabrielsen, 1985, 1994; Haas, 1985).[28] As mentioned before, in the course of the century, the trireme – a specialised and expensive warship – was increasingly adopted, adding to the cost of war considerably and entailing state navies (Morris, 2009). Single individuals could no longer be expected to supply ships in sufficient quantity.[29] Several of the earliest attested Athenian wars involved some sort of sea-power and are probably to be dated to the late seventh or early sixth century.[30] It is also possible that Athens possessed at least some triremes early in the sixth century.[31] In other words, Solon's reforms gave incentives for public spending at a time when the naval powers of the state can be assumed to have been something of an issue, as pointed out by Lyttkens (1997). Liturgical spending would have facilitated the transition from private to publicly owned ships.[32]

As a consequence of Solon's political reforms, rich Athenians had incentives to spend in a visible way for the benefit of the city-state. Was this his intention, i.e. did he foresee and desire this development? Our interpretation depends on what we know of Solon's motives and his ability to correctly predict the effects of his reform. Since Solon was a member of the old nobility, it is noteworthy that the liturgical expenditure would initially have fallen mainly on the non-aristocrats, with the aristocracy belonging to the beneficiaries.

With respect to Solon's motives, we have enough evidence to make it a viable hypothesis that his intentions with the reform included the emergence of liturgical spending. He showed a personal interest in several of the potential avenues of spending: (1) He was engaged in the question of water supply. (2) In his youth, Solon urged the Athenians to take action against the island of Salamis, which implies naval power (Andrewes, 1982a, p. 373). (3) He may have instituted a public religious festival (Davies, 1988, p. 379; Jacoby, 1944).

Overall, I think it is also reasonably plausible that Solon could have foreseen that his reforms would provide an incentive for publicly visible spending. After all, in later tradition, Solon was regarded as one of the seven wisest men in Greece (*The Oxford Classical Dictionary*, p. 1397). Reasonably he must have asked himself how his fellow citizens would react to such a drastic change in the rules of political competition. Spending of a political nature was a well-known phenomenon, although in more private forms. It would probably have been clear to him that the rich non-aristocrats would eagerly seek ways to demonstrate their wealth-based right to political influence and that this might entail spending on public projects, including some he himself had in mind.[33] A word of caution may be appropriate however: we should perhaps not look too much for far-sighted consequences of the actions of someone trying to find a reasonably satisfying solution in a revolutionary situation.

5.2 Tyranny paving the way for Kleisthenes

To set the stage for Kleisthenes, a few comments on the activities of Peisistratos and his sons are necessary. We know that elite factionalism did not end with Solon. There were problems with the election of archons several times in the following decades. After two shortlived attempts (the first in 561), Peisistratos established a tyranny in Athens in 546. His dynasty then ruled Athens for 36 years.

Peisistratos' motive for taking power was probably straightforward: to further his own interests.[34] Like other early tyrants, his rise to power was a reflection of aristocratic rivalry. Peisistratos arranged matters so that the poor could borrow from the state and thus became less financially dependent on the elite. He also provided a means of jurisdiction not involving the local nobility. These measures, and the support of new public religions, can all be seen as ways of breaking the power base of potential rival rulers (the fellow aristocrats) and at the same time tying the farmers to the Peisistratids.

Peisistratos introduced a 5 per cent tax on produce. It appears that Peisistratos used the tax mainly to secure his position. He paid his bodyguard, maintained friendly relations with other states, gave loans to farmers, etc. As other tyrants of his age, Peisistratos spent on public goods. He adorned the city and fostered public cults, as mentioned above. This reduced the power of the old nobility, which had a considerable hold over traditional religion. The public activities strengthened the tie between the state and the common citizens and increased the legitimacy of Peisistratos' rule. Such investments can be very profitable for a ruler by reducing the cost of enforcement (North, 1981).

In 510, Peisistratos' son Hippias had to flee from Athens. In the ensuing struggle, Kleisthenes of the Alkmaionid family lost against his fellow aristocrat Isagoras. As we saw in Chapter 4, Kleisthenes then turned to the common people for support, which prompted Isagoras to call in the Spartans. They tried to expel not just Kleisthenes but an additional 700 families. However, the council resisted and was joined by the people: the Spartans and Isagoras were the ones who had to leave the city.[35]

5.3 Kleisthenes – the political entrepreneur

There are two dominating views of Kleisthenes in the literature. One is that Kleisthenes was no friend of the *demos* and that his interests throughout were to further his own position and that of his family (the Alkmaionids). The other suggestion is that Kleisthenes was a selfless visionary democrat.[36] Such diverging views are already present in our ancient sources.[37]

The initial struggle between Kleisthenes and Isagoras should in all likelihood be seen as a straightforward return to the aristocratic competition for power (Ostwald, 1988, p. 305; Ober, 1996, p. 37; Osborne, 1996a, p. 294). The Peisistratids had formally left the Solonian constitution intact and the "political institutions [...] were, in early 508, still quite rudimentary and were still dominated by the elite" (Ober, 1996, p. 38). Struggle and competition for power were outstanding characteristics of the Greek elite in the archaic and early classical periods (Murray, 1993; Osborne, 1996a).

The natural assumption is that Kleisthenes aimed at establishing himself and the Alkmaionids as the leading family in terms of power and status. As leaders in the enterprise against the Peisistratids, this would have been the ambition of the Alkmaionids on their return from exile. As we shall see, this is also consistent with Kleisthenes' actions.

The fact that Kleisthenes turned to the people only *after* being worsted by Isagoras also clearly suggests that his original motive was personal power. That he turned to the people is hardly evidence of democratic or altruistic visions – he presumably had no other way of finding a rival power base that would allow him to turn the scales against Isagoras in the short run (a satisficing solution).[38] While it is true that Kleisthenes' actions inaugurated a process that produced the democracy of the mid-fifth century, this is likely to have been an unintended consequence.

There are two things that need an explanation in connection with Kleisthenes' rise to power. One is what Kleisthenes could suggest that gave him the upper hand against Isagoras – the archon in power. Second, what could it be that later motivated the citizens at large to take part in a violent riot against Isagoras and the Spartans (again an unprecedented occurrence)? As emphasised by Osborne (1996a, p. 294), there is nothing surprising in the struggle between Kleisthenes and Isagoras in view of the previous history of aristocratic factional conflict. What is new is the role played by the people. It is true that history has witnessed some by all appearances spontaneous revolutions (Cairo in 2011, Berlin in 1989, Paris in 1789, etc.) but these stand out precisely by being exceptional. As emphasised above, it is generally important to look at individual incentives, not just at collective rationality. The free-rider problem of collective action (Olson, 1971) suggests that it would be gratifying if we can find actors with strong incentives that could motivate them to take part in a violent uprising (and against the dreaded Spartans to boot, even if probably only a few of them were present).

In my view, and given the rational-actor perspective, most of the explanations proposed in the literature fail to provide a strong incentive for the support of Kleisthenes and the uprising against Kleomenes, even though the dissolution of the council implies that there would have been no lack of willing aristocratic leaders (none are mentioned in our sources however). Osborne (1996a, p. 294) suggests that there are three main alternatives. Military considerations were important, and some see a reorganisation of the army as the relevant mechanism (ten new tribes served as the basis for the army). In somewhat tangential support of this view the Athenians beat off a coalition of Spartans, Boeotioans and Chalcidians in 506. However, neither this nor hostility against Sparta seems to provide *individual* benefits of sufficient magnitude.

Osborne's third candidate is the constitutional changes enacted by Kleisthenes. The *deme* reform broke up the traditional social structure of Attica. As mentioned in Chapter 4, many scholars agree that an important reason for the *deme* reform was to undermine the authority of the old nobility and to reduce or eliminate their influence over the common people. For example, members of one aristocratic family would now be living in several *demes*, and the *demes* were distributed in such a way that the political influence of old cult centres was broken. While this may have looked like important benefits to Kleisthenes (see below) it is unlikely to have galvanised the people, even if ideological concerns can sometimes motivate behaviour.

Some authors argue that the people were incited to action by the prospect of more democratic rule. Against this I would argue, first, that the prospect of more democratic rule would have been too nebulous a benefit to suffice as an incentive. Second, Kleisthenes' reforms were probably *not* particularly democratic. It seems clear that Kleisthenes did not aim to put the effective control of the state in the hands of the common people because he left most of the aristocratic institutions intact. Furthermore, "he did not undercut the oversight powers of the Council of the Areopagus, abandon property qualifications for officeholding, or introduce pay for government service" (Ober, 1989, p. 73). Indeed, it has been said that a salient feature of Kleisthenes' thinking was "an absence of anything that was necessarily democratic about his administrative provisions" (Snodgrass, 1980, p. 198). One may add that any explicitly democratic reforms would probably have been met with widespread aristocratic opposition, not just from the supporters of Isagoras.

Ober (2007) argues that we are dealing with a spontaneous popular uprising against Isagoras and Kleomenes, and that this uprising constitutes the origins of Athenian democracy. It changed the political environment (the view of the world) and was a necessary (not sufficient) condition for the subsequent emergence of democracy. The prior conditions that made the revolution possible were the "strong principle of equality", the co-evolution of land warfare and agriculture, and the civilian consciousness fostered by the Peisistratids. Similarly, it has been argued that when the elitist ideology collapsed after 525, the general acceptance of middling values made democracy a real possibility and when an oligarchy fell apart as it did in Athens, democratic institutions were a possible response (Morris, 2000).

There is in fact, however, one other very good candidate for explaining the popular support for Kleisthenes and for causing a riot against Isagoras and the Spartans. The answer, I believe, is that citizenship appeared as a major issue once again, a solution proposed by Manville (1997) and Lyttkens (2004) that has not been given the attention it deserves.[39] As already mentioned, after the fall of the Peisistratids (and presumably before 508/7) the Athenians enacted a revision of the roll of citizens (*diapsephismos*) according to Aristotle's account (*The Athenian Constitution*, 13.5). The proposal for a *diapsephismos* is not surprising since it would have served the interest of the traditional nobility to restrict entry to the elite, just as before Peisistratos' rule. This measure created a great number of discontented persons – those already disenfranchised or threatened to be.

A revision of who had really the right to call himself a citizen would have been a process controlled by the aristocratic families through their authority in the old tribes.[40] In this situation "inevitably, powerful men took the lead in putting citizens to the test, and they would have endeavoured to protect the status of their own followings, and to strike out against the followers of their opponents" (Manville, 1997, p. 183). Hence the *diapsephismos* would quickly have become part of the fight for leadership in the *polis*. Furthermore, Manville (1997, pp. 177, 183) emphasises that there were no centrally agreed rules for the implementation of the *diapsephismos*, which opened possibilities for arbitrariness and manipulation. This lack of formal procedure meant that not just those who had immigrated under the Peisistratids but more or less *anybody* could be at risk. Precisely the "notion that any 'outsiders' might be able to become members of the polis [by the end of the sixth century] threw open to suspicion the origins of almost everyone" (Manville, 1997, p. 183). The group threatened by the *diapsephismos* would have been of military importance, it probably included many hoplites and in particular it would have included some of the former mercenaries of Peisistratos.[41] The loss of citizenship was no minor matter. It implied the risk of slavery, perhaps that your ownership of landed property was illegal and perhaps expulsion (at some point ownership of landed property was restricted to citizens).[42] The formal legal status of being a resident alien (*xenos* or *metoikos*) probably did not exist at that time.

Consequently, a promise to remove the threat of the *diapsephismos* and to institute instead a formal procedure for determining citizenship which was far removed from the control of the old aristocracy, and one that promised enfranchisement to those who had entered Athens under the Peisistratids, is likely to have held great appeal for a large segment of the population. This looks like an issue of sufficient magnitude to overcome the free-rider problem of collective action, especially for such relatively well-defined groups as those recently disenfranchised, but also among all those who worried about the future. Hence it can explain Kleisthenes' popularity and the uprising against Isagoras and Kleomenes.[43] In fact, Lyttkens (2004) suggests that the *diapsephismos* does not just provide a better explanation for the support of Kleisthenes than other suggestions in the literature, but that it is probably also the *only* alternative that implies sufficiently individual incentives.

To top everything, Kleisthenes himself may also have been at risk in the *diapsephismos*. His mother was the daughter of Kleisthenes, tyrant in Sikyon, hence she was not Athenian by birth. Since we do not know the principles (if there were any) of the *diapsephismos*, it is perfectly possible that Kleisthenes had to be prepared to be excluded from the citizen body (in particular in view of the curse on the Alkmaionids). It surprises me considerably that this fact about Kleisthenes descent is rarely mentioned when scholars try to explain his actions.

Kleisthenes' reform offsets the direct effects of the *diapsephismos*, as he "saw to it that many non-Athenians and even freed slaves were inscribed in the new demes" (Hansen, 1999, p. 34.). Aristotle's description of events (*The Athenian Constitution* 21.4) supports the suggestion that citizenship was the most important issue of the *deme* reform at the time when it was enacted and that it is the spark that ignited the popular support for Kleisthenes. Aristotle reports that the intention of the *deme* reform was to ensure that the inhabitants of Attica would "not call attention to the newly enfranchised citizens", and that Kleisthenes introduced the 10 new tribes in order to "mix up" the population so that "more might take part in the government" and to avoid "investigation by tribes" (*The Athenian Constitution* 21.1–2).

It could be argued that the *deme* reform is a complicated and roundabout way to put a stop to the *diapsephismos*, but that is not necessarily so. What Kleisthenes needed was an institutional structure that made the *diapsephismos* impossible both at the time and for the future. This disqualifies all solutions that could be changed by a single decision in the Assembly – instead there had to be vested interests in the status quo. The *deme* reform fits the bill by giving considerable power to local communities – power they would be unwilling to relinquish, in particular because it could mean a renewal of the *diapsephismos*.

Furthermore, Kleisthenes could draw on a similar reform of the tribal structure enacted by his grandfather in Sikyon (Herodotos 5.68.1). Such a blueprint would have been very convenient and a huge saving of decision costs and time, and constituted likely a satisficing solution (I would not be surprised if this turned out to be the reason why this particular policy was chosen by Kleisthenes).

The new process put the determination of citizenship beyond the immediate control of the old aristocracy and ended the fundamental arbitrariness, thus alleviating the common threat of losing citizenship. From now on, citizenship was to be decided by fellow *demes*-men in the *deme* assembly and the procedure was being formalised. The implication of what Aristotle tells us is that the majority of the members in the *demes* were willing to accept as a citizen anyone with a reasonable claim to belonging in Athens, which makes sense, given that the alternative might put many (indeed anybody) under suspicion. Moreover, it is probable that appeal was possible to central courts and the council from the start of the deme process (Manville, 1997, p. 188), which in that case means that the ultimate authority was no longer in the hands of the local nobility. This possibility of appeal to a collective body would arguably have appeared to be a safeguard against arbitrariness, even though the (still elected) Council would presumably continue to be dominated by the traditional elite (and assuming that logrolling was not a problem). At least initially, one would expect a preponderance of Kleisthenes' supporters in the Council, and they would presumably support Kleisthenes' policy of negating the *diapsephismos*.

Another important effect of the *deme* reform was, as mentioned above, that it reduced the influence of the nobility over the population at large through ties of kinship, religion, etc. This was arguably an important additional benefit from Kleisthenes' point of view. Remember that Kleisthenes had just lost to Isagoras in the traditional type of aristocratic game for power. Even with Isagoras out of Athens he probably had to reckon with opposition from the remainder of his faction. At least the Spartans thought it was a viable policy to try to reinstall Isagoras (Herodotos 5.74.1). Presumably there was also a Peisistratid faction, striving to bring Hippias back (there certainly was some years later, but they may have kept a low profile in 508). It is not surprising that Kleisthenes tried to find something better than to revert to the situation before 508/7. His reform created a system that retained aristocratic power in principle, and which he could hope would make himself and the Alkmaionids the most powerful aristocrats in Athens; the *deme* reform promised to strengthen his relative power in the aristocratic competition by making free agents of the poor majority but also making them indebted to him.

According to Aristotle (*The Athenian Constitution* 22), it was Kleisthenes who introduced the famous procedure of ostracism a few years after the *deme* reform. It went like this. Once a year, at a meeting of the Assembly, it was decided whether the citizens wanted an ostracism that year. If the vote was in favour, the next voting took place about two months later. Those who so wished could then vote for the banishment of one individual. If on this occasion more than 6,000 votes were cast, the person who got most of the votes had to go into exile for 10 years, but without loss of property, citizen rights, etc.

Aristotle states that Kleisthenes' primary motive for making this law was a desire to banish one Hipparchos, a relative of Peisistratos (*The Athenian Constitution* 22.3–4). This statement is sometimes disbelieved by modern scholars (perhaps because the ostracism did not happen as planned), but I see no reason to doubt Aristotle on this. Such a measure is certainly consistent with my interpretation of Kleisthenes' motives and actions, since the threat of ostracism may have been seen as an important instrument in the factional struggle. The threat from the Peisistratid faction, for example, is evidenced by the fact that the Spartans later tried to bring Hippias back (Herodotos 5.91.1 and 93–94). Since Spartan help was needed to overthrow the Peisistratids, it is a reasonable assumption that the Peisistratids were not particularly unpopular in Athens. Lewis (1988, p. 302) notes that when "Cleomenes began to besiege the tyrants [...] [he was] supported by 'those of the Athenians who wanted to be free', a phrase which hardly suggests a mass rising [against the Peisistratids]".[44] We will come back to the use of ostracism in section 5.4.

While the *deme* reform reduced the influence of the aristocracy in general over the population, Kleisthenes had reason to hope that his own influence would remain strong. The terminology used by Herodotos (5.66.2) – that Kleisthenes took the people into partnership by making them his *hetairoi* – could imply that he hoped to use the support from the multitude to create a relatively lasting power base. With the new political structure, Kleisthenes and the Alkmaionid faction could hope to dominate the archonships and be effective rulers of Athens. This was largely an unprecedented situation, and no one could reasonably predict how long the support for Kleisthenes would last.[45] Furthermore, just as with Solon, we have a decision maker (Kleisthenes) with a potentially very short planning horizon. He needed something that would allow him to gain the upper hand in the aristocratic struggle *immediately*, and if it had beneficial long-term properties, so much the better.

Kleisthenes' policy is a logical continuation of Peisistratos' efforts to reduce the ordinary people's dependence on the nobility and tie them to himself instead. The example of the Peisistratids suggests that Kleisthenes would have been well aware of this aspect of his reform. Kleisthenes was around in Athens during the rule of the Peisistratids, as evidenced by the fact that he served as archon in 525/4. Finley (1983, Chapter 2) argues that Peisistratos, Kleisthenes and Perikles shared the aim of making the poor independent of their traditional local lords.

Tyranny was instrumental in bringing about democracy in Athens

Overall, Kleisthenes' success would hardly have been conceivable if Peisistratos had shown less political acuity. For more than a generation, his policies (travelling judges, state loans, public cults, etc.) had weakened the hold of the nobility over the common people.[46] A significant, gradual change in the informal rules that governed the behaviour of the common people is to be expected, as well as a change in how ordinary Athenians perceived the world, with traditional elite rule no longer regarded as inevitable. Similarly, Ober (1989, pp. 68–69) argues that Kleisthenes realised that the poor were "free agents" after the fall of the Peisistratids, and that he showed remarkable skill in exploiting this leaderless power base.

By their actions, the Peisistratids had unintentionally prepared the ground for Kleisthenes. While it would have been obvious to them that their policy would loosen the ties between the population at large and the elite, they could not reasonably foresee that this in combination with their citizenship policy (or rather their immigration policy) would provide an opportunity for an aristocrat to seek the support of the population at large to gain the upper hand in a traditional aristocratic struggle, a struggle which was destined to re-emerge, because the political institutional framework had not been changed.

Another possibility would be that Kleisthenes realised that popular rule could have unpleasant long-term consequences, but that he considered the short-term benefits to be sufficiently attractive to settle the matter. Any long-term consequences would probably have seemed relatively unimportant to him anyway – his discount rate would have been very high. In this context it is worth noting that Kleisthenes was not a young man – Davies (1971, p. 375), puts his age at somewhere between 53 and 65 years in 507.

It was argued in Chapter 4 that Kleisthenes' breach of the informal rules for aristocratic competition began a process where the aristocratic competition for power gradually undermined the position of the members of that same elite. That Kleisthenes' manoeuvring set the Athenians on a path that led them to adopt far-reaching democratic institutions was arguably not his intention. He would not have been in favour of a development that ultimately deprived the aristocracy (and the Alkmaionids) of their political power. It seems reasonable to assume that he may have realised that other leaders could follow his example and turn to the common people for support in the Assembly, and that there was a risk that they would concede privileges of various sorts to them. However, neither the extent nor the pace of democratising could reasonably have been foreseen, and the development was encouraged by "exogenous" events (the Persian wars, the Athenian Empire). It is also possible that the potential consequences were overlooked because Kleisthenes' immediate and pressing need to find weapons against his political opponents precluded consideration of other aspects of the situation. Merton (1936) suggests precisely that "immediacy of interest" is a source of unintended consequences.

The ensuing process towards democracy illustrates the unpredictable nature of the long-term effects of institutional change. As a consequence of their internal competition for popular support, members of the elite gradually introduced the changes that eventually undermined their own dominant position as a group, as discussed in Chapter 4. That this could be the consequence was likely to have been perceived only in the late stages of the development. Similarly, in a single-ruler context, Barzel (2000) shows how democracy may evolve out of dictatorship without any group purposely setting out to create democracy, and he argues that democracy evolved in England as "the incidental byproducts of wealth maximisation by the King and by the subjects" (p. 48).[47]

5.4 Understanding the Areopagos – another failure of self-regulation?

Appointment by lottery and the status of the Areopagos

In Chapter 1, I began my story of institutional change in Athens by noting that in 487/6, a lottery system was introduced for the appointment of archons in Athens. Remember that he archons were the most powerful officials of the Athenians. The lottery system was used to select the nine archons from an elected shortlist of 100 citizens.[48] Only those belonging to the highest (or the two highest)[49] of four property classes could be elected. As before, ex-archons took a seat in the powerful council of the Areopagos.

The lottery system came to be a significant characteristic of the political machinery in Athens in the fourth century: 500 councillors and 600 other magistrates were yearly selected by lot. The remaining 100 or so magistrates were chosen by election, including the military commanders. Selection by lot was complemented by the rules of rotation, ensuring for example that you could not be a magistrate in two consecutive years (Hansen, 1999, p. 113). Appointment by lottery also came to be viewed as "the democratic way" in ancient Greece.[50] Lottery gave everybody an equal chance of being selected, whereas election favoured those who were prominent in society in terms of status, wealth, or family background. Lottery also prevented the rise of powerful bureaucrats.[51]

Using a lottery system to select those given the authority to govern the state is a very strange idea to the modern mind. To draw another anachronistic parallel, it is as if in the United States the Republican and the Democratic parties each elected a group of ten candidates, and subsequently the President and the Vice President of the US were selected randomly from these groups (come to think of it and looking back in history, perhaps not necessarily a bad idea from a European perspective).

I believe that appointment by lottery must originally have seemed like a strange notion to the Athenians as well. Election had probably been used to appoint archons for more than 100 years, and it is a natural way to select the most suitable persons for important posts. Hence we need to find a rather specific incentive for some actors to advocate the introduction of a lottery system. Tridimas (2011) shows that under some circumstances two competitors for office may agree to having the issue settled by lot rather than insisting on an election. Modern literature otherwise seems to devote more effort to discussing *when* the lottery system was introduced than to contemplating the fact that this peculiar institution was introduced at all.

From our rational-actor perspective, the position of the powerful council of the Areopagos deserves particular attention. The Areopagos, as mentioned above, had the authority to oversee the laws and the magistrates of the Athenians. It seems highly unlikely that such a reform as lottery could have been introduced against the will of the majority in the Areopagos. It is important to consider in this context that the selection of archons was not just an appointment of short-term officials, in practice it was equally an election for life to the Areopagos. The use of the lottery system inevitably meant that the status associated with the post of archon was reduced and this must also have been obvious from the start. "This maneuver naturally reduced the standing of the archonship and, by extension, that of the Areopagus council" (Neer, 2004, p. 71).[52]

To use lottery would have changed the citizens' view of the archons and of how Athenian society functioned. A system where the highest officials of the state are appointed in a partially random manner implies that these positions require considerably less ability and skill than the previous election procedure suggested. In a rational-actor perspective it seems highly improbable that individual members of the Areopagos would have consented to a measure that lowered the esteem that the archonship enjoyed – a position that all members individually had held – unless something specific and important was at stake.[53]

When contemplating how the introduction of this system was viewed at the time of its inception, one should not be fooled by the relative unimportance of the archons later in Athenian history. The archonship would come to lose its political importance (partly as a result of the lottery procedure), but the position was still important when appointment by lottery was introduced in 487 (see below). For example, in 508/7 the intensive power struggle within the elite ended with the winner (Isagoras) becoming archon. Additionally, the famous Themistokles[54] was archon in 493/2.

It is better to be selected by lot than to be elected and ostracised

In order to understand the introduction of the lottery, we need to consider the immediate background. After the fall of the Peisistratids in 510, violent internal conflict re-emerged, including a military intervention from the Spartans. It also induced the aristocrat Kleisthenes to turn to the common people for support against his peers.

It must have been obvious that intra-elite conflicts at this level posed a significant threat to the position of the traditional elite in Athens. For example, if one aristocrat had turned to the common people for support, the risk must have been obvious that others would follow his example. Ancient Greece had been producing impressive thinkers for quite some time (Anaximenes, Parmenides, Pythagoras, Thales, Xenophanes and others) suggesting that unconstrained mental exploration into such consequences was well within the mental capacity and belief system of the Athenians. In short, the position of the traditional elite was likely to suffer from the intra-elite conflicts.

Shortly after the victory against the Persians at Marathon in 490, the internal struggle among the Athenian elite once again reached dangerous levels.[55] In 489 Miltiades, traditionally viewed as the architect behind the victory at Marathon and one of the most prominent individuals in Athenian politics, was condemned in a political trial and fined 50 talents. In 487, ostracism was used for the first time and Hipparchos, a former archon, was sent into a 10-year exile. The use of ostracism was "a setback for all aristocrats" (Neer, 2004).

> the battle of Marathon [...] two years after the victory the people now being in high courage, they put in force for the first time the law of ostracism [...] the first person banished by ostracism was one of his [Peisistratos'] relatives [...]. But directly afterwards, in the next year, in the archonship of Telesinus, they elected the Nine Archons by lot.
>
> (Aristotle *The Athenian Constitution* 22.4–5)

It seems reasonable to suggest that it was the threat that such conflicts posed to members of the elite that prompted them to try to devise a mechanism that would reduce the level of intra-elite conflict. Appointing archons by lot was clearly such a mechanism, and would arguably have been recognised as such at the time. It removed the most important offices from the immediate contest for power. "By the use of the lot magistracies would cease to be attractive weapons in the struggle for power" (Hansen, 1999, p. 236). These posts would from then on have been expected to circulate among the leading families, a way of regulated power-sharing. Hence appointment by lottery would have been an attempt at elite self-regulation, similar in this respect to the introduction of written law in the seventh century and elected magistrates around 700 (Lyttkens, 2008). This looks like something the elite might have been able to agree upon. It is no coincidence, I would argue, that Miltiades' trial and the first ostracism were quickly followed by the introduction of the lottery system in the year immediately after Hipparchos' exile. This could thus be another instance of "Davies' rule" – that major institutional changes occurred in Athens because somebody was trying to prevent something unpleasant from happening.[56]

We may add a few observations. First, with the law on ostracism in place, and now also being put into effect, it might have seemed like a good idea for enterprising Athenian leaders to avoid the conspicuous position as eponymous archon. Second, the members of the Areopagos probably counted upon being able to influence the appointment of archons sufficiently to maintain the aristocratic nature of the council in the foreseeable future: it was their task to scrutinise potential magistrates before they were allowed to take up office (Hansen, 1999; Rihll, 1995). Third, such a lottery system would have placed more power in the hands of the Areopagos in the medium term, because it would have meant that less prominent individuals became archons, arguably increasing the relative power of the Areopagos itself (mitigating the long-term loss of status).[57]

If I am right about the intentions behind the lottery reform, the measure was in many respects a failure. Ostracism continued to be used, until the renewed threat from the Persians forced unity upon the Athenians. The elite continued to advocate democratising measures to please the citizen majority, as discussed in Chapter 4 and above. They also found new arenas for their internal competition.

The ten generals were elected, and this office became a long-term basis for status and power, with Perikles as the best-known example. The archonship, on the other hand, ceased to be politically important in Athens, probably not least because the lottery system suggested to the citizens that the ability of the archons was not as great as they used to believe.

The introduction of the lottery system likely had profound long-term consequences for Athenian society by changing the citizens' view of the world: if it was okey-dokey to appoint the highest officials of the state in a partially random manner, this clearly implied that the requirements in terms of ability were modest. Presumably this was what provided the basis for the notion that *anybody* could hold offices of the state, another version of a "strong principle of equality".

The practice of appointment by lot was consequently extended to the council that prepared issues for the Assembly, minor magistracies and jurors. Compared to this, the rules of rotation represent a conceptually smaller change. These downstream consequences were reasonably unintended (or at least unwanted) as far as the traditional elite is concerned.

Other explanations for the introduction of lottery do not explain the attitude of the Areopagos

All other explanations for the introduction of lottery in my view fail to take sufficient account of the curious behaviour of the Areopagos, i.e. that it apparently did nothing to prevent this political innovation.[58]

One tradition connects the introduction of the lottery system for selection of magistrates with Solon's reforms in 594. The association of Solon with the lottery system is on good authority, as explicitly stated by Aristotle in *The Athenian Constitution* (8.1). However, it is just as explicitly contradicted by another great authority, no less than Aristotle in *Politics* (1273b35–41) with the statement that election of magistrates was retained by Solon as an aristocratic element in the constitution.

Hence one has to fall back on other evidence. Lottery may have been introduced by Solon to mitigate the consequences of the endemic rivalry within the elite. Second, it has been suggested that Solon introduced the lottery system in order that those outside the traditional aristocracy would stand a real chance of entering the elite.[59] In my view, however, precisely this characteristic argues against an introduction of the lottery system by Solon. A very slow process for changing the composition of the elite would have been much preferred by the Eupatrids.

A major problem with dating the introduction of appointment by lottery to Solon's time is that it implies that the *polemarchos*, one of the nine archons and the one who commanded the army at least until the board of 10 generals was instituted in 502/1, would have been selected by lot (Hansen, 1999, p. 52). It is hardly conceivable that the Athenians would have found it acceptable to fight battles under the command of someone selected by lot (in the classical period, the Athenians held strictly to the principle that the generals should be elected). This fact speaks strongly against an introduction of the lottery system for archons before 502.[60]

It has been suggested that Themistokles introduced the lottery procedure (in 487) in order to eliminate the archonship as a source of power for his political opponent,[61] but there is no evidence that Themistokles was behind the reform (Badian, 1971; Rhodes, 1993, p. 274). I very much doubt that he could have persuaded his friends and colleagues – all ex-archons – to accept a reform for factional purposes that would reduce the status of archons.[62]

Badian has argued that the introduction of a lottery system in 487 was a "measure of relatively minor administrative reorganization".[63] First, he argues that there was no significant difference in the kind of men who held the position as eponymous archon before and after 487 – they were all relatively undistinguished. Themistokles, for example, he argues, was undistinguished when he held the position as archon in 493/2, and his alleged building activities in Piraeus were less important than believed and probably took place later.[64]

Second, he emphasises that Herodotos explicitly states that the polemarch had been chosen by lot at Marathon in 490. Badian's suggested solution is that the archons at the time of Marathon were elected, but then drew lots among themselves as to who should occupy which particular post (as the Romans did in similar circumstances). Personally, I am inclined to agree with those who argue that we know far too little about Athenian politics during the first half of the fifth century to be certain about the relative importance of the men we happen to know were archons.[65] Even if Badian's suggestion that Kleisthenes introduced the lottery system within the group of archons is correct, I would argue that he severely underestimates the importance of the change that the reforms of 487 represented. We would still need to find a motivation for the Areopagos to accept such a downgrading of the members of their own council.

5.5 Institutional change by design and by chance

The introduction of the lottery system as an appointment principle in ancient Athens shows once again that intra-elite competition and attempts to (self)regulate that competition are potent driving forces in institutional change. Further, it shows not only that an institutional change may fail to produce the intended results, but also that a perhaps seemingly minor change, through a striking combination of Murphy's Law, unintended consequences and serendipity, may fundamentally change the structure of the political market.

According to fourth-century Athenian writers (but not Herodotos) the development towards democracy began with Solon's reforms around 594 BC.[66] As we have seen, however, it is debatable whether these reforms actually moved Athens in a democratic direction. At the same time, it appears that the reforms did not hinder and in some ways actually contributed to the rise of tyranny. Peisistratos in his turn introduced reforms that later enabled Kleisthenes to enlist the common people on his side in the power struggle with Isagoras, an action that was instrumental in the subsequent development of democratising institutions. As far as more immediate effects are concerned, it therefore turns out somewhat paradoxically that it was Peisistratos the tyrant – not Solon the renowned sage and reformer – who contributed to a democratic turn of events in Athens. Neither Solon, Peisistratos nor Kleisthenes need to be credited with democratic visions, contrary to the suggestions of some modern commentators.

The Athenian experience illustrates the mutual influence between institutional changes and gradual changes in behaviour as individuals adapt to new circumstances and to the changing behaviour of others. For example, behaviour changed as a result of both Solon's and Kleisthenes' actions, eventually leading to new changes in the institutional structure. Both the belief systems and the informal rules that had sustained traditional aristocratic rule changed significantly over this period.

Even if individuals strive to act rationally and in accordance with their self-interest, their actions may have both surprising and undesirable consequences, as illustrated by these 150 years of Athenian history. The rise of tyranny was in direct conflict with Solon's intentions. The Peisistratids, on their part, could probably not have foreseen (nor desired) how their actions would contribute to a set of circumstances that made it logical for Kleisthenes to build a power base by appealing to the population at large (and also logical for him to succeed). Kleisthenes, finally, probably realised that his actions to a certain extent jeopardised the aristocratic dominance in Athenian society, but could not have foreseen the extent to which it would do so. The eventual outcomes were the result of cumulative effects of competitive interaction within the elite, and the issue of citizenship may have been crucial for the rise of both Peisistratos and Kleisthenes. The development of democracy in Athens is a story of how members of the elite in different ways contributed to the institutional changes that eventually undermined their own dominant position as a group. This is a healthy reminder in view of the inevitable temptation within the rational-actor paradigm to see a close connection between the intentions behind an action and its consequences.

To understand how different societies make the transition to becoming a functioning democracy is a matter of continuing and contemporary interest and the rational-actor paradigm, the concept of unintended consequences, and the link between loss aversion and institutional action, shed additional light on that process of institutional change in ancient Athens.

6   Taxation – a ubiquitous phenomenon if there is one

Taxation has already figured prominently in the account in the previous chapters. It is already looming on the horizon in the process of state formation in the ninth and eighth centuries, since taxation of trade is likely to have become increasingly important, and taxation of trade implies authority over a territory rather than over people. Furthermore, the reasoning of Bresson (2007) implies that it was the relatively unique absence of extortionary taxation of the poor by the rich elite that set ancient Greece on a self-sustaining path of trade and specialisation. Next, revenue considerations may have been part of Solon's motives for reforming the Athenians institutions the way he did, and taxation is one of the fundamental factors when political power is shifted back and forth between population groups in the archaic and classical periods. The changes are consistent with the notion that it is important to credibly commit not to use one's power to abuse property rights through taxation or other sorts of confiscations. Finally, the issue of credible commitments can explain why the rich were given responsibility for tax collection in the fourth century.

That taxation is a recurrent theme is not surprising, nor is it mere chance. Few things tells us as much about a society as the nature of its taxation. From the way taxation is organised and administered and from how the actors in the economy react to these taxes we learn about the relationship between the state and the rest of the population.[1] The distribution of the tax burden and the tax-financed benefits tells us much about who rules in a society and how they do it. The degree of tax avoidance tells us how individuals view each other and whether they trust those in power.

One of my favourite dictums is that "it might be an exaggeration to claim that 90 per cent of all human behaviour can be *explained* by taxation, but it is surely no exaggeration to claim that 90 per cent of all human behaviour is *affected* by taxation". Hence I was greatly pleased when I found the following quote from Benjamin Franklin a few years ago:[2] "In this world nothing is certain but death and taxes." In other words, no analysis of the institutions in a society would be complete without a comprehensive study of taxation, its structure and the effects on the economy. A further illustration of the salience of taxation comes from Athenian law in the Classical period: upon entering office the councillors in Athens swore "not to imprison any citizen prepared to give bail, except traitors, enemies of the democracy *and tax-collectors*" (Hansen, 1999, p. 255, my italics).[3]

It is a safe bet that if you witness a strange practice somewhere in the world, the reason is to be found in taxation. A few examples from Sweden illustrate this:

1. Travelling in the countryside of southern Sweden a few years ago, I noticed that flax suddenly was being grown – a suspicion immediately formed that this was due to EU subsidies (a negative tax) – and this was subsequently confirmed in discussions with farmers. In 2011 it was corn that suddenly permeated the Swedish countryside instead.
2. Swedish economists (Ohlsson, 2011) recently discovered that the number of high-valued gifts increase by a tremendous amount in the 1940s. This was evident from the increase in the revenue from the tax on gifts. Had the Swedish population all of a sudden developed a new genetic trait of generosity? Nope, instead a political debate had begun on whether there ought to be an increase in the property tax, so for tax reasons it seemed prudent for a lot of people to distribute their wealth among family members.
3. Until recently, rumour has it that it was common practice – especially among elderly Swedish citizens – to go to the bank on one of the last days of December to make a huge withdrawal from their bank account, then keep the money at home (usually as a banker's draft) over the new-year celebrations,[4] and finally return to the bank one of the first days of January to deposit the money again. This way the tax authorities were not informed about this part of their wealth, because the banks only submitted a statement of accounts for 31 December. Not surprisingly, the tax authorities reputedly got wise of this practice and began investigating December withdrawals.
4. Eliasson and Ohlsson (2011) show that in Sweden those with taxable estates were 10 per cent more likely to die on 1 January 2005 rather than on 31 December 2004, compared to those without taxable estate, which is interesting in view of the fact that the inheritance tax was abolished from 1 January 2005. It seems that not only are taxation and death the two certainties in life, they are also correlated.

This chapter deals with three interrelated issues. The first is to characterise Athenian taxation – the tax structure, level of taxes, levied on whom, methods of tax collection, etc. This is important because taxation greatly affects what happens in the rest of the economy. It will be argued that the structure of taxation is largely explained by transaction costs and the degree to which different groups pose a threat to those in power. The second issue is the development over time of taxation in Athens, which shows how different sectors in the economy interact. The third issue is the effect that taxation had on Athenian society.

6.1 The constraints on taxation

Competition for power

As noted in Chapter 1, my view of the state is the predatory one, the state as an agency of a group or class with the function of extracting income from the rest of the constituents (North, 1981, 2005). The Athenians were also well aware that politics was an arena of conflicting interests (see section 4.4).[5] In Athens, during the classical period politicians increasingly had to propose measures that were to the advantage of the poor majority.

In general, a ruler (the one who controls the state apparatus) is constrained by the opportunity costs of the constituents. The competition from potential rival rulers serves as a constraint on ruler behaviour in general and taxation in particular; the competition may be internal or external, explicit or implicit. A ruler's ability to tax different groups in a society is limited by their relative bargaining power (political, economic, and coercive).[6] "Rulers are always predatory but they cannot always do as they please" (Levi, 1988, p. 46).

Rival rulers can come in different forms. In the archaic period in Greece, tyrants frequently came to power with outside help. Hence such interventions clearly would have been among the imaginable outcomes for any political leader or ordinary citizen. An important restriction on public policy in classical Athens lay in the ever-present threat that the rich and oligarchic element would enlist aid from another state (notably Sparta) to overthrow the government. Spartan intervention had occurred in 508/7 (and after) and it occurred again after the Peloponnesian War.

The structuring of the tax system may also confer influence to various actors in the economy, and the ruler needs to take this effect on the stability of his position into consideration. Levi (1988) argues that revenue maximisation will turn out to be a good empirical approximation of the ruler's objective throughout history and still today. The reason is that whatever the ruler's objectives, revenue is usually necessary to attain them. The ruler may be the main beneficiary of the revenue collected, but will also need to keep the support or at least acceptance of sufficient parts of the population. Alternatively, the ruler may primarily be an agent acting on behalf of powerful groups in society (but even if he is such an agent, he is likely to have ambitions of his own).

The discussion in Chapter 4 showed that there are limits to the taxation (or extraction more generally) of rich and poor in a society, as either group may find it advantageous to revolt or change the political rules if they are pressed hard enough. Changes in political power and violence potential determine who is going to tax whom. In view of the ruler's interest in raising taxes, the ability of the ruler to commit *not to increase* taxation greatly affects the political and economic activities in society. In particular, it determines the allocation between open and hidden economic activities.

Transaction costs

Transaction costs are important determinants of the structure of taxation. Transaction costs of taxation include the cost of identifying those who should pay the tax, measuring the tax base (the entity which is being taxed, e.g. property, income, etc.), the cost of collecting the tax, and the cost of policing everyone: the taxpayers, the tax collector, and so on.

The ruler in society can usually be presumed to prefer higher net revenues to lower and hence to prefer a system with low transaction costs, *ceteris paribus*. Furthermore, the ruler will sometimes prefer an inefficient institutional structure (e.g. badly defined property rights) if that reduces the transaction costs of taxation sufficiently to increase the net revenue from taxation (North, 1981). Similarly, I would add that the ruler will benefit from a system that transfers the burden of the transaction costs to other parties in the economy.

As we shall see, many aspects of the Athenian tax system served to economise on transaction costs, which suggest that the more detailed organisation of Athenian taxation by and large can be explained as a desire to reduce or minimise these costs.

Tax compliance

Tax compliance is of course fundamental. In a simple "crime and punishment" model, the taxpayer simply calculates the net wealth that will result with tax-avoidance and tax-compliance, and chooses the alternative with the greatest expected wealth. In doing so, the expected cost of tax avoidance is the size of the punishment in case of detection, weighted by the probability of detection. Levi (1988) suggests, however, that taxpayers sometimes *choose* to pay their taxes even when the probability of detection is low. Such "quasi-voluntary" compliance can occur when the taxpayer gets something of reasonable value to him from the ruler in return for his money *and* believes that everybody else will also pay. Once again the belief system is of paramount importance, as well as factors that affect those beliefs.

It is a formidable challenge to try to change everybody's beliefs so that one can switch from tax-avoidance as the primary strategy to quasi-voluntary compliance. This has been obvious in the transition economies and in the current (2011–2012) problem-countries in the EU.

Quasi-voluntary compliance greatly reduces the cost for the ruler of enforcing compliance. Note that the ruler has to make it credible that the level of taxation will not increase (unduly) and that the level of benefits will not decrease (unduly). Exogenous changes, such as the loss of the Empire for the Athenians, can erode the basis for quasi-voluntary compliance, e.g. by making it unlikely that the level of taxation will remain unchanged in the future. The notion of quasi-voluntary compliance provides a link between micro behaviour and macro changes and it seems to explain much of actually observed behaviour.

Illegal tax evasion is one way to avoid paying taxes. Another – and legal – way is to physically leave (or not enter) the area of the authority that demands tax payments, or more generally not taking part in the taxed activity. If you are a trader you can bring your goods to another location, and you can also bring yourself to another location.

6.2 The structure of taxation in Classical Athens[7]

Taxes on trade[8]

The most important source of revenue for many city-states was trade, which was taxed whenever possible. There is some uncertainty about the extent of such taxes in Athens in the classical period, but the list includes: import and export dues at the harbour of 1–2 per cent, a separate import tax on grain of 2 per cent, a toll at the city gates, a tax on goods auctioned out by the state, and perhaps a general sales tax at the city market (Gabrielsen, forthcoming).

By ensuring that transaction costs were minimised in the agora, the city-state also facilitated taxation of that trade. Similarly, some city-states limited foreign trade to one port.[9] This may have helped the trade in some ways, but it would definitely also have increased the possibilities to tax the trade. Predatory rule once again.

The yield from these taxes varied with the military and political position of Athens, such as the existence of the Empire. In terms of internal factors, as an increasing part of the population came to rely on the market for their needs, the yield from these taxes ought to have increased during the fifth century.[10] To this one must add that Athens served as an entrepot for much of our period, but the extent of transit trade must have varied considerably.

The harbour dues were sold to tax farmers for 36 talents in 401/0 (Andokides 1.133–134), a few years after the Peloponnesian War, when this kind of revenue must have been at low ebb. Towards the end of the fourth century, Lykourgos reputedly managed to increase Athenian state revenue to 1,200 talents. This likely depended a lot on an increase in the taxes on trade (Bergh and Lyttkens, 2011) – in the second half of the fourth century trade was considerably facilitated by institutional changes (see Chapter 7).

On the use of tax farming (avoiding transaction costs: lesson one)

The Athenians relied heavily on tax farming for collection of their taxes. Each year all regular taxes were auctioned out to the highest bidder (not just the harbour dues).

There are several factors to consider in an evaluation of the relative merits of tax farming. First it is important to realise that the use of tax farming entailed a choice. The ancient Greeks were perfectly capable of developing complex bureaucratic procedures when they wanted to. The Athenians, for example, incurred considerable costs in the process of auditing officials who handled their money.[11] However, tax farming was probably preferable both in terms of transaction costs and to avoid permanent tax officials.

Jones (1974, Chapter 8) argued that tax farming was used when the yield of a tax was unpredictable, so that it would have been difficult and costly to audit an official.[12] Kiser (1991) adds that the principal (the ruler) will prefer his agent (the tax collector) to be the residual claimant when supervision is difficult; the tax farmer will then have incentives for efficient tax collection and will not take bribes from the taxpayers. Jones further noted that under competitive conditions the winning bid among the tax farmers will represent the highest estimate of the *net* yield of the tax, adjusted for collection costs and a "reasonable" profit. Hence tax farming does not in principle relieve the state budget of the collection cost or the cost of checking the taxpayer, but if there is competition among the tax farmers then this will tend to minimise these costs. If the ruler has risk aversion, an additional advantage of tax farming is that it provides a guaranteed return (Kiser, 1991). Competition will ensure that the party with the smallest risk price will acquire the contract (the best insurer).

There is always a risk that tax farmers exploit the taxpayers, especially if the tax liability of the individual is not well defined. This could be a problem for the ruler, and so it may be necessary to police the tax farmers. However, Athenian tax farmers always risked public prosecution and Jones (1974, Chapter 8) believes that this served as an effective inhibition on them.

An important aspect of the Athenian legal system was that it largely depended on private initiative. "There was no public prosecutor: the system was 'accusatorial', i.e. based on accusations by private individuals" (Hansen, 1999, p. 191). Consequently the control of tax collectors was left to private initiative (i.e. that some private individual took it upon him to accuse the tax collector) and hence the state budget was largely relieved of the cost of control.

In general, private suits could be brought only by the injured party, while public prosecutions (*graphai*) could be brought by any citizen (Hansen, 1999, p. 192).[13] In several categories of trials, the accuser received a substantial financial reward if he was successful (e.g. three-quarters of the property being withheld from the state[14]). However, the system of private accusation also covered some cases where a successful prosecutor received no financial reward. So it rested on other incentives, and, for example, MacDowell (1978, p. 62) notes that "to do harm to one's enemies was considered by most Greeks a perfectly proper aim". We should also note that in some cases the prosecutor could be punished if he failed to get one-fifth of the votes of the jury (Hansen, 1999, p. 192).[15]

There is also an obvious risk that a tax collector colludes with the taxpayer (a more direct relationship than usually assumed in the capture theory of regulation). The problem increases if it is necessary to have permanent – rather than temporary – tax officials. However, with tax farming, this ceases to be a problem as long as there is competition between tax famers. Once again tax farming economises on transaction costs.

Whoever collects a tax acquires some degree of power from his position. In Chapter 4, it was argued that it was politically important to transfer the control of the property taxation to the rich elite in the fourth century. Similarly, Levi (1988, Chapter 4) has pointed out that tax farming confers bargaining power upon the tax farmers, but that rulers sometimes do a trade-off between relative bargaining power and transaction costs. Hansen (1999, pp. 235ff.) argues that the organisation of the political institutions of the Athenians clearly shows that they wanted to avoid a powerful bureaucracy. This was, for example, a major reason for choosing magistrates by lot.[16] The Athenians were well aware that powerful bureaucrats would entail a reduction in the power of the Assembly, i.e. a reduction of the sovereignty of the people.

However, this principle does not seem to explain all cases where tax farming was used. If a tax could be collected by an official appointed for only one year this would seem to be unproblematic. The problem appears if it becomes necessary to re-elect the official. The implication is that tax officials would be acceptable long as their tasks were not too complicated. For example, it would seem that per capita taxes could easily be collected by temporary officials. In contrast, taxes on trade are somewhat complicated to collect – they require measurement, some knowledge of wares and materials, etc., and may have been too difficult for a temporary tax official. Hence the bureaucracy argument suggests that tax farming would be preferred because arguably the alternative was permanent tax officials.

Taxes on wealth (avoiding transaction costs: lesson two)

In democratic Athens, the poor majority was not likely to tax itself extensively, nor would a politician who tried to advocate such a policy have been successful. The obvious alternative was to tax the rich minority. Even though the distribution of wealth was perhaps relatively egalitarian in a comparative perspective, this group possessed a large part of the potentially taxable resources.[17]

There were both formal and informal taxes on wealth. In Chapter 4, we encountered the peculiar institution of *liturgies*. In the classical period, it was considered a duty and an honour for a rich Athenian citizen to perform a liturgy – to finance and manage certain functions for the common good. Performing a liturgy entailed both personal service and expenditure. The trierarchy was a military liturgy: to commission and command a state-owned warship for a year. The other liturgies concerned the religious festivals, and the best known was to stage a dramatic production (*choregia*). In the fourth century there were about 100 festival liturgies each year (Davies, 1967). In the fourth century, there was also a liturgy concerned with the collection of the property tax (the *proeisphora*). In the fourth century, it became accepted that some trierarchs hired substitutes to escape the personal performance part, so that the trierarchy could take the form of a pure expenditure (Gabrielsen, 1994, pp. 95ff.).

The Athenian case is best known, but the existence of liturgies was not confined to Athens (Andreades, 1979; Gabrielsen, forthcoming). The *choregia* is first attested with certainty at Athens in 502/1, when the practice of inscribing the names of victorious *choregoi* on stone began (Capps, 1943; Davies, 1967,

1992). The trierarchy is attested for Samos in 494 and for Athens and other states in 480. By that time it appears that the trierarchy represented a uniformly applied solution to the financing of naval warfare.[18] However, as argued in Chapter 5, it is not unlikely that spending of a liturgical nature had occurred long before these dates, and I will return to this question below.

Only the richest Athenians had to perform liturgies. The level of wealth required for ascription into the liturgical class lay somewhere around 3–4 talents in the fourth century (Davies, 1971, pp. xxiii–xxiv).[19] The liturgical class was small – probably only a few per cent of the population. The liturgists likely numbered somewhere around 300–1,200 individuals. Most scholars lean towards the higher number (Gabrielsen, forthcoming; Möller, 2007). This figure may have increased in the second half of the fourth century, perhaps to more than 4,000 persons, because by then it was common to share the burden of a trierarchy (see below), and at the same time there was a rule that you were exempt from liturgies for two years after having performed a (part of) a trierarchy.[20]

The known costs of trierarchies range from around 4,000 to 6,000 drachmas.[21] Originally a single person assumed responsibility for a trireme. Unfortunately we do not know to what extent the existence of the Athenian Empire relieved the rich Athenians of this kind of burden. It is a safe guess, however, that the Peloponnesian War strained the resources of the wealthy Athenians, not only those of the Athenian allies.[22] Towards the end of the War the *syntrierarchy* was introduced, whereby the burden of a trierarchy could be shared among two or more persons.[23] The costs for the other liturgies range from 300 to perhaps 3,000 drachmas.[24] Faced with these figures on expenditures, it is worth remembering of course that the figures given by the orators must be suspected of bias as the speaker usually was trying to convince people that he had been very generous. In the fourth century a person was not obliged (or not allowed) to undertake more than one liturgy simultaneously. Similarly, there was also a rule of exemption between liturgies. The exemption lasted one year for the festival liturgies, while for the trierarchy it probably began as a one-year exemption, but the exemption period had be extended to two years in the second half of the fourth century. It is not clear if these rules already applied in the fifth century (Davies, 1971, p. xxix; Rhodes, 1982).

These figures mean that even a cheap liturgy cost nearly as much as a skilled workman would earn in a year. The usual presumption is that the daily wage rose from around 1 drachma towards the end of the fifth century to around 2 drachmas towards the end of the fourth century (Loomis, 1998; Scheidel, 2010).[25] To finance a liturgy a rich man would often have to spend a sizeable amount of that year's income from his property, reduce his savings, sell some property, or borrow from his friends.[26]

The liturgies entailed almost no transaction costs for the state. No money was ever collected because those who performed the liturgies carried the cost directly. The informational costs entailed in measuring wealth would have been substantial and the Athenians always avoided it.[27]

There were almost no measurement costs or enforcement costs because the Athenians relied on private initiative to assess the assets of the liturgical class. By the procedure known as *antidosis* a person who was appointed to perform a liturgy could challenge another he considered better able to afford the expense.[28] The challenged person either had to take over the liturgy or to accept an exchange of property with the instigator of the procedure. If the challenged person refused both to perform the liturgy and to exchange property, a court would decide which of the two parties had the greater obligation to perform the liturgy. Thus only if the two parties failed to reach a private agreement did the public responsibility go further than making a note of the *antidosis* challenge. However, even when the issue ended up in a court the authorities did not gather any independent evidence (incur any measurement costs); Gabrielsen (1987a) argues that the trial probably rested only upon the evidence produced by the contestants.

Having been appointed to perform a liturgy, it was punishable to avoid it. Enforcement largely rested on private initiative, as described above. The Athenians complained about "sycophants", i.e. persons "who gained profit [...] by misusing every citizen's right to bring a public action and blackmailing those he prosecuted or threatened with prosecution" (Hansen, 1987, p. 224). This way of attaining compliance made the possibility of blackmail unavoidable. The prosecutor must be given part of the defaulter's tax debt in order to have an incentive to seek him out and, unless this is 100 per cent of the tax debt, there is scope for bargaining between the parties.

The pressure on a rich individual to perform liturgies and gain goodwill was strengthened by the risk that a political trial would lead to heavy fines or outright confiscation of property. In the courts the jurors were chosen by lot among ordinary citizens. It is a recurrent theme in the ancient literature that the poor in a democracy might exploit the rich in this way. The revenue from the courts could make a large contribution to state revenue, but it is not known to what extent rich persons actually suffered in the courts (Ober, 1989, pp. 200–202). In an oration spoken after 338

> there are three examples of how the Athenian courts did *not* fall into the temptation of condemning a number of rich mining-concessionaires. On the other hand, [...] in those very same years, the richest of all [...] Diphilos, was condemned [...] and his fortune of 160 talents distributed among the citizens.
>
> (Hansen, 1999, p. 315)

The sum of 160 talents can be compared to total public (peacetime) revenue, which was 130 talents in the 350s, increased to 400 talents in the 340s and to 1,200 talents in the 320s. The risk that the courts were used to soak the rich is relevant in particular from 462, when the Areopagos lost much of its judicial power to the Assembly and the popular court. Before that date it is unlikely that the general population could materially sanction non-liturgists with the aim of increasing public revenue.

The liturgies can be characterised as an informal property tax (no list of those liable, no specified tax rate etc.).[29] The rich Athenians also had to pay a regular property tax from time to time – the *eisphora*. If not before, the *eisphora* was introduced in Athens in 428/7 when 200 talents were collected according to Thykydides.[30] It was a tax on capital, usually used in times of war. The Athenian state had no budget in a modern sense. Instead there were a number of expected expenditures and to each of these certain sources of revenue were allocated. The allocation of revenues to different purposes (the *merismos*) had the status of a law (*nomos*). Normally, no deficit was possible – government expenditure was strictly limited to the amounts actually in the hands of government officials. Any extraordinary or unexpected expenditure thus had to be met by extraordinary revenues.[31]

Since war implied extraordinary expenditures, the Athenians needed a means to temporarily increase revenue, hence the *eisphora*. During the following century the *eisphora* was a normal feature of the economic and political life of the Athenians. Unlike some other city-states, the Athenians appear to have used an *eisphora* only for military purposes (Gabrielsen forthcoming). Finally, from 347/6 to 323/2, it was used as a regular annual tax of 10 talents a year, though the Assembly could still impose extra *eisphorai* (Brun, 1983, pp. 49–55). It is probable that a greater number of people paid the *eisphora* than those who performed liturgies, perhaps 3,000–3,500.[32]

When the tax was levied the Assembly also specified the tax rate – probably around 1 per cent. There was in all likelihood an exemption limit, at least in practice, so that only persons with wealth exceeding a certain level were likely to be liable. The tax was probably roughly proportional to the value of a man's wealth, and all wealth – movable and immovable – was in principle included. Each man assessed himself on oath. Obviously the scope for tax evasion was considerable, for example by transferring some of one's property to less visible kinds (coins, deposits with private banks, etc.). As with the liturgies, the Athenians relied upon private initiative to prosecute tax defaulters, and awarded the prosecutor part of the money recovered. However, the state could also engage itself in such activities, as evidenced for example by the commission led by Androtion to collect *eisphora* arrears (Demosthenes 22.60).

As shown by Levi (1988), it is typical to find extra taxes levied in times of war. A war raises the rulers' discount rate and the tax subjects are temporarily willing to pay more in order to finance a war effort. It is also easier to persuade people to pay a tax when they are certain that the revenue will be used for the specified purpose. The Athenian taxpayers could feel confident about the *eisphora* when it was used during the Peloponnesian War because the foreign policy situation was well known to them. Conversely the ruler will meet demands for tax reductions when the war is over. The *eisphora* is a very good example of all this: for several generations it was not allowed to become permanent but was voted on specifically on each occasion that it was needed.

In the fourth century Athenian property taxation was gradually formalised. In 378/7, the citizens liable for the *eisphora* were divided into 100 symmories and a general reassessment was made, where the property of the Athenians was estimated to 5,750 talents (Hansen, 1999, Chapter 5). This was probably also the time when the *proeisphora* was introduced; the 300 richest citizens (the *proeispherontes*, three for each symmory) could be called upon to advance the total amount of the *eisphora* to the state and thereafter to reimburse themselves from the other taxpayers. Some 20 years later (in 358/7) a symmory system was introduced or extended to cover those liable to perform trierarchies.[33] The interpretation of these measures will be discussed in connection with the overall development of property taxation over time (see below).

Per capita taxes (avoiding transaction costs: lesson three)

It is commonly argued in the modern literature that the classical Greeks regarded taxation of citizens or their property as degrading and as a sign of tyranny (Möller, 2007), and that they tried to avoid it whenever possible. Gabrielsen (forthcoming) sees this as a myth, and Migeotte (2003) has collected evidence to show that direct taxes were used in various *poleis*. Indeed this is what we would expect from our perspective. Those in control of the state apparatus take the opportunity to tax the other groups in society. So for example, we find in Athens direct taxation of the wealth of the rich minority (but no tax on the produce of the majority). And there was no restraint with respect to taxation of non-citizens or to those who practiced "disreputable trades".

In Athens, the metics paid a yearly per capita tax (*metoikion*) of 12 drachmas for men and six drachmas for independent women. The tax roughly corresponded to 12 days' earnings for an ordinary citizen. Prostitutes (both male and female) also paid a special tax – the *pornikon* (Aischines 1.119–120). Finally, freedmen may have had to pay a special tax (*triobolon*). None of these groups had any say in the Assembly.

Not surprisingly, those who were subject to special taxation in Athens were those with the least bargaining power. Female prostitutes had no power qua being female and furthermore were often metics or freedwomen (Pomeroy, 1975, p. 89). A citizen who prostituted himself lost his political rights (Aischines 1.28–32). Freedmen were not citizens and hence had no political power. However, some freedmen became economically important and received citizenship (e.g. the banker Pasion). The taxation of rich metics – who were important economically – may seem odd. Overall, however, a wealthy metic was less heavily taxed than rich Athenians (Lyttkens, 1992). They paid the *eisphora* but at a lower rate, some festival liturgies (possibly all) but *not* the trierarchy (Gabrielsen, forthcoming). This accords well with the ease with which they could leave Athens. In any case 12 drachmas may have seemed like a small price to pay for access to the thriving Athenian market.

The rules for the *metoikion* economised considerably on transaction costs. In terms of measurement, a per capita tax requires only identification of the tax subjects and metics had to register themselves. It also appears to have been the metics' own responsibility to pay the tax to the tax farmer – hence no collection costs for the authorities. As for compliance and enforcement costs, we know from the law and economics literature that there is a negative correspondence between the size of the penalty for non-compliance and the probability of detection that is necessary to achieve in order to enforce compliance. The penalty for not registering as a metic and not paying the *metoikion* was extremely severe – a tax-evader could be sold as a slave.[34] It seems unlikely that non-compliance would have been common – it would have been a very profitable business to search for tax evaders. The amount they could be blackmailed for would be limited only by their total wealth.[35] The cost for detection was limited since the metics usually lived in the city. The *metoikion* will have brought in a useful sum, though not overwhelming, perhaps some 45 talents of a budget of 400 talents in the middle of the fourth century.[36]

Both the *metoikion* and the *pornikon* were farmed out. Three are several possible explanations for this. It could be because competition then minimised transaction costs. Tax farming was not, I would argue, necessary to avoid powerful government officials, because the *metoikion* was a simple tax that could easily have been collected by an official with one-year tenure.[37] The best explanation seems to be that it would have seemed easier to extend one functioning system to another area rather than create a new system for the purpose of collecting this particular tax – a case of satisficing behaviour.

Much less is known about the *pornikon*. One might guess that it was a per capita tax like the *metoikion*. In that case it seems likely that tax farming reduced the transaction costs for a given revenue. How much revenue the *pornikon* produced seems like a field open for speculation:

1   It depends on the tax rate, where only the total income of the prostitutes sets an upper limit.
2   The income of the prostitutes in turn depends on the price of the service and the demand.[38]
3   The latter depend a lot on, for example, whether a part of the slave-population should be included among the customers (as seems likely). Hence depending on the assumptions on these issues, the yield from this tax can easily vary from 15 to 150 talents.

The guiding principles of taxation in Athens

The Athenian tax system largely relieved the public budget of transaction costs. The liturgy system functioned without the money ever entering the public purse, and it was left to private initiative to ensure that those best able to afford it also carried the burden. The *eisphora* also relied on private initiative to define the tax base and (eventually) also for tax collection. Most taxes were farmed out and competition will have ensured that costs of tax collection were minimised. Head taxes, finally, are obviously always easy to administer. At the same time an overall impression is that the system totally disregarded the burden that fell on private actors, which is consistent with the predatory view of the state as being interested in the net revenue of the state and little else. The system also avoided creating powerful bureaucrats that might become rival rulers.

Sometime after the Sicilian expedition (415) the Athenians tried to replace the tribute in the empire with a 5 per cent tax on exports and imports throughout the empire (Thukydides 7.28.4; Andrewes, 1992). At a guess the tribute was increasingly being resisted, and the Athenians hoped that a tax would be less offensive and meet with more compliance.[39]

It is regularly noted that the aim of the taxes on trade was simply to raise revenue and not to conduct any other economic policy. Indeed, the impression one gets from the overview of the different taxes above is that the Athenians seized the opportunity to tax all transactions and items they could identify with reasonable ease, i.e. where the transaction costs were low. This impression is strengthened by the existence of some other taxes. In the days of Aristotle, a measure of olive oil was to go with amphorae to the winners of sporting events during the Great Panathenaia festival. This oil was obtained through a general levy on the oil production of farmers on whose land the sacred olive trees grew.[40] To finance the cult of Apollo, the Athenians in 434 introduced an annual tax on those who performed military service (Schlaifer, 1940). Another example comes from Hippias' time as tyrant: he reputedly sold to house-owners the right to have a second storey and to have a door that opened outwards, etc. (Ps. Aristotle *Oeconomica* 2.2.4). In the words of Vincent Gabrielsen (forthcoming): "no activity, or trade, or commodity, or group of individuals, or kind of possessions was likely to escape the watchful eye of the state". Gabrielsen also provides further examples of specific Greek taxes from various city-states, as does Andreades (1979).

The taxes on property faced particular constraints, as they had to be balanced against the current or potential power of the rich to veto the taxation or simply try to topple the democracy in favour of a more elitist government. We now we look at how that balance was struck over time.

6.3 Development over time

Taxation in the archaic period

In archaic Greek society, we may assume that the members of the elite demanded contributions from the local population, providing protection and governance in return. However, as we noted in Chapter 3, compared to other societies at that time, the common citizens in a Greek city-state were allowed to keep a substantially larger part of their production.

When we discussed the consequences of Solon's reforms in 594, I argued that one of these consequences may have been the appearance of liturgical spending. The areas where such spending seems likely to have appeared are notably among those areas where the liturgy system evolved in the fifth century. Both the navy and the religious festivals are areas where new sources of finance would have been welcome in the early sixth century, and where we may suspect that rich Athenians would have been spending to show off their wealth.

Then enter Peisistratos and his sons on the stage as tyrants. During their reign, voluntary spending to establish political rights (or political ostentatious spending in general) was relatively less motivated, but if ostentatious spending – perhaps also for the common good – had become incorporated into the status game within the elite it may nevertheless have continued spontaneously. Furthermore, since Peisistratos and his sons are generally supposed to have relied on mercenaries throughout their reigns (Herodotos 1.64; Andrewes, 1982b, pp. 397–399), it is perhaps not unlikely that they could demand contributions, for example, from some of those who were allowed to hold office.[41] There is a Hellenistic text which reports that Hippias allowed those expecting to perform trierarchies or other liturgies to contribute a sum in cash instead (Ps. Aristotle *Oeconomica* 2.2.4). Since no near-contemporary source mentions a connection between Hippias and the trierarchy, this statement is generally disbelieved by modern authorities.[42] However, if you believe as I do that there is a clear possibility that spending of a liturgical nature emerged already long before Hippias' reign, then you are probably more predisposed to regard the Hippias–trierarchy connection as a realistic possibility.

The Peisistratids introduced a 5 per cent tax on produce (Aristotle *The Athenian Constitution*, 16.4; Thukydides 6.54.5; Andrewes, 1982b, pp. 407–409). This is the first formal tax we know of in Athenian history, and it was abolished after the fall of the Peisistratids. Finley (1981, p. 90, n. 34) suggests that tax grievances were a reason for the overthrow of the Peisistratid dynasty, but this is only based on general plausibility, the fact that both Thukydides and Aristotle mention the tax, and that it was abolished with the fall of the tyranny. The main factor behind the fall of the Peisistratids, as I argued in Chapter 4, was more likely the loss of revenues from northern Greece due to the Persian expansion, the concomitant increase in war expenditure, and the fact that whoever ruled Athens could look forward to a more prosperous future due to the finds of silver.

In stark contrast to tax grievances being a factor behind the *coup d'état*, it is possible that the 5 per cent tax in practice represented a tax *reduction* for the ordinary farmers, as pointed out by Harris (1997). The reason is that under the Peisistratids the common people perhaps no longer had to pay tribute to their local chieftains, as they presumably had been forced to do under traditional aristocratic rule. The previous tribute may well have been a greater burden than the Peisistratid tax (e.g., it may have been one-sixth of the crop, the situation of the *hektemoroi*).[43]

After the fall of the Peisistratids, several effects kick in. Because the Peisistratids had reputedly kept the Solonian constitution intact, the issue of the property qualification must have come to the fore again after the fall of the dynasty in 510, when offices were once more open to everybody who could prove their eligibility. Spending to demonstrate wealth was now as important as before.

The abolition of the 5 per cent tax implies an acute lack of public funds (and the personal incomes of the Peisistratids were no longer available). This lack of resources ought to have been conspicuous. As noted in Chapter 4, it seems likely that the military expenditures had gradually increased for several decades, especially with the use of triremes. The foreign situation was threatening, with the expelled tyrant Hippias being friendly with the Persians (Ostwald, 1988, p. 338). This would make anyone who were willing to undertake public expenditure very popular in Athens.

To the extent that spending of a liturgical nature had taken place under the Peisistratids it is likely that it was seen as rather less than voluntary. When charitable behaviour becomes compulsory and expected the status element associated with the activity reasonably falls. Hence we can imagine a disinclination on the part of the elite to continue with liturgical spending just when it was needed more than ever.

This suggests a new view of the fact that in 502/1 the practice of inscribing the names of the victorious *choregoi* on stone began. In our economic perspective, the most straightforward interpretation is that this reflects a need to increase the status element in liturgical expenditure. The formalisation of the liturgical system can be seen as the creation of a market for honour, with the government selling positions of honour in order to increase its implicit revenue.[44]

In 502/1 we meet the most important festival liturgy (*choregia*) in a formalised and "fully developed" form (Davies, 1992, p. 29). The trierarchy was soon to follow. The navy is an area where the shortage of funds after the fall of the Peisistratids must have been particularly obvious. The Athenians were unable to defend their coast in *c.*506 against Aegina, a potential ally of Persia. The increasing use of the costly trireme made it impossible to rely on privately supplied ships for the fleet, as originally had been the case. When, by the time of Salamis, an individual turns up with his own ship it is seen as exceptional (Herodotos 8.17; Haas, 1985, p. 40).

The trierarchy solved the problem of financing the fleet by splitting the costs for a ship between the state and a trierarch. Originally, such a split may have taken place ad hoc. At some point, the system we know from the fourth century must have been introduced, i.e. with the generals being responsible for appointing the trierarchs.[45] The main candidate for the formalisation of the trierarchy is in connection with Themistokles' shipbuilding programme of 483/2.[46] However, we know that in 502/1 the Athenians began electing a board of ten generals (*strategoi*).[47] Conceivably appointing trierarchs might have been one of their duties from the start (in which case the trierarchy could have begun the same year as the *choregia* was formalised).

The incentive to spend for the benefit of the population in general was soon enhanced by the actions of Kleisthenes in 508/7, described in Chapters 4–5. Kleisthenes broke the informal rules of aristocratic competition for power, and started a chain reaction which led the aristocrats to introduce democratising measures in order to gain the upper hand against their fellow aristocrats (thus in the long run eroding the basis for aristocratic power). These events produced a new interest among the leading class in securing the support of the general public and would have encouraged liturgical spending.

It will always remain a possibility that liturgical spending appeared for the first time after Kleisthenes' reforms, with which the formalisation of liturgies has quite rightly been associated.[48] As I see it, a problem with that explanation is the relatively short period of time between 508/7 and 502/1. On the political side, one should remember that it took more than a generation of further changes in attitudes and in the constitution before we reach the fully developed democracy of Perikles' time. It seems more natural to begin the practice of inscribing the names of the *choregoi* on stone if spending of a liturgical nature had already been established for some time. In other words, the formalised version of liturgies probably did not appear out of the blue.[49]

This account suggests that liturgical spending may have emerged as an effect of Solon's reforms, continued under the rule of Peisistratos and his sons in a somewhat less than voluntary form, was encouraged by an increase in the status value of liturgies in 502/1 – formalising the institution and noting the undertaking for posterity – and finally received an increased impetus by the changing nature of elite competition that followed in the fifth century.

The classical period

The liturgies do not represent a straightforward tax on wealth, as a rich man could derive some personal benefits from a liturgy and volunteers were important throughout the classical period. There was clearly an honorific element involved; people sometimes paid out more than they had to on their liturgies, as lavish spending could be useful both politically and in front of the popular courts (but see below on the need to pay more than required). A trierarchy might even be profitable if, for example, it gave the trierarch opportunities to acquire property in conquered areas. Hence it is not difficult to explain how this institution could function once it was in place, just as rational explanations have been found for large-scale generosity in other societies (Johnsen, 1986; Lundahl, 1983).

Because of the honorific element it is conceivable that recruitment of liturgists originally did not require any enforcement. As time passed, I would argue that the payment of liturgies came to depend instead on quasi-voluntary compliance: even though there was considerable possibility for evading one's duties and it was often individually rational to do so, the wealthy chose to finance liturgies because they received something in return for their expenditure and they believed that others also contributed. Such a cumbersome system as the *antidosis* procedure could not have worked unless there was widespread quasi-voluntary compliance.

It is also obvious however that there was an element of taxation. The liturgies ceased to be voluntary, even if they had started that way. They became instead a financial burden which a rich man could not or dared not avoid, and "the trierarchy was primarily viewed and treated as a fiscal entity" (Gabrielsen, 1994, p. 44). For the fourth century there is ample evidence that people tried to avoid some of the obligations.[50] While it was still "standard practice to boast publicly of liturgical performances [...] in reality some of these boasts concerned services which the braggart had been compelled to discharge" (Gabrielsen, 1987a, p. 37). Aeschines provides an example of how the father of the other party in a trial is accused of tax evasion:

> I will now show you that his father had not a little ready money, which the defendant has squandered. For the father, afraid of the special services to which he would be liable, sold the property that he owned [...] – a piece of land in Cephisia, another in Amphitrope, and two workshops at the silver mines, one of them in Aulon, the other near the tomb of Thrasyllus.
>
> (Aeschines 1.101)

Since we do not have the same kinds of sources (in particular forensic speeches) for the fifth century as for the fourth, it is perfectly possible that there were similar attempts to avoid liturgical burdens in the earlier period. As argued in Chapter 4, other developments make it likely that the propensity to try to escape taxation increased in the fourth century compared to the fifth. Tax compliance regarding taxation of wealth became more problematic after the Peloponnesian War and in the fourth century. There are several reasons for this.

First, Davies (1981) has suggested that the rich Athenians became less interested in the Athenian wars. In the fifth century, with the Athenian Empire, they could anticipate acquisitions of land and property in other states and they had overseas investments to protect. This was no longer the case after the dissolution of the Empire.

Second, public display of generosity was becoming less important politically (which is not to say that the incentive disappeared completely). The composition of the leading class changed over time. Originally the rulers belonged to the old aristocratic families and spending for public welfare (whether as liturgy or taxes) brought honour, social standing, and a recognised position as a leader of the people. Our evidence could be taken to show that the contributions gradually ceased to bring political support and honour.[51] In the second half of the fifth century new men appeared on the political scene, but they were still men of wealth. One finds that

> Down to and including Perikles all Athenian leaders [...] had been aristo-crats and landowners; after him they were often of lower birth – just as wealthy [...] their power was based much more on their ability to persuade people in the Assembly.
>
> (Hansen, 1999, p. 39)

In the fourth century noble ancestors largely ceased to have a role, and we even find men of modest means among the politicians (Ober, 1989, Chapter 6.E; Davies, 1981, Chapter 6). So there was less to gain informally from appearing rich. By then people also complained that it had become dangerous to be rich. Earlier, wealth was a thing to boast about, but now the wealthy risked taxation, blackmail and lawsuits (Isokrates 15.159).

Third, there was also a change in a formal institution that made payment of, for example, liturgies less interesting. In 457, the third property class was admitted to the archonship. Hence you no longer needed to be recognised as belonging to the top two property classes, which made public display of wealth pretty much irrelevant for the purpose of proving your eligibility (in addition to which the archonship itself was less important after the introduction of the lottery in 487). The fact that the reform of 457 gradually ought to have caused problems with, for example, the financing of liturgies has not been noted. One reason could be that this effect was countered for a while by the tribute from the Athenian Empire, which meant fewer burdens on the rich Athenians.

Fourthly, as the use of liturgies to finance festivals and, in particular, the war effort made liturgies a commonplace phenomenon and almost compulsory, it is very likely that in order to get honour and status from the expenditure you actually needed to pay *more* than legally required (Ober, 1989, pp. 241–242). This may explain why we find individuals doing just that, or at least saying that this was what they had been doing (Lysias 21, 25.12–13). In other words, just performing a liturgy may have largely ceased to bring status. This is equivalent to an increase in the implicit tax rate. In this sense what we have after the Peloponnesian War could be a parallel to the situation after the fall of the Peisistratids – the market for status was no longer functioning in the way the rulers desired, and the rich were on the look-out for new ways for gaining prestige. These effects may also explain why we see new forms of generosity emerging and expanding in the fourth century, such as the government asking for voluntary gifts to specific purposes (*epidoseis*; see Gabrielsen, forthcoming).[52]

Fifth, the loss of the empire also meant that the wars would have to be financed with internal revenue (no tribute). There were also fewer rich citizens, and the population was smaller. This implies higher rates of taxation.

Sixth, the running of the democracy was becoming more expensive – the remuneration of magistrates was discontinued, but Assembly pay was introduced – the first 6,000 to arrive at an assembly meeting received payment, originally of one obol but quickly raised to three obols for a total expenditure of perhaps 45 talents per year (Hansen, 1999, pp. 315–316) and later increased again (Hansen, 1999, p. 150). The *theorika* was a payment of two obols per day (Loomis, 1998, pp. 225–226), introduced in the middle of the fourth century, originally as "theatre money" to allow all citizens to afford entry to the theatre on those festival days when tragedies and comedies were performed. It is gradually extended to other festivals. With 30,000 citizens, and assuming everybody received the payment (one can easily imagine the rich abstaining), it would cost 1.7 talents for each day it was paid. At a guess, and since it was viewed as "the glue of democracy" (Hansen, 1999, p. 316), the yearly total expenditure was around 70 talents (Bergh and Lyttkens, 2011).

Seventh, the changes in the economic life and in the composition of wealth made tax evasion easier. A rich man's land holdings were no longer restricted to one deme and, more impotently, wealth was no longer tantamount to landed property. Instead there were coins, precious objects, slaves etc. Several of these forms were much easier to conceal than landed property (in fact probably all of them).

Finally, I would argue that as time passed and market relationships proliferated, the Athenians came to be more and more economically rational, and also expected such behaviour from their fellow citizens (see Chapter 7).

Against this background, it seems likely that the relatively extensive evidence of tax evasion that we find in the fourth century does indeed signify a shift in tax compliance. Given the described development we would expect the degree of quasi-voluntary compliance to fall as some taxpayers found that the terms of their implicit bargain (tax payment vs. benefits received) deteriorated. The other prerequisite for such compliance is a belief that everybody pays. Hence the mere fact that the orators began publicly complaining of non-compliance may have significantly contributed to such behaviour. From the end of the fifth century and onwards, it is a frequent theme in the speeches held in the courts that people evade their civic obligations, do not perform liturgies, do not pay the *eisphora*, and conceal their wealth.

The incentive to hide some of your wealth (transfer resources from agriculture to trade and other monetised activities) could be very high for the individual (Lyttkens, 1992). The reason is that you either paid liturgies and the *eisphora* or you did not. When you became known as a liturgist, *all of your wealth* was suddenly taxed. We hear of no system for deducting a part of your wealth before starting to calculate your tax liability. In practice, with liturgies you either were one of those who were regularly appointed or you were not. Davies has suggested that the limit was 3–4 talents – above that you were unlikely to escape liturgical duties. This should obviously not be thought of as an exact limit, but persons with wealth above 3–4 talents would in the long run be unlikely to escape liturgical duties. The likelihood that you have to finance liturgies is arguably increasing both in your level of wealth and in additions to your wealth.

This means that if you were unlucky, even a small increase in your wealth could push you into the group of persons being expected to perform liturgies. Therefore the implied marginal rate of taxation on an increase in wealth could be very high indeed.

Assume, for example, that belonging to the liturgical class entailed an average tax of 1 per cent per year on your wealth (Lyttkens, 1992). Assume further that an increase in wealth from three to four talents (18,000 to 24,000 drachmas) with a 100 per cent probability moved you into the liturgical class. The implied marginal wealth-tax on that extra one talent is 4 per cent (1 per cent of 24,000 divided by 6,000). This is at least higher than what we have had in Sweden the last 100 years. If the return on capital is 8 per cent, and we think of the liturgy as a tax on that return, the implied marginal tax rate on the associated increase in return from capital is 50 per cent (1 per cent of 24,000 drachmas divided by 8 per cent of 6,000 drachmas)!

Even if nobody at that time had heard the expression "marginal rate of taxation", I am confident that the Athenians were perfectly capable of grasping that it could be a very good idea tax-wise to ensure that you ended outside the liturgical class, and also that they had a good working knowledge of how much of their wealth they needed to conceal to accomplish that. This has as much to do with common sense as making the observation that prices tend to rise when there is excess demand. Even if 100 per cent probability is an obvious exaggeration in the calculation above, the fact remains that the incentives for tax evasion could be substantial for someone with wealth close to the critical level.

We saw in Chapter 4 and in section 6.2 that the collection of the *eisphora* and the allocation of liturgical duties were formalised in the fourth century. This change in tax administration goes hand in hand with the transfer of powers from the Assembly to other bodies where the rich would have greater influence (in particular the Areopagos). As I argued in Chapter 4, the latter changes were necessitated by the fact that the poor could no longer credibly commit not to increase taxation of the rich.[53] The need for the majority to commit not to increase the taxation of the rich after the Peloponnesian War was probably the reason for transferring tax collection to the wealthy, thereby giving them implicit but considerable control over the use of the tax.[54] The formalised position of the *proeispherontes* and their small number would encourage co-operation among them and give them considerable power over the administration of the tax. If they wished they could probably sabotage any attempt to use it. It follows that the rich seem to have had much more influence over the use of the *eisphora* after the reform than before. Such a transfer of power was probably a *sine qua non* for the rich to accept the situation in general, and also – by the way – to accept the formalisation of the tax.[55]

In contrast the traditional explanation for the reform in 387 (symmories, *proeisphora*, assessment) is as a way of obtaining a more accurate list of the wealthy inhabitants (Davies, 1981, App. 1; Rhodes, 1982). More importantly, it constitutes a substantial departure from the previously occasional character of the *eisphora*. With the reforms of 378/7 a permanent organisation to collect the tax had been constructed. This potentially reduced the cost of using the tax considerably and would probably not have been conceivable unless the rich were given control over tax collection.[56]

6.4 Effects of taxation on the Athenian society and economy

Taxation had important effects on Athenian society. First and most fundamentally, by requiring monetary payment, the taxation pushed the population – and in particular the rich – into the market economy. Arguably both the liturgies and the *eisphora* entailed monetary outlays. By requiring monetary outlay, the taxation must have induced a shift towards economic activities that gave a monetary return, such as trade and production for the market, and away from a focus on land holdings, self-sufficiency and status. That taxation served as a push factor as regards economic activities parallels the similar conclusion for the Roman Empire by Bang (2008).

The move towards the market led to specialisation – Harris (2002) documents more than 160 different occupations in Athens. Specialisation and trade in turn led to economic growth. This way the tax system arguably increased the long-term prosperity of the Athenians. It also helped change the individuals' view of the world, including their perception of their compatriots (more on this in Chapter 7).

Two other effects of the taxation also served to increase the market reliance and hence specialisation. On the one hand, if you tax the wealth of a person, you take away some of his consumption possibilities. If that person – prior to taxation – had chosen an optimal allocation of his time between leisure and work, then taxation will lead to a change in optimal behaviour. Common sense tells us that he is very likely to increase his work so as to make up for some of the loss in consumption possibilities, even if that means less leisure (if there is no change in behaviour, then at the margin, one hour of leisure will be worth less than the increase in consumption that will follow from one hour of work[57]). Hence a tax will tend to increase the labour supply of the affected individuals and thereby gross domestic product (GDP) as conventionally constructed. This is a so-called income effect.[58] Clearly in the Athenian case it is taxes on wealth that are the most relevant category in this context (taxes on income were few and particular, see above). Both the *eisphora* and the liturgies would have had an income effect, increasing labour supply (in the case of liturgies, mitigated by their honorific aspect).

On the other hand, the activities that gave a monetary return were by and large also the activities that were easy to hide from taxation. When we take account of the possibility for illegal tax evasion, there is also a substitution effect between having your wealth in easily taxable forms versus easily concealed forms. The incentive to hide your wealth because of the tax system had very similar effects to the need for a monetary return. The incentives to avoid taxation made it attractive to move economic activities from the traditional land holdings to more "invisible" activities such as trade, lending, commercial enterprises, etc. (and it encouraged the development of banking).

Finally, we should point out that the per capita taxes, such as the *metoikion*, also had an unambiguously positive effect on labour supply, since there was a clear income effect.

6.5 Concluding remarks

The structure of Athenian taxation suggests that tax policy was informed by an understanding of the political and economic ramifications of taxation. The Athenians could not raise taxes on trade without peril because then trade would disappear. They could not raise taxes on the metics because then the metics would disappear. And they could not raise taxes on the rich because then the democracy would disappear.

Hence it is an impressive fact that the tax system seems to have functioned remarkably well, so well indeed that the Athenians tried to replace the tribute with a tax on trade throughout their empire. Despite the complaints about tax evasion, the liturgy system functioned well enough to let the Athenian enjoy a vast number of festivals. The liturgies together with the *eisphora* allowed the Athenians and to conduct warfare on a remarkable scale. In the fourth century, the Athenians were at war 396–386 and 378–338 with occasional year-long intervals. Pritchard (forthcoming) has estimated, for example, that the average yearly military expenditures in the period 378–370 came to 522 talents, a sum that most probably exceeded the total public revenue in peace time.[59]

The structure and effects of Athenian taxation also implies that there was overall a very rational attitude towards matters economic, both on the part of those who taxed and among those who were the objects of taxation. The Athenians were very adroit in avoiding spending public money on transaction costs of taxation. In general, they also seem to confirm to the predatory hypothesis of Levi (1988) – doing their best to increase tax revenue in any way they could come up with. At the same time, when as individuals they were the tax subjects, they were quick to transfer their property to invisible forms. An additional objective seems to have been to avoid creating powerful bureaucrats.

The widespread participation among the citizen body in running the state (the result of the Athenian political rules of rotation, etc.) must have given them a pretty good idea about the limits possible for their tax system, and the likely reactions among the citizens and metics. After the loss of the Empire and several times in the fourth century, they were able to manipulate their tax system to avoid a total breakdown in the implicit contract between rich and poor. They were aware both of taxation as a manifestation of the conflicting interests in society, and of their common interests in fostering trade and of using taxation to appropriate some of the resources that were engaged in that trade (Xenophon *Ways and means* 3). By experience if nothing else they had learned that trade and the concomitant specialisation made them better off than ever before.

7 Institutions and markets

Discussions of the development of democracy increasingly emphasise that there is no mono-causal relationship between economic development and institutional change. Rather, there is a complex interplay between these two processes, where different societies may end up on different paths due to particular early circumstances.[1] As formulated by Greif (2005, p. 727): "neither the assertion that liberal political institutions lead to markets nor that markets lead to liberal governance are supported by theory or history. Markets and political institutions co-evolve through a dynamic inter-play between contract-enforcement and coercion-constraining institutions."

For the Athenian case, Ober (2008) argues eloquently that it was the particular form of democracy found in ancient Athens that enhanced the economic performance of the state, and enabled the Athenians to outdo their rivals in prosperity. He argues that there was a widespread agreement among the Athenians that the very existence of their *polis* faced considerable risks from external rivals and internal civil wars. This led to a common view among the citizens that Athens must be sufficiently powerful to withstand such threats. There was thus an integrating interest – an overwhelming preference shared by the Athenians for a rich and powerful state.[2] There was also a set of institutions that ensured widespread participation in the running of the state and increased the likelihood that the Athenians shared the same view of how their world functioned.

It is commonplace nowadays to emphasise that certain institutions promote efficient economic behaviour and growth (e.g. secure property rights), and the Athenians introduced a great number of efficiency-enhancing institutions, as we shall see, institutions that were also conducive to an expansion of the market sector in society. Over the years, less attention has been paid to the fact that the influence also runs in the other direction, that is, from increased reliance on market relationships to institutional change.[3] In this chapter, we will begin by looking briefly at the relative success of the Athenians and the fact that this development was characterised by an increasing reliance on the market. Then we will look at the institutional changes that encouraged market relationships, and finally how the emergence of market behaviour may have fed back into the institutional structure and its effects. This should be envisaged as a mutual dependence: the institutional changes encouraged the growth of the market sector, and at the same time the effect of the market on individual behaviour arguably had repercussions on institutional development.

7.1 A prosperous democracy

Morris (2004) has estimated that real income per capita increased by 50–100 per cent in ancient Greece over the period 800–300, corresponding to a yearly per capita growth of 0.07–0.14 per cent. This means that the economic growth outpaced the almost tenfold increase in population. Some data suggest that the increase in prosperity was even larger. Morris (2004, p. 720) notes, for example, that by "300 the typical Greek house cost something like five to ten times as much as the typical house had around 800". An increase in real incomes is of course what we would expect as a result of the increase in trade and specialisation that we know took place.

While the Greek *poleis* in general experienced improved living standards, it seems likely that Athens prospered more than its competitors. Ober (2008, Chapter 2) argues that the Athenians outdid their rivals in terms of prosperity, measured as aggregate material flourishing or its constituent parts: fame, territory size, international activity, public buildings.[4] Athens "was the outstanding competitor in […] a highly demanding environment" (p. 39). The *poleis* were always ready to imitate institutional arrangements from each other and generally kept a close look at what the "competitors" were doing.[5]

The Athenians also benefited from having silver mines and – for much of the fifth century – from their empire. Ober (Chapter 2) shows that state capacity was also remarkable in Athens during periods without imperial power; the late classical era of 354–322 was, for example, unquestionably prosperous. Furthermore, Ober (p. 73) notes that some other *poleis* also possessed outstanding mineral resources without achieving a performance in state capacity on the Athenian level.

Scheidel (2010) estimates that the real daily wage in Athens increased from 8–9 litres of wheat in the late fifth century to 13–16 litres in the late fourth century, i.e. by some 50–100 per cent (assuming that wages were the same in Athens as in nearby Eleusis, which seems likely). In this calculation Scheidel uses the level of nominal wages, which increased from 1 drachma per day to 2.5 drachmas per day, to which he adds information about the price of wheat. Scheidel's calculation is perhaps the first acceptance of the most straightforward interpretation of this increase in the nominal wage – namely that it also represents an increase in real wages.[6] For example Loomis (1998), in his excellent survey of wages in Athens, does not include this possibility in his discussion.

Previously the increase in the nominal wage level from one to 2.5 drachmas has often been discussed in terms of inflation.[7] In ancient Athens at this time, inflation would mean a reduced relative price of silver. This is a conceivable consequence of the fact that the Athenians expanded mining operations from 350 to 330,[8] but unless something very strange occurred on the grain market, Scheidel's results suggest that the rise in nominal wages at least partly represented an increase in real wages.[9] An increase in the real wage does not seem implausible. Increased productivity of labour may have occurred for a variety of reasons – better management, improved methods in agriculture, etc. (Bresson, 2007).

Whether similar developments took place in other *poleis* is impossible to say, but Ober's collection of evidence suggests that the Athenian increase in real wages was not typical for the average *polis*.

That Athens experienced an increase in (at least) nominal wages is also suggested by the level of assembly pay. Such payment compensated ordinary citizens for loss of income when attending a meeting. Many decisions by the Assembly required a quorum of 6,000 attendants, and the payment was one way of ensuring that the necessary number attended (in the fifth century the Athenians had used punishment for non-attendance). Presumably only the first 6,000 to show up received the payment. Assembly pay in the early fourth century was three obols and in the late fourth century it had been raised to one drachma for an ordinary meeting, which lasted a few hours, and 1.5 drachmas for the main meetings (of which there were ten per year) which took longer, perhaps a whole day (Hansen, 1999, p. 150). Assuming that sitting in at the Assembly is more pleasant than working (though this would possibly depend on the weather and hence the season), the implication is that wages were above rather than below assembly pay, i.e. that wages exceeded 1.5 drachmas per day in the late fourth century.[10]

Athenian prosperity in the late fourth century is furthermore clearly indicated by the expansion of the Athenian fleet during the fourth century, from 100 ships in the first decade to 400 in the age of Demosthenes (Hansen, 1999, p. 111). Similarly, the public revenue of the Athenians increased during the second half of the fourth century from 130 talents to 1,200 talents (Demosthenes 10.37–38; Hansen, 1999, p. 260). The biggest contributor to this increase in income is presumably taxes on trade, with the proceeds from leasing out the silver mines coming perhaps in second place.

7.2 A marketish economy[11]

Somewhat unsurprisingly, the growth in prosperity was paralleled by an increased reliance on market relationships in ancient Greece. Trade expanded at least from the eighth century with concomitant specialisation (Osborne, 1996a, b; Thomas and Conant, 1999; Morris, 2002; Reed, 2003). In the late seventh century, "a handful of Greeks were aggressively pursuing gain all across the Mediterranean and doing very well out of it" (Morris, 2002, p. 32). Osborne (1996b, p. 42) argues that already in the first half of the sixth century, archaic Greece "was marked by a 'conglomeration of interdependent markets' in which production and prices in producing and consuming cities were linked".[12] Probably by 500, major Greek cities such as Athens were permanently reliant on imported grain,[13] and olive oil and wine were exported by a number of Aegean states (Davies, 2007, p. 343). In the classical period, the Greek city states formed a network of trading partners with extensive international division of labour and accompanying productivity gains (Bresson, 2008, p. 176). This still does not necessarily mean that we should think in terms of one great Mediterranean market economy in the modern sense; the latter would imply that wages and prices, *mutatis mutandis*, were equalised across states and regions (and there is a lack of evidence of such conditions).

At least by the late fifth century, it is evident that market forces are at play and that people are aware of this. Several remarks in the comedies of Aristophanes make it clear that prices fluctuate with supply and that people react to it, e.g. rushing to buy cheap sardines in *Knights* (640ff.). The fact that the Athenians tried to stabilise grain prices also shows that people were aware of price fluctuations.

In the fourth century, land was being bought as an investment to improve and resell, as described by Xenophon:

> My father [...] never allowed me to buy a piece of land that was well farmed; but impressed me to buy any that was uncultivated and unplanted owing to the owner's neglect or incapacity [...] did your father sell when he got a good price? [...] he sold of course...] but he would promptly buy another that was out of cultivation.
>
> (Xenophon *Oeconomicus* 20. 22–26)

Furthermore, deliberate investment for profit becomes visible in the form of urban rental property (Davies, 2007, p. 357). Loomis (1998) shows that there was no such thing as a "standard wage" – the same for everyone and irrespective of occupation. On the contrary he demonstrates substantial variations in wages in the fifth and fourth centuries, variations that can easily be explained by variations in the demand and supply of labour.[14] Also by the fourth century, there were private banks in Athens that took deposits and lent to private entrepreneurs. "The bank is a business yielding a hazardous revenue from money which belongs to others" (Demosthenes 36.11). In Athens, private individuals could borrow from *deme* sanctuaries (Chankowski, 2005). However, if you wanted to earn interest on your deposit you probably had to go to the private banks with your money.

Reliance on the market was not restricted to the rich. "In bad years most and in normal years many Athenians had to buy their cereals" (Hansen, 1987, p. 12).

> Extensive specialization of labour made it inevitable that the average Athenian [...] would have dealings with those outside the restricted circle of family, neighbours, and friends. When he bought and sold, he thus had to enter the world of market relations.
>
> (Harris, 2002, p. 76)

Athenian exports included not only olive oil and wine, but also ceramics and other manufactured goods (Amemiya, 2007, p. 86). Harris (2002) documents the existence of no less than 160 different occupations in Classical Athens. "The extensive level of horizontal specialisation was [...] generated not by the elite's tastes for luxury goods but by the widespread demand for a broad range of commodities" (Harris, 2002, p. 78). The building and maintaining of a substantial fleet contributed to the growing specialisation (Halkos and Kyriazis, 2010). In the fourth century, we meet one Phainippos who prefers to produce wine on his well-watered lands, a crop that could provide cash (Osborne, 1991). As mentioned in section 1.4, Herodotos tells a story about the Persian ruler Cyrus which clearly implies that the agora was an important market place by his time (if not before).

This overall picture has recently led some of the economists that have studied the period to conclude that Athens was "a vibrant market economy" (Bitros and Karayiannis 2008), that "fifth and fourth century Athens had an extensive monetary and market system" (Amemiya, 2007, p. xi), and that "the Athenian economy was market dominated and highly monetized" (Halkos and Kyriazis, 2010). Similarly, Christesen (2003) argues that individuals in fourth century Athens displayed instrumental, income-maximising behaviour. What seems indisputable is that there was increasing trade and specialisation, and a movement towards a monetised market economy. The pace and scope of this development are open to debate, but the direction seems clear. It should be envisaged as a gradual process, beginning no later than the seventh century and possibly accelerating after the Peloponnesian War and even more so around 330–320.[15]

Following the approach of Isager and Hansen (1975) (and with essentially the same result), Bergh and Lyttkens (2011) show that the Athenians relied heavily on trade. The importance of trade in the lives of the Athenians is quantified by looking at the value of imports. The calculation goes as follows: we know that in 401/0, the tax farmer who gained the contract for the import/export dues of 2 per cent paid 36 talents and still made "a small profit" (Andokides 1.133). One should note that this was shortly after end of the Peloponnesian War, when the volume of trade probably was unusually low.[16] If the profit rate is 5 per cent, the total volume of trade implied is $(1.05 \times 36)/0.02 = 1,890$ talents. Assuming that 50 per cent of this was transit trade and that we should add 500 talents worth of grain imports (which was taxed separately), total imports plus exports amounted to $500 + (1,890 \times 0.5) = 1,445$ talents or 8,670,000 drachmas. With 50,000 free adult males (citizens and metics), this corresponds to 173 drachmas per adult male or 89 per cent of his income from his own work, assuming 195 working days at one drachma per day (or 77 per cent if people work 225 days per year, or 49 per cent with 350 working days).[17] The reliance on imports hardly decreased during the course of the fourth century.

The margin of error is obviously very large in a calculation of this kind. However, it is worth noting that it places the reliance on markets in the same order of magnitude as Hansen's calculations of the import of grain to Athens – two-thirds of the population fed by imports.

Taxation, we noted in Chapter 6, had the important repercussion that it pushed the citizens – in particular the elite – into market relationships for want of cash, and later taxation encouraged monetary wealth because such wealth was invisible and was unlikely to attract taxation. In other words, taxation served both as push and a pull factor to get people into the market sphere.

7.3 A democracy with efficient institutions

Prosperity, trade, specialisation and an increased reliance on market relationships characterised classical Athens. Yet another unsurprising finding is that this development was encouraged by a series of institutional changes.

For economic efficiency there are two major concerns regarding the institutional set-up in a society – the size of transaction costs and the security of property rights. Obviously the two are interrelated because, for example, if property rights are not well defined then transaction costs will rise.

Transaction costs

Among the early important changes was the introduction of coinage.[18] This may originally have taken place for other reasons than trade (e.g. taxation, status, financing state expenditure, paying mercenaries, etc.), but in any case it quickly included small denominations (Kim, 2002), and must greatly have encouraged trade by reducing transaction costs. This effect of coinage must have been obvious almost from the beginning, and was instrumental in stimulating trade and growth over a wide Mediterranean region (Bresson, 2008, Chapter 2).

The first coins were made of electrum (an alloy of gold and silver). This coinage was relatively soon replaced by silver, probably because it was impractical for several reasons (Bresson, 2009). The gold and silver content of the electrum coins could be manipulated, which creates transaction costs because traders need to ascertain the value of the coins. The small denominations were physically too small to be practical, such as the 1/192 coin, 2.5 mm in diameter and weighing 0.08 g. Yet even in these small denominations the electrum coins were too valuable to be useful for everyday transactions.[19]

Over time the Athenians came to have access to what was extremely sound money. Athenian coins – the famous "owls", tetradrachms in silver with Athena on one side and her owl on the other – were the greenbacks of the eastern Mediterranean (Engen, 2005). Athenian coins are found over large distances, and sometimes the Athenian coins are imitated by other states – not necessarily with fraud in mind; the imitations often contain the same amount of silver as the originals. The owls were used also in transactions where neither party was an Athenian.

In 375/4 the so called law of Nikophon was enacted in Athens (Engen, 2005). A magistrate was given the task of taking out of circulation debased Athenian-looking coins. Traders were thereby ensured that Athenian coins obtained in Athens were of certified value, which encouraged trade. Compared to other *poleis*, the Athenians for a long time retained a less aesthetically pleasing and archaic coin, presumably in order to build upon its reputation.

Ober (2010) suggests that classical Athens benefited greatly not only from egalitarian *polis* institutions that encourage human capital formation, but also from institutions that reduced transaction costs, such as standardised weights and measures and standardised and publicly available laws. In addition to having magistrates that checked the quality of the coins circulating in the agora, the Athenians appointed other magistrates who supervised the weights and measures used.[20]

Additionally, fraud in business deals was outlawed in Athens (Demosthenes 20.9). Bresson (2008, Chapter 1) emphasises that the Athenians in particular, but also other city-states, took measures to ensure that the agora was a "legal space" (*un espace de droit*) where transaction costs were minimised, thus contributing significantly to economic growth. Bresson also argues that other rules applied for transaction conducted outside the agora, so that each party had to take more precautions, which increased transaction costs.

By ensuring that transaction costs were minimised in the agora, the city-state also facilitated taxation of that trade, as we noted in the previous chapter. Similarly, some city-states limited foreign trade to one port.[21] This may have helped the trade in some ways, but it would definitely also have increased the possibilities to tax the trade. Predatory rule once again.

Property rights

The importance of secure property rights for economic performance is now invariably emphasised not only in new institutional economics but also in mainstream economics. An individual needs to have his property rights protected against on the one hand other private parties, and on the other hand against the government.

Traders who moved between cities or other societies in the ancient world faced the risk of having their person or their goods seized. There were of course bandits and pirates, but also the risk of being a foreigner in a legal dispute with a citizen of the town in question.[22]

Several mechanisms were developed to deal with these risks. Traditionally there were ties of friendship between citizens of different *poleis*, essentially a continuation of the same practice among the elite in the Dark Ages. In the classical period, a *polis* – Athens say – could appoint a citizen of another *polis* to be *proxenos*. This title meant that the *proxenos* acted as sort of ambassador for Athenians who visited his *polis*. In return the *proxenos* received privileges in Athens. There were also bilateral agreements between different *poleis* that ensured that traders would have legal right in the *polis* where they were not a citizen. Twenty or so such agreements between Athens and her allies and other cities have been preserved, and there are examples from other city-states (Migeotte, 2009, Chapter 4). I will not deal in detail with the mechanisms of exchange; these are thoroughly investigated in Bresson (2008).

In the second half of the fourth century, changes in Athenian legislation were undertaken in order to facilitate commercial activity, in particular for foreigners

(Bresson, 2008, pp. 16–18; Burke, 1992; Migeotte, 2009, p. 154). This was apparently an Athenian innovation. The procedures for hearing commercial disputes were altered and the law was changed to admit individuals to litigation without regard to their nationality. This meant that foreigners were for the first time allowed to appear in court and present their own case (previously having depended on some Athenian citizen to argue their case). In addition, it allowed for adjudication within a month. Both these changes entailed a reduction in transaction costs by reducing the uncertainty in the commercial relationship.

We turn now to the protection an Athenian citizen had against the state. Taxation has been dealt with in the previous chapter, and only marginally concerns us here. An important reform – attributed to Solon – was the right to appeal the decision of an archon. As argued in Chapter 5, this should probably be conceptualised as a piece of elite self-regulation, like many of the other early laws in various *poleis* (Osborne, 1996a). This early legislation developed into established procedures for challenging the activities of the magistrates in general (Hansen, 1999, p. 221).

Similarly, the first action of an archon when he took up office was to swear that "all men shall hold until the end of his office those possessions and powers that they held before his entry into office" (Aristotle *Athenian Constitution* 56.2).[23] In other words, the importance of protecting property rights is established yearly by the highest-ranked official. It seems to me that this may also go back in time and be another instance of elite self-regulation – members of the elite and their property were protected from the actions of those of their peers who happened to be in office.

Both of these principles are potentially very important for the security of property rights for ordinary citizens, but they depend on the functioning of the judicial system. The right to appeal against the decision of an archon, for example, looks very different depending on which kind of court the case ends up in.

Before Peisistratos, the judicial power resided with the elite and the ordinary citizen was probably dependent on the local chiefs. Hesiod (*Works and days* 30–39) complained around 700 that the aristocrats "gave crooked sentences for the lure of gain". By his system of travelling judges, Peisistratos made the ordinary population less dependent on the local landlord and likely strengthened their property rights. In 462 the Areopagos was deprived of most of its powers, which were transferred to the Assembly and to courts manned by ordinary citizens.[24]

When we come to the period when jurors were selected by lot and paid for their service, i.e. sometime after *c.*450, the poor majority is safely in the saddle (and are presumably in majority in the courts[25]) regarding legislative and judicial matters, including security of property rights.[26] There were established procedures for dealing with conflicts regarding property rights and other contractual issues. In 403/2 the Athenians established a rule that magistrates were only allowed to use written laws.

Nevertheless, rich Athenians faced a risk that their property rights would not be respected in a judicial conflict. As mentioned in section 6.2, the ancient literature has preserved frequent complaints that the poor in a democracy might exploit the rich in political trials. A trial could lead to heavy fines or outright confiscation of property. The revenues from the courts make large contributions to public revenue, but we do not now to what extent the poor soaked the rich in this way. Probably the best interpretation is that this was not a problem in normal times, but in crisis situations it could perhaps be somewhat risky being rich if you end up in a court.[27] This adds a further incentive to keep your wealth out of the public eye. In modern societies the problem is usually the opposite, in that the rich have an advantage in courts.

Chance, design or spontaneous solution

So we find several efficiency-enhancing institutions being introduced in Athens in the archaic and classical periods. It lies near at hand to argue that the escalation of trade increased the demand for helpful institutions, and that once these institutions were in place, trade expanded even more. However, if we are to argue that these institutional changes occurred because there was a need for them in the market, we also need to make a credible argument that the Athenians understood what they were doing. Despite pessimistic statements about the economic understanding of the ancient Greeks, it is evident that the Athenians came to understand a great deal about the links between the institutional structure and economic performance, at least in the fourth century. Otherwise how should we understand the law of Nikophon safeguarding the value of Athenian coinage, or the laws enabling foreign merchants to appear in court and have their cases resolved within a reasonable space of time? Around 355, Xenophon explicitly points to the quick settlement of commercial disputes as a source of prosperity to Athens:

> If prizes were offered to the magistrates for the just and prompt settlement of disputes, so that sailings were not delayed, the effect would be that a far larger number of merchants would trade with us [...]. It would also be an excellent idea to reserve seats in the theatre for merchants [...] the rise in the number of residents and visitors would of course lead to a corresponding expansion of our imports and exports, of sales, rents, and customs.
>
> (Xenophon Ways and means 3.1–3)

The Athenians were aware of the beneficial effect of trade on the prosperity of their *polis*. Furthermore, Plato was aware that specialisation led to greater efficiency and to a general increase in wealth (Bresson, 2007, p. 113; Harris, 2002, p. 72). That this proves to be the case is hardly surprising: here we are more or less in the realm of common sense and simple empirical observation – these observations do not require advanced economic analysis. We may also note that Plato (*Laws* 11 916a–c) suggests that there should be a period of 12 months during which the buyer could cancel the purchase of a slave with epilepsy (and six months for other illnesses). An inscription from Abdera from around 350 attests the existence of this kind of legislation (Bresson, 2008, p. 38). These measures significantly reduced the buyer's commercial risk and transaction costs.

I do not wish to propose that the ancient Greeks understood every aspect of the economic forces they were dealing with. They did understand several relationships that you can readily observe, such as the fact that prices fluctuate in response to variations in supply, or that trade is encouraged if traders are assured a fair deal in court. They probably did not understand fully the effects of import or export taxes. What they definitely did understand was tax revenues.

In addition to public measures, the market provided some spontaneous institutional innovations. The most obvious example is the development of banks, which occurred in spite of the lack of limited liability arrangements. Falling partly outside the scope of existing laws and regulations in Athens, the banks also came to rely on informal norms and long-term relationships (Cohen, 1992).

To safeguard the quality of goods, spontaneous market solutions included the development and protection of brand names. For example, already in the fifth century (at the latest) there was an international consensus that the wines from Chios and Thasos were the best of Greek wines. Consequently, high-quality wines from Thasos were sold in small amphorae unlike others on the market.[28]

The importance of efficient institutions

Overall, it seems likely that institutional quality contributed significantly to the prosperity of the Athenians, even though there are obviously many factors involved in economic growth and growth was not confined to Athens. To take an obvious example, the import of cheap energy in the form of slave labour was probably one of the most important factors in the material success of ancient Greece.

Using the Economic Freedom Index as a way to measure institutional quality, Bergh and Lyttkens (2011) found that Athens in the second half of the fourth century displayed a high degree of economic freedom.[29] On a scale from one to 10 (with higher values representing higher freedom), ancient Athens scores 8.9. This admittedly anachronistic exercise places ancient Athens between Hong Kong and Singapore – the two top countries in the index AD 2008. In general Athens scores high on all the different dimensions of the index, with a few notable exceptions, such as the regulation of the grain trade. It is also important to note that the restricted rights of women and slaves are not easily fitted into the index, so it measures economic freedom from the perspective of the male citizens only.

The main area where trade was regulated by the Athenians (and by other states) was in grain. One law forbade anyone living in Athens or Attica (whether citizen or metic) to lend money to a ship importing grain into any other place than Athens. Another law forbade anyone living in Athens or Attica to transport grain to any other harbour than Piraeus, and two-thirds of the grain had to be disposed of in Athens. The grain trade was the only one regulated in this way.

Furthermore, there were price controls ensuring that prices would not soar too high (Bresson 2000, Chapter 8; 2008, Chapter 4), and occasionally the state would subsidise grain. Magistrates controlled that "unground corn in the market is on sale at a fair price, and next that millers sell barley-meal at a price corresponding with that of barely, and bakers loaves at a price corresponding with that of wheat" (Aristotle *Athenian Constitution* 51.3). Also, grain retailers are not allowed to buy more than a certain quantity of grain at a time, to prevent speculation. Sometimes individuals are lauded for selling at not much above the usual price, despite there being a shortage. This suggests that such benefaction was not standard practice. It also implies that subsidies are not always available or adequate.

While these measures reduced the level of economic freedom, they cannot reasonably be characterised as irrational or as necessarily inefficient. The costs of transportation were so high in antiquity that famine could strike in one area even if there was an excess food supply nearby. In this situation it appears entirely rational to try to guarantee a supply of food. The main problem appears to be that Athenian farmers may have been put in a lose–lose situation: if the harvest was bad, their incomes would fall, in particular as the prices were perhaps not allowed to rise to equilibrium levels. If on the other hand the harvest was good, they were hit by the fact that they were not allowed to export, so local prices would be very low.[30]

7.4 The feedback loop – market relationships, economically rational behaviour and institutional change

Ancient Greece in general and Athens in particular consequently witnessed three gradual, simultaneous and interdependent developments: income growth, increasing trade and specialisation, and a movement towards a monetised market economy. These processes were encouraged by institutional changes (coinage, taxation, etc.). At the same time, however, the development arguably had repercussions on people's behaviour, their belief system and their moral attitudes. The influence from the economic domain to other social domains is the subject of this section.

The old world based on informal relationships and activities focused around the aristocratic household was disappearing. Instead we find individuals who are becoming increasingly free agents, and market relationships are becoming important in the everyday life of the Athenians. I find it inconceivable that this process could go on without a concomitant change in the individual's view of the world and in his preferences. In economic analysis, preferences are usually assumed to be stable. This assumption may sometimes be reasonable, and it is certainly a convenient analytical tool. However, it is not a good approximation of reality – there are many reasons to expect that both preferences and the view of the world are changing with the experiences of the individual (Fehr and Hoff, 2011; Lichtenstein and Slovic, 2006).

A reasonable hypothesis is that over the three centuries 600–300, an increasing prevalence of market transactions (in contrast to giving and lending from family, friends and neighbours) gradually made people think and behave differently, and also, equally importantly, to expect another kind of behaviour from their fellow citizens than the traditional one. In view of the lack of relevant evidence, the discussion below is necessarily speculative. However, as these mechanisms constitute an important part of the jigsaw puzzle, there is good reason to consider them.

The literature on social capital has emphasised that there are two kinds of trust: thick and thin trust, alternatively labelled personalised trust and generalised trust. The former (thick) trust is the trust that exists between friends and family and people you know well, the other concerns trust towards people in general. Generalised trust is important for economic development, as it is a feature of many economic relationships. Kenneth Arrow (1972) has pointed out that there is an element of trust in every economic transaction. On reflection this is obvious. There is no way you can write complete-contingency contracts with those you do business with,[31] so important parts of a business agreement depend on trust that the other party will honour the contract. Otherwise transaction costs would be prohibitively high; it is simply too costly to deal with people you don't trust. Market relationships depend on individuals not acting according to a narrow definition of their economic interest, so that they play "trust" even though in a one-shot game it would increase their net income to play "defect". This is why, for example, companies try to establish long-term relationships with their trading partners. Opportunistic behaviour becomes much less likely if there are repeat transactions between the same parties.

In a market economy you do not hesitate to do business with someone you have never met before. For example, you can go into a shoe store you have never visited before to buy a pair of shoes, and if the sales person says that they are made of leather you tend to believe him. You do not expect a person with whom you transact to take every opportunity to deceive you.

Arguably, not only market relationships but also democracy builds on trust to a considerable extent. Democracy is potentially only stable if the minority trust that the majority will not use their position to, for example, create laws or change the constitution so that political power is permanently transferred to them (so that it is no longer a democracy), or to raise the level of taxation for the minority.

In real life – as distinct from a game-theoretic model – it is difficult to make a totally credible commitment. Whether a commitment is credible will, for example, often depend on the private information of different actors, and anyone party must trust that the hidden information does not dramatically alter the situation.

A likely hypothesis therefore is that the gradual democratising of Athens in the fifth century was facilitated by the fact that everyday market relationships had made the Athenians somewhat used to the thought that it was possible to trust people beyond the narrow group of friends and relatives. This should not be taken to imply that the other factors discussed in Chapter 4 lose their significance. For example, remember the cushioning effect of tribute from the Empire during the formative years of the democracy, 508–450, and the fact that taxation of the rich could be kept at relatively low levels for most of the fifth century. It is quite likely that all the factors were necessary ingredients in the development of the "radical" democracy in Athens.

Some empirical evidence offers at least weak support to this hypothesis. It has been shown in experimental economics that market integration and prosocial behaviour are positively correlated. Take the case of the so-called "Ultimatum game". There are two parties, who get to share a specified sum if they agree on how it should be split. The first of the parties suggests a split. The other party has just two options: either they accept the split suggested by the first party, in which case the money is distributed as suggested, or they can refuse to accept the proposed split, in which case neither of the two parties will receive anything. Let's say the total sum is £100 – 100 British pounds. If the first party is economically rational, and believes that the other party is so too,[32] then they will suggest the following split: they take £99 for themself, and leave just £1 (one!) to the party who just can say "yes" or "no". If party number two is also economically rational, they will accept this very uneven split (after all one is more than nothing). However, many individuals find such an uneven split unacceptable and prefer to refuse the split. It turns out that proposers anticipate this, and that the suggested split often leaves between 25 and 50 per cent of the sum to the second party. This is an example of prosocial behaviour.

In a few experiments, researchers have gone beyond the usual rat population (university students), and have conducted the same ultimatum game-experiment in widely differing and comparatively simple societies.[33] What they find, interestingly enough, is that the degree of prosocial behaviour increases in the level of market integration in the society. Market integration is measured in these experiments as the percentage of calorie intake that is obtained from the market. With this measure ancient Athens would count as a relatively highly market integrated society, judging by, for example, the share of grain (two-thirds) that was imported to Athens. This could suggest a comparatively high degree of prosocial behaviour.

The direction of causality is not clear in these experiments, and one would like to see more studies to be sure about the validity and generalisability of the results. This being said, however, it does not seem far-fetched to suggest that an experience of market relationships changes behaviour in the direction suggested by the experiment, and that this carries over to other similar situations and provides a basis for trusting behaviour.

In ancient Athens, the widespread participation in running the state also contributed to the transparency of the system and to making it credible that the majority would not abuse its political power. In the fourth century, as mentioned above, the male citizens numbered perhaps around 30,000 and Assembly meetings (of which there were 40 a year) were generally attended by at least 6,000 citizens. Hansen (1999, p. 313) calculates that the rules regulating rotation on the council and magistracies ensured that every third citizen served at least once on the council, and that the pool of magistrates must have been well above 1200 citizens. This popular participation likely had far-reaching consequences, and was instrumental in enabling the Athenians to adapt their institutional structure to changing conditions and to maintain a social equilibrium between the elite and the common citizens (Ober, 2008). The widespread participation meant that the system was transparent for the population as whole, which greatly facilitated trust and added to the stability of Athenian democracy.

There was one group of people, however, that seemingly was not to be trusted in Athens. The Athenians were extremely careful to establish institutions that enabled them to prevent magistrates (and anybody else who handled public money) from enriching themselves at the public's expense, and rules that meant politicians were held accountable for the advice they gave.

> The Athenians had the characteristic of being honest with themselves about themselves. [...] they went on the basis that, given the chance, every one of them would have his hand in the till and make a profit out of political activity, and they took every possible means to limit the chances.
>
> (Hansen 1999, p. 310)

The overarching principle behind the extensive rules and regulations was "that absolutely nobody is to be trusted" according to Davies (1994, p. 204), who attributes this characterisation to David Lewis.

As far as the magistrates are concerned, there was an obvious 1/N problem. If the official enriched himself at the public's expense, the money went directly into his purse. Furthermore, being only one citizen of many (e.g. N citizens, where N is a couple of tens of thousands), any problem due to missing public funds only affected him slightly (to the degree of 1/N). This is not like a business deal, where you gain by establishing a reputation for honesty. In fact, the Athenians desire to avoid powerful bureaucrats and therefore limit their time in office to one year will have exacerbated the problem – there was no gain for the individual official in obtaining a good reputation during his one year in office because he could not make a career out of it anyway (he could only serve as official every second year).

The experience of running the state system made the Athenians aware that the risk of a revolution or *coup d'état* were not the only problematic policy issues. The democracy could be undermined simply by stupid decisions in the Assembly, or decisions that were proposed by a speaker who had some personal hidden agenda, so that the decision might be good for him but very bad for the Athenians in general. The threat of revolution could be handled by the use of ostracism – potential tyrants could be expelled for ten years. To deal with the other problems, the Athenians began using another procedure, the *graphe paranomon*. Under this heading, anybody who had proposed a decree could be accused of proposing a decree that was

> unconstitutional, formally or informally, or that it was undesirable and damaging to the interests of the people [...] the notion of illegality was extended

in the course of the fourth century to breach of the (democratic) principles underlying the law.

(Hansen, 1999, p. 206)

So even though the Assembly had voted in favour of the suggestion, you could be punished up to *one year after* having made the proposal. At the same time, to avoid excesses, the person who made the accusation would be punished himself if he withdrew the accusation or failed to get at least 20 per cent of the votes in favour of the accusation. The *graphe paranomon* seems to have replaced ostracism as a way of disciplining politicians from around 415.[34] These safeguards against bad decisions were probably instrumental in sustaining the democracy through the fourth century.[35]

The attitude towards those who had been selected to act as magistrates depended also on another aspect of the emergence of market relationships. This is that the experience of individualistic market relationships (the logic of the market) encourages self-interested behaviour and an individualistic ethos,[36] i.e. more of what we would call "economically rational behaviour", and less "embededness".

Language and thought processes are intimately linked. It is therefore interesting to note a change in language. The word "agora" originally signified a public meeting place, but as noted in Chapter 1, by the middle of the fifth century a new verb, agorazo, "I buy" had appeared (Davies, 2007, p. 335). A new word – an innovation in language – is a tangible indication of a change in the view of the world (as George Orwell showed with "Newspeak" in *1984*). It implies that the citizens' view of the society surrounding them had changed compared to the time when the agora was only a meeting place.

Consequently, the individual in ancient Greece would increasingly expect economically rational behaviour from fellow citizens – looking after their own own interest – whether in business transactions, politics, as taxpayers, or in public administration. This is an example of intertransactional linkages, to use the term introduced by Greif (2006, p. 48). Compare Thukydides' (1.70) description of the Athenians: prone to innovation, inclined to take the utmost advantage of any possibility, constantly on the lookout for new opportunities. That "economic rationality" gradually evolved in Greece does not mean that it describes all behaviour at any time in this period; but then it does not describe all behaviour in modern society either.

Such changes may have been further encouraged by the increasing level of income in ancient Greece. When selecting a course of action in everyday life, individuals in most situations follow their habits, acting in an unreflective manner, otherwise life would be unmanageable (Hodgson, 1997). Sometimes, however, the individual makes conscious efforts to engage in explicit and calculated decision making on the basis of expected costs and benefits associated with different alternatives. The latter strategy corresponds to "economically rational behaviour". In modern society, there are several reasons to believe that those with fewer resources at their disposal are more prone to rely on habits

(Lindbladh and Lyttkens, 2002). For example, explicit decision making is costly, and those in low social positions have accustomed themselves to the fact that it just seems meaningless to devote resources to that activity.[37]

The implication of these considerations is that a general increase in prosperity is likely to produce more of explicit decision making and more of economically rational behaviour. This is probably particularly important in times of rapid changes in society, as is the case now and as arguably was the case in the late archaic and classical periods in ancient Greece.

The changes in attitudes and behaviour, as well as changes in what kind of behaviour people expect from others, have important implications for the effects of different institutional set-ups and for the incentive to change institutions. For example, the basis for compliance with the property taxation in Athens was eroded as the act of tax compliance became more of a consciously calculated decision for the rich, rather than being something which followed automatically (by habit) with one's social position. In a first stage, the basis for compliance likely shifted from custom to quasi-voluntary compliance.[38] The latter change had probably taken place at least by 400, because we hear numerous stories from the law courts of individual tax evasion in the fourth century (see Chapter 6). The emergence of economically rational behaviour arguably also increased the demand for market-enhancing institutions, such as those introduced in Athens to facilitate commercial activity.

7.5 Concluding remarks

The Greeks in general and the Athenians in particular developed institutions that in the modern world would be considered conducive to economic growth. Indeed, in terms of economic freedom, Athens compares favourably with the most successful countries of our time (Bergh and Lyttkens, 2011). Furthermore Ober (2008, 2010) argues that Athens outdid her contemporary rivals in terms of prosperity and that per capita income was higher in classical Athens than in other pre-modern societies. We cannot prove that the institutional characteristics of ancient Athens were the major cause of this prosperity, but it seems fair to conclude that the institutional set-up in all likelihood contributed to the outcome.

The Athenians benefited from institutions that enhanced efficiency in market exchange. Additionally they faced taxation that both pushed and pulled people into the market sector, which served to enhance specialisation and growth. There was a mutual relationship in that the trading sector gained in importance because it was supported by the institutional structure, and at the same time, the greater the reliance on trade, the stronger the incentives to improve the institutional set-up. The development of the market affected the process of institutional change.

It seems reasonable to assume that the gradual emergence of market relationships changed the individual's perception of the world and of other people. There is a significant difference between on the one hand trying to be a self-sufficient farmer, grow all you need so that you can minimise the need for buying things, and on the other hand relying on the market for a supply of most things you need in everyday life (such as grain). In the latter case, you deal with other people, some of whom you do not necessarily know. The experience from market relationships – which depend on trusting more or less anonymous actors – probably facilitated the democratisation of Athens and also helped to stabilise the democracy after the Peloponnesian War.

8 Economic analysis of institutional change in ancient Athens – the past meets the present

The time has come to summarise the conclusions from the analysis of institutional change in ancient Athens. By applying modern economic theory to these issues we get a partly new perspective on the ancient society, and concomitantly we learn about the mechanisms of institutional change. The Athenian case is interesting in its own right in view of the renown of the Athenian democracy, but a study of Athenian history and experiences of institutional changes also provides lessons and hypotheses for the modern world. It helps us discern mechanisms that might otherwise remain poorly understood.

8.1 Institutional change, economic rationality and unexpected consequences

New Institutional Economics provides a useful framework for analysing institutional change in ancient Greece. It provides a consistent theoretical framework and it sometimes suggests new interpretations of the issues and evidence. The presumption that it would be possible to analyse the process of institutional development in terms of *rational choice* has also been supported. Individual decision making in ancient Greece comes out as being consistent with (and seems to reflect) boundedly rational satisficing behaviour. Behaviour is economically rational in the sense of representing self-interest – there is, for example, no need to assume egalitarian ambitions for members of the elite, as has occasionally been done in the literature.

Rationality of course does not rule out *unintended consequences* of purposeful actions. Such consequences indeed seem ubiquitous in the modern world and characterise important parts of the Athenian experience as well. Hence it is always precarious to argue backwards from identified consequences to hypothesised motives for an action. The assumption regarding motives needs to be based on other empirical evidence or theoretical reasoning. What we know (or what seems reasonable to assume) about the motives of individual decision makers in ancient Athens definitely suggests that unintended consequences appear again and again. Institutional change is a process characterised by rational decisions and unexpected consequences.

Several factors contribute to the likelihood that consequences will be other than the decision maker had hoped for. The timespan within which a course of action has to be determined is often short. Solon and Kleisthenes are outstanding examples. In both cases it must have been imperative to find a solution quickly. At a guess, each of them needed at least a partial solution within a few days (or hours). In order to be chosen, the action taken by no means necessarily had to be optimal. But it needed to be satisfactory and available in time, i.e. in time to avoid the unpleasant consequence that loomed ahead. In such a situation, many potential consequences are likely to be ignored because of the necessarily limited analysis of the decision maker. This is particularly likely to occur if the consequences are a long way in the future and therefore carry very little weight. Being pressed for time is also a recipe for unintended consequences, as are situations where some factor(s) attract such a great immediate interest as to dwarf all other aspects (Merton, 1936).

The fact that a series of democratising measures were decided upon by the Athenians, eventually leading to the radical democracy of late-fifth-century Athens, was arguably not in the interest of the members of the Athenian elite, irrespective of whether we think of the Eupatrids or the extended elite after Solon's reforms. This most likely is true not only for the elite as a group, but also for individual members such as Solon and Kleisthenes. The only reason for them to advocate democratising measures was to strengthen the position of the elite in general and/or to improve their own personal strategic bargaining position.

8.2   Institutional change and individual incentives

In my economic perspective, formal institutions only change if someone has an incentive to change them. Institutional change is a process that requires resources, not least because there is always some vested interest in retaining the old institutional structure. Organisations have been created in response to the existing institutions, people have invested time and other resources in learning about the institutions and the rules of the game they create, etc. In the long run, the institutional set-up in a society is likely to be to the advantage of those who govern that society.

Institutional change will normally only be attempted if circumstances change. This may occur for several reasons. One has to do with the process of institutional change itself. It takes time for individuals to adapt their behaviour to a new institutional setting. Hence the effect of an institutional change may take a considerable time to materialise. Furthermore, there will be chain reactions – when some individuals adapt to a new institution, this change in behaviour will cause other individuals to change their behaviour because their environment has changed, and so on. This is in contrast to a model which assumes that individuals immediately behave optimally with respect to new institutions. To add to the complexity of the situation, in my implicit model, not only do individuals learn only gradually, but the feedback they receive does not necessarily make their belief system more correct.

A gradual adaptation among the actors in the economy is likely one of the reasons why it took 48 years after Solon's reforms before Peisistratos managed to topple the elite leadership and establish a long-term tyranny in Athens (15 years to his first attempt). One reason for this was arguably that there had been a one-time shift of resources to the common people, making them better off, and so it would naturally take some time before they were heavily in debt again. It probably also took some time before it became apparent that the abolition of slavery for debt was a mixed blessing (Chapter 5).

A factor of great importance is the beliefs people have, both regarding how the world actually functions and with respect to normative views about what exactly constitutes a just and proper society. Obviously we can only get a good idea of what people believe to be in their own best interest if we have a reasonably accurate idea about how the same people believe that their society functions. For example, an important development must have been the gradual insight that there were alternatives to traditional elite (oligarchic) rule. As we have noted, the tyrants probably helped bring about this change by providing an alternative mode of governance. In our modern democracies, a major issue is how you make voters feel that it is important that they vote, when we know that it is very unlikely that the individual vote will have any influence on the outcome.

This means that by his very existence and position, Peisistratos changed the conditions for elite power, and helped make free agents out of the Athenian poor, thus enabling Kleisthenes to win them over to his side. Similarly, to the extent that there was a growing egalitarian spirit, fostered at least partly by the development of hoplite fighting, the effect on people's belief system may again have been to make non-elite rule an imaginable solution. The development suggested by Morris (2000) of a strong principle of equality was precisely a belief about the world they lived in – the notion that governance of the whole society should not be entrusted to any particular party or small group of citizens (Chapter 4).

An important change in ancient Greece in the archaic and classical periods was the gradual emergence and eventual proliferation of market relationships. As I have argued, this must have *changed the individual's perception of the world* and of the society surrounding them, in particular what kind of behaviour to expect from their fellow citizens and others. They also came to realise the importance of trade for the prosperity of the city-state. In consequence they established institutions that facilitated trade. The logic of the market also formed their perception of how to construct the rules of administration and politics. They carefully scrutinised the behaviour of those engaged in such activities, expecting them to behave economically rationally.

8.3 Institutional change and uncertainty

North (2005, p. 4) makes the important observation that the "deep underlying force driving the human endeavour [is] the ubiquitous effort of humans to render their environment intelligible – to reduce the uncertainties of that environment".

One such mechanism is very apparent in the Athenian experience (Chapter 5). Several times it so happened that group-belonging became important for your position vis-à-vis your property rights and other rights. Situations when this became an issue were for example after Solon's reforms; if you were a citizen then you could not be enslaved for debt within Attica and you had – if you were rich enough – certain political privileges.

Solon's reforms must have made an issue of who was a citizen not only among the poor who feared slavery, but also among the rich inhabitants of Attica. A likely effect was conflicts over who was to be counted as citizen, with manipulation of the rules being the name of the game. Similarly at the time of the conflict between Kleisthenes and Isagoras, there was a proposal to purge the citizen body of those who had no right to be counted as citizens. And once again manipulation of this issue must have become a strategy for power. The thing to note here is that both of these situations were fraught with uncertainty for the individual citizen, and this was precisely so because there was no well-defined criterion for who was a citizen and who was not. Perhaps predictably, both situations led to major social upheavals and institutional change, as we have seen, associated with the rise of Peisistratos and of Kleisthenes to power.

The current trends in society towards individualisation – where the individual is increasingly expected to take responsibility for everything in life, from you children's education to your own cancer – and towards globalisation both contribute to uncertainty in our lives, an effect that is particularly obvious for the less privileged in society. This may be an important factor behind, for example, the international trend towards obesity (Offer *et al.*, 2010) and use of alternative medicine (Lyttkens, 2011). It seems likely that globalisation was a keenly felt phenomenon in ancient Greece, with increased reliance on trade and thereby on conditions far away from you, with a mighty empire just below the horizon. Therefore a fruitful field for future research would be other attempted ways of coping with that uncertainty.

8.4 Change for the better or for (avoiding) the worse

When we turn to our ancient laboratory, we find that institutional change can take at least three different forms. A first and common reason for institutional change is, according to "Davies' law", that people (individuals) are trying to *prevent something unpleasant from happening.*[1] Examples from ancient Athens include, for example, the actions of both Solon (trying to stop a revolution) and Kleisthenes (trying to stop Isagoras from becoming archon). So there is much to be said in favour of Davies' (2003, p. 320) conclusions regarding the decision process that eventually led the Athenians to adopt *demokratia* "insofar as it had any unifying principle at all, that principle [was] the perceived need to *prevent* this or that unpleasant or undesirable development or practice from continuing or from gaining a foothold". I would argue that this principle covers not only the reforms of Solon and those of Kleisthenes, but also the introduction of a lottery to appoint archons. Arguably it may also have been the main reason behind the attempts at elite self-regulation in the archaic period (introduction of written law, of elected officials, etc.).

This principle – that there seem to be stronger incentives involved in preventing a downward turn in fortune – receives empirical (and theoretical) support from the work of Kahneman and Tversky (1979) and Kahneman (2011), who emphasise the importance of reference point bias and suggest the existence of loss aversion, which means that a loss is felt stronger than a corresponding gain. A reference point – defined as the status quo – will also be instrumental in determining what constitutes a satisfying solution.

Note also that these kinds of decisions typically are taken in a great hurry, because one has waited until the last moment. The recent (in 2011) financial crises in several of the members of the EU are a case in point: Portugal and (modern) Greece, for example. Action is not taken until the crisis threatens to lead to a breakdown of the whole of the EU. Or when one is beginning to suspect that we may end up with some countries being placed under international administration. There seems to be no lack of illustrations of this principle in modern times, once you put on the right eye-glasses. Another EU example is that it has been notoriously difficult to reform the common agricultural policy, which is so clearly inefficient. At the same time, huge sums are presently being dished out to the Greeks, who have been mismanaging their affairs but whose collapse would produce a series of political crises in the EU.

Similarly, in his analysis of the future of the Swedish welfare state, Borg (2009) concludes that radical reorientations of public policy have historically primarily been motivated by a desire to avoid a major crisis or total breakdown. He offers Swedish housing policy and public pensions as examples. In the latter case it was obvious in the 1970s (and probably earlier) and documented that pension structures were not sustainable in the long run (Kruse and Ståhlberg, 1977). Nevertheless the pension reform was not agreed upon until 1994 (launched in 1999), when breakdown was becoming imminent (Kruse, 2010).

A second type of institutional change is the *incremental changes that follow from day-to-day elite competition for power*. In ancient Athens, competition within the elite stands out as the most important engine of change. This arguably is how we should view the period of democratising measures that takes us from Kleisthenes' not-so-very-democratic constitution to the fully developed democracy of the 450s. Competition for power is also the underlying force that drives elite self-regulation (Chapters 3–5).

A third type of institutional change is something of an exception, but a very interesting exception. It is exemplified in ancient Athens above all by the changes enacted after the Peloponnesian war, changes that transferred some political power to the elite. The changes did not cause any major upheaval and, on the contrary, probably saved the Athenians from elite coups for a long time.[2] In other words, we are witnessing a society that demonstrates a great deal of *flexibility* in its institutions, the potential to reform the institutional set-up and create a more efficient society (more on this anon).

In all of this, taxation appears as the perhaps most consistently important societal factor. As noted in Chapter 6, *taxation is ubiquitous*. The possibility for the state to use taxation (and other means too of course) to transfer resources from one part of the population to another part (guess who) makes the control of the state an issue of fundamental importance for a society. It emphasises the importance of credible commitments. To what extent can those who control the state credibly commit not to increase the tax burden (or other burdens) on the rest of the population? This as we have seen may explain the emergence of democratising reforms and de-democratising ones, as well as changes in the structure of taxation.

While there is an influence from institutions on economic performance, there is also a relationship between the development of the market and market relationships to institutional change in various spheres of activity.

8.5 Long-run stability *and* useful flexibility

If hurried decisions with unintended consequences are the archetypical characteristics of institutional change in many circumstances, one may wonder if any factors exist that enable a society to reform its formal institutions in reasonably good time and with time to make a comprehensive a priori analysis of the likely consequences. Similarly, while stable rules of the game are in principle a beneficial factor, it can also be important for a society to be flexible, to be able to reform its institutional structure when the old institutions are no longer viable, i.e. to show what North (1990) calls adaptive efficiency. Rodrik (1999, 2000) has emphasised that a vital quality of a society is the ability to cope with shocks and making adjustments without causing violent domestic conflict. He suggests that participatory democracy is a meta-institution for building good institutions.

Let us briefly recapitulate the main features of the Athenian democracy. The political decisions were taken in the assembly, where all (male) citizens could participate, speak and vote. The Athenian state apparatus was run by 1,200 magistrates, the great majority of which were appointed by lottery for one year. Courts were also manned by lottery. Lottery was considered the democratic way of appointment because it gives everybody an equal chance of being selected. Magistrates were paid so that even the poor could serve. A citizen could only serve once in a lifetime in a particular post and he could sit on the council twice. The council prepared issues for the Assembly. The consequence of this, in particular the rules of rotation, was that one-third of all adult male citizens over 18 served on the council at least once and the pool of magistrates must have been well over 1,200 in a society with 30,000 citizens (Hansen, 1999, p. 313). If there ever was a democracy that deserved the adjective "participatory", this is it.

Ober (2008) argues that this widespread participation in politics was the decisive factor for the leading position of Athens in term of material conditions, coinage and literature. The Athenian model implied that information, knowledge and experiences were collected from all parts of Athenian society. The system became predictable for the citizens at the same time as it entailed a great deal of flexibility. This was why the Athenians managed to reform their institutions in difficult situations (Ober, 2008).

The widespread participation that followed with the rules of rotation had the important implication that the system became more predictable for the inhabitants (Ober, 2008). In this sense, the rules of rotation are, I would argue, an institutional response to the uncertainty that people experienced in their lives. Remember that there were 1,200 magistrates each year. This in a population of 30,000 eligible males. This must surely mean that each year everybody knew somebody who was a magistrate and usually they must have known several such persons.

Turning now to modern times, many commentators have suggested over the years that the Swedish welfare state is not viable in the long run. On one hand there will be increasing demands for welfare expenditures, not least because of the ageing population. One the other hand, globalisation and economic integration leads to demand for tax cuts (tax competition between countries). The problems associated with high marginal tax rates have also become more obvious with the passage of time. However, despite all this and the negative predictions, the welfare state has survived with largely unchanged expenditures and average tax rates (in all the Nordic countries).

Bergh and Erlingsson (2008), however, show that the Swedish welfare state has in fact undergone a metamorphosis. In the 1980s the economy was highly regulated, there were many government monopolies, and according to the Economic Freedom Index (Gwartney *et al.*, 2008) Sweden was far below countries such as France, Holland, Italy and the USA, as well as below the other Nordic countries. By 2003, however, Sweden had moved to a top position in the Index. The facts behind this development are that many markets have been deregulated and government monopolies abandoned (capital, electricity, telecomms, pharmacies, aviation, taxis, etc.). Those who lived in Sweden 30 years ago (including yours truly) easily forget how extensively Swedish society was regulated. In 1982, when the leading conservative politician Ulf Adelsohn arrived in Sweden from a holiday in Hong Kong he proudly showed the reporters a fancy wireless telephone he had bought. He was then immediately reported to the police by the Swedish government telecommunications agency, which had a government monopoly on selling telephones!

The most remarkable reform is in many ways that concerning the pension system. Against all odds (theoretically, it ought not to have been possible) it was possible to construct and switch to a system that is sustainable in the long run (Kruse, 2009), mainly because of a very long transition period.[3]

It is particularly striking that these reforms have been carried through with the agreement of both political blocs. Different parties have been unanimously in favour, at least in practice if not necessarily in their public rhetoric. Bergh and Erlingsson (2008) argue that it is the Swedish system with government commissions that has been instrumental in achieving this unanimity and flexibility in the system. The decisions have been firmly based on social science research, and the deliberations in the commissions have entailed close contacts between the research community and the political sphere. All major political parties are represented in the commissions.

This also means that the reforms and the welfare state have built on experiences from different parts of the political spectrum. Therefore the reforms have been politically stable which has facilitated planning for all private parties, individuals and organisations. Within the commissions there has been scope for discussions out of the limelight, thereby facilitating the development of a common view of how the world functions. The reason for bringing up this issue here is that significant parts of this story sound very much like Josiah Ober's analysis of Athenian democracy and why that was so successful.

We have here – or so it seems to me – two parallel success stories, namely contemporary Sweden and ancient Athens. Both have found unique solutions to the mechanisms of institutional change, solutions that have given these societies flexibility. This has enabled them to reform their institutions in ways that have secured their continued existence. Both in Sweden and Athens the system is based on gathering information from very different parts of society and on creating a setting that allows a common view of what is going on to develop. Both had features that ensured widespread participation in the process of policy making.

The Athenian democracy finally disappeared in the social upheavals that followed the conquests of Alexander the Great. Sweden should be happy as long as nothing similar happens here and as long as the system of government commissions prove immune to political manipulation.

In conclusion, the objective of the individual in his life-game is primarily to prevent loss, not to achieve gain. Athens is an example of a society that for a considerable time was able to make both marginal and non-marginal institutional changes that worked well. Contemporary Sweden is another. Among the characteristics of a society that are conducive to such relative successes are political systems that rely on widespread information-gathering (so that many viewpoints are represented) and opportunities to reach a consensus on how the world works.

Glossary

Ancient Greece

Terms that only appear once in the text are explained at that point and are not included here.

Agora   Originally a public meeting place, in particular used for various political functions. Over time also an important market place.

Antidosis   Exchange of property. If someone nominated to perform a liturgy considered someone else better being able to afford it, he could challenge the other person to either undertake the liturgy or agree to an exchange of property with the initially nominated person.

Archon   A magistrate. The plural "archons" in an Athenian context usually designates the nine highest state officials. The singular "archon" usually designates the highest state official after whom the year was named (the archon eponymous).

Areopagos   Short for The Council of the Areopagos (the hill where the council met).

Basileus   1. King (but this is somewhat misleading for the Homeric period, cf. Chapter 3). 2. One of the nine archons (*see* Archon).

Choregia   A liturgy (see liturgy) – to equip and train a dramatic or lyric chorus for a performance at one of the festivals.

Deme   Kleisthenes divided Attica into 139 demes, geographical, political and administrative entities. Every citizen was a member of one deme.

Demos   People, but please see the discussion in section 1.6.

Drachma   Unit of currency (4.3 g. silver). According to the Attic standard, six obols = one drachma, 100 drachmas = one mina, 60 minae = one talent. Consequently one talent = 6,000 drachmas.

Eisphora   Property tax.

Eupatrid   Literally the "well-fathered". Came to be used exclusively in Athens, initially to denote an aristocracy of birth.

Hektemoroi   "Sixth-parters". Usually assumed to designate small-time farmers in Athens who before Solon had to pay one-sixth of their produce to the elite.

Hetairoi   Companions, comrades, warriors, followers.

Liturgy   Public service for the state, e.g. the trierarchy (a naval liturgy), the *choregia* (a festival liturgy) and the *proeisphora* (a liturgy for the collection of the *eisphora* (qv)).

Metic (*metoikos*)   Resident foreigner; a foreigner who had stayed for more than a month in Attica had to register, pay the metic tax (*metoikion*) etc. He had no political rights.

Metoikion   Per capita tax paid by resident foreigners: 12 drachmas per year for a man and six drachmas for a woman.

Obol   See drachma.

Polemarchos   One of the nine archons (see archon), who commanded the army at least until the board of ten generals (*strategoi*) was instituted in 502/1.

Polis (pl. *poleis*)   1. City. 2. City-state. A *polis* usually comprised a city and its hinterland.

Pornikon   Tax on prostitutes.

Probouleutic   Denotes a system whereby an issue was introduced in the Assembly only after being prepared by the council.

Proeisphora   Advance payment of the property tax. It was regarded as a liturgy (see liturgy).

Proeispherontes   Citizens appointed to perform the *proeisphora* (qv).

Talent   *See* drachma.

Thetes   1. Day labourers. 2. The citizens who belonged to the fourth property class.

Trierarchy   A liturgy (qv) – to equip and command a warship for one year.

Xenos   Foreigner, passing by or resident, in which case he or she would be labelled metic (qv).

Economics

Ceteris paribus   A favourite analytical tool in economics. It means *other things being equal*. For example, looking at only the isolated effect of the change in one factor and keeping all other factors constant. It is a great help when you want to discuss an issue such as the effect on labour supply of an increase in income taxation. In messy reality, of course, the *ceteris* are never *paribus*, and so it becomes more difficult to discern the effects of a change in any one factor.

Collective action problem   A sort of multi-player version of the prisoner's dilemma (qv). A situation where a group of individuals would benefit if they all acted in some specified way, but where each individual has an incentive to free-ride on the behaviour of others, because he will receive at least part of the advantages of the beneficial behaviour of others even if he personally makes no contribution. It is not possible to reward the players individually. Therefore we may end up with nobody contributing. For example, everybody gains if your country wins a war, but everybody has an incentive to get the other citizens to do the fighting. So nobody on your side fights and your country is taken over by some less individually rational people. The problem tends to be greater the larger the size (N) of the group involved.

Logrolling   denotes a system where different actors trade votes with each other. So, for example, I could promise to vote for your suggestion to provide publicly financed baby-sitting, it you promise to vote for my suggestion to furnish the Swedish military with nuclear bombs. This way both suggestions will carry a majority vote even though none of them would do so if everybody voted after their preferences. Cf., e.g. Rosen (2005, pp. 118–120).

Mutatis mutandis   *The necessary changes having been made.* Again a very useful tool for condensed writing (and possibly condensed thinking).

NIE   New Institutional Economics

Prisoner's dilemma   The prisoner's dilemma is a standard prop of economists' thinking. Briefly, it is used to denote a situation where two or more parties can reach a comparatively good situation by co-operating, but if for some reason they cannot co-operate (or if they do not trust each other and therefore behave as if they could not communicate, it is after all economics we are talking about), then they both suffer a bad outcome. The standard textbook version is a situation where two crooks can get off with light sentences if neither of them tell on the other, but each of them can get off even better if he tells on the other (and he is the only one of them telling on the other). Additionally, if someone tells on you, then you get a heavy sentence. If these two crooks cannot communicate and are rational they will both tell on the other, and both of them end up with heavy sentences. Cf., e.g., Frank (2006, pp. 454ff.).

Transaction costs   The costs of measuring the valuable attributes of what is being exchanged and the costs of protecting rights and policing and enforcing agreements.

Vested interest   1. A strong personal concern in a state of affairs, system, etc., usually resulting in private gain. 2. A group or person that has such an interest.

Notes

Preface

1 Why I landed in economics is a story on its own, and certainly unexpected given my family background. Since the ubiquity of unforeseen consequences is a major theme in this book, I might mention that it was an unexpected consequence of meeting my wife-to-be.

1 Ancient Greece, institutional change and economic analysis

1 While the Athenians applied a principle of strict equality among the male citizens, they applied an equally strict principle of inequality between the genders. Formal political influence was restricted to male citizens. And then of course there were slaves…
2 Tangian (2008) shows that the democratic institutions in Athens guaranteed a high level of representativeness.
3 This is the city of Lund in southern Sweden: like Athens it is an important centre for higher education. In Athens there were approximately 30,000 male citizens in the fourth century (Hansen, 1999) which together with women and children make up around 100,000 inhabitants. This citizen population in Athens was complemented by *c*.40,000 resident foreigners (metics) and an unknown number of slaves. The same applies to Lund, *mutatis mutandis*, with more than 46,000 students taking the place of the metics (or slaves?).
4 That this was the case is forcefully argued by Ober (2008).
5 Amemiya (2007), Bitros and Karayiannis (2008), Fleck and Hanssen (2006), Halkos and Kyriazis (2010), Kaiser (2007), Kyriazis and Metaxas (2010), Lyttkens (2006), Lyttkens (2010a), Pitsoulis (2011), Tridimas (2011) to name a few dealing with ancient Greece.
6 I use the expressions "*polis*" and "city-state" interchangeably. It should be noted, however, that whereas city-state implies an autonomous status, there are a variety of examples of dependent *poleis* (Hansen, 1997, 2004c).
7 Cf., for example, Hansen (1999), Manville (1997), Morris (2000), Ober (1989, 1996, 2008), Osborne (1996a), Raaflaub, Ober, and Wallace (2007).
8 Whether Athens was in any sense also the "first democracy" is a moot question. It depends inter alia on what we (and the ancient authors) mean by democracy. Cf. Robinson (1997) on early democratic changes in other city-states.
9 Revised and updated in Finley (1999). See sections 1.3 and 7.2.
10 This my personal experience at seminars and conferences, dinner parties, during coffee breaks etc. (i.e. "anecdotal evidence" in seminar vernacular). For the record, there is of course nothing less surprising to me than the fact that people take an interest in the ancient world.

11 North (1990, p. 3). There are many different definitions of "institutions" in economic analysis, for example, game-theoretic definitions of institutions as equilibria, cf. Aoki (2001) or Greif (2006).

12 On the importance of transaction costs, the obvious references include Coase (1937, 1960), North (1981) and Williamson (1985).

13 Though in the Athenian case taxation may in fact have increased the efficiency of the economy, see section 6.4.

14 In practice, these objectives are interrelated. Both power and wealth bring status. Wealth may bring power while at the same time power often provides opportunities to acquire wealth.

15 It is often argued that it is easy to accommodate Simon's argument in a traditional utility-maximising framework – what you need to do is just to include the cost of additional information in the model, the probability of finding superior solutions, etc. If you do, then there will be a limit to the extent that a utility-maximising individual will search for superior alternatives. While one could argue that this would still confront the individual with enormous computational problems (the world of Asimov's *Foundation* is not here yet), the more important argument is to me that it is conceptually wrong to try to save the maximising format with yet another (fundamentally mistaken) maximising framework. Such attempts to save the traditional approach are strongly reminiscent of the epicycles of the ancient astronomers, whereby they tried to save the model of the universe, with the earth stable in the centre and the sun and the planets circling around it, by postulating the existence of more and more complex systems of circles (an overinvestment in the protective belt if you speak Lakatosian). I do not subscribe to the extreme positivist versions of economics as in Friedman (1953) and believe firmly in the importance of realistic assumptions (Sugden, 2000).

16 Cf., e.g. Schoemaker (1982), Seidl (2002), Kahneman and Tversky (1979).

17 Kyriazis and Metaxas (2010) apply the notion of satisficing behaviour to path dependence and institutional change in ancient Greece.

18 Raaflaub (2007b, p. 13): "Athens, as by far the best-documented ancient democracy, can become for us [a] historical laboratory."

19 In contrast to the postmodernist position, I believe that we can actually learn something about historical societies – historical studies do not only tell us things about ourselves and our own time.

20 Cf. also Morris (1994) and Bresson (2007, Chapter 1), on the debate and the background in the writings of Weber, Polanyi, and others. The substantivist vs. formalist debate replaced the earlier modernist vs. primitivist debate, where the latter focused on the different scale of economic activities now and in antiquity.

21 Bresson (2007) notes that "*homo economicus*" is also conspicuously absent in the modern world.

22 See, for example, Aoki (2001), Greif (1994, 2006), North (1990, 2005).

23 Slater (2009) points out that the temples on Delos appear to be anything but administratively competent. In general, I would be surprised at finding a publicly owned enterprise that tried to be socially efficient. For example, most (if not all) major government investments in communication infrastructure in Sweden the last couple of decades have been preceded by economic analyses that have shown them to be inefficient. This has not prevented them from being put in motion. Or take the behaviour of Homeric heroes (Donlan, 1994) – in an economic approach we would not be discouraged by the fact that their utility function seem to have status and power as important arguments. Cf., e.g. Auriol (2008) on a market for status positions.

24 An extended description of the growing importance of market relationships is provided in section 7.2.

25 Morris (2002), Osborne (1996a, b), Reed (2003), Thomas and Conant (1999).

26 Sanctuaries also performed banking functions, in particular in Athens (Chankowski, 2005).

27 Bresson (2008, Chapter 1), Aristotle *The Athenian Constitution* 51.3–4, Demosthenes 20.9.
28 In other words, the pendulum seems to be swinging back. We might easily overshoot the target, just as Finley did, but a healthy antidote is provided by Bang (2008).
29 A nice illustration of the differences in paradigms is the use of the expression "in a recent article/book/paper NN argued that..". In economics, this "recently" indicates that the work in question is not older than three years or so. In medicine, the same expression signifies that the work is perhaps at most 3–6 months old. In ancient history, "recently" can refer to a book published 10 years ago.
30 The terminology at this point owes its inspiration to Sellar and Yeatman (1975); this in itself is also a Good Thing in my opinion. Sellar and Yeatman (1975) distinguish between Good Things and Bad Things (and some things that are neither).
31 At least this is the research strategy that most economists would pay at least lip service to. There are two important qualifications to this statement. On one hand, a part of the economics literature is purely theoretical, never moving beyond anecdotal evidence. On the other hand, the current trend in much of the empirical literature is not to be too explicit about the theoretical model, letting the implicit model be characterised indirectly by the data available and in that sense approaching an inductive research strategy. As noted in Lyttkens (2009), footnote 15, "while there is too little theory in empirical work, there is also too little realism in economic theory". And anyway, epistemologically speaking, I believe that McCloskey (1983) was largely right, so what economists are engaged in is in fact storytelling, persuasion and rhetoric (and I hope that my stories will convince you). Perhaps I should also warn the reader that (*pace* Popper) falsification as a strict scientific criterion is pretty meaningless in the social sciences: we can never know which particular part of a theory or empirical specification has been falsified, given the huge amount of assumptions and hypotheses involved in the usual kind of empirical test. The situation is somewhat different in experimental economics, though there are other problems there, such as whether the laboratory situation really tells us anything about real life. The possibility of falsification is nevertheless something worth striving for.
32 Historian, archaeologists, and philologists have their own differences of opinion (Morris, 2000).
33 The problems with the evidence concerning Solon and his activities are discussed below (sections 1.6, 4.2, 5.1).
34 This footnote is in honour of Sellar and Yeatman (1975) who argue that "history is what you can remember". The Swedish group ABBA won the Eurovision song contest in 1974 with the song "Waterloo", and there is no end to the historical confusion that could have emerged. For example, some people might think that they remember that the famous Swede Arthur Blücher (or was it Wellesley), inventor of the water closet ("water-loo"), married the French dancing queen Josephine, nicknamed boun-apetit because of her healthy appetite, and so on.
35 Andrewes (1982a), Hansen (1999, pp. 31, 50, 164), Osborne (1996a, pp. 217–220), Blok and Lardinois (2006a, b).
36 For example, Solon speaks of having liberated the black earth by removing the boundary stones (*horoi*). These stones have been suggested to mark the land as being held as security for debts, as being border stones between Athens and Eleusis, and as representing a figurative of speech and not being actual stones at all. The person writing the Solonian poems is variously seen as an historical character, a Homeric-type poet, or a fourth-century invention. Cf., e.g. Andrewes (1982a), L'Homme-Wery (2004), Blok and Lardinois (2006a, b, Introduction and Chapters 1–6), and Owens (2009).
37 Herodotos 1.29–34, 2.177.
38 Cf., e.g. Hansen (1999, pp. 49–52), Andrewes (1982a).
39 Plutarch wrote one of his famous double biographies about Solon and Publicola.

40 Neither of which, unfortunately, were primarily interested in the internal politics in Athens or the institutional structure. Herodotos' concern was the Persian wars, and Thukydides focused on the Peloponnesian War.

41 The initials of these four characters together make up "ASEA", a famous Swedish manufacturing company (now part of Asea Brown Boveri). ASEA is an excellent mnemonic device to remember the names of these authors, one of many useful things my terrific older sister taught me to get by in life. Other such things include maths, physics, how to make a handstand and so on.

42 In Homer it can also mean the rural part of the population, cf. Owens (2009).

43 To give names seems unwise. If no one is mentioned, no one is forgotten (a traditional and very useful Swedish saying).

44 Blamire (2001), Pébarthe (2000).

45 So, for example, Rhodes (2006) leans towards the suggestion that what Solon did was to "filter out" the highest class from three already existing classes.

46 As noted in section 1.5, the issue is not one of using or not using a theoretical framework, as this is needed in both approaches.

47 In other words, I suspect that if you think there is an undisputed fact, it only shows that you have not searched the literature enough. An analogous situation confronts any person who claims to be perfectly healthy – it is someone that has not undergone sufficiently careful medical examinations. The latter I have humbly coined as "The Lyttkens principle" (my other main field of research is health economics).

48 Working with such a dual perspective is happily – if I have got my friends from the history department right – also reasonably in vogue in historical circles.

49 To be specific, I assume that rationality of this kind is present when major decisions on institutional change are taken. This should not be taken to imply that all decisions are subject to this kind of cost–benefit calculation. On the contrary, most decisions follow from unreflective habitual behaviour, as noted above.

50 Cf., e.g. Aoki (2001, pp. 267–270), Boudon (1982), Merton (1936), North (1990, p. 104), Smith (1776, III. IV.17 and IV. II.9, pp. 422, 456), Weesie and Wippler (1986).

51 While it is sometimes relatively straightforward to argue the case that a consequence is negatively valued by a particular actor, it is obviously much more difficult (impossible) to argue that its occurrence was totally unforeseen in the sense of not being envisaged even as a remote possibility.

52 If we describe consequences as being "unintended" we also imply that the actor has tried to achieve some future outcome with his actions. For those in low social positions, however, any cost–benefit calculus dealing with future outcomes may seem meaningless, as things "never turn out that way anyway" (Lindbladh and Lyttkens, 2002).

53 I will argue (Chapters 4–5) that this is true only in a very indirect sense, since his political reforms pushed Athens away from the kind of democracy that later developed. In my view, Solon's most important legacy was that he prepared the ground for the tyranny of Peisistratos, which in turn enabled Kleisthenes to disassociate the ordinary citizen from the traditional elite.

54 A case study is provided in Lyttkens (2012).

55 It is of course always possible to define the current situation in a way that incorporates the road to get there.

56 In the stimulating work of Margaret Levi (1988) the predatory theory is taken one step further in that it is argued that the state likely will attempt to maximise revenue, because whatever the ruler's objectives, revenue is likely to be needed to achieve them. See below.

57 In other words, not "I think, therefore I am" but "I am, therefore I am efficient". Incidentally, my version of this would be: I am being taxed – therefore I am. See Chapter 6.

58 Moreover, in several areas of Greece the *polis* structure never became established, representing instead the so-called *ethnos* type of state. Cf., e.g. Austin and Vidal-Naquet (1977, pp. 78–81), Hansen (1997).

2 Historical background: ancient Greece from the demise of the Mycenaean society to the death of Alexander the great

1 Luckily though some teachers refused to be pc.
2 For more detailed accounts, see, for example, the various volumes and chapters in the *Cambridge ancient history*, 2nd edn. Useful overviews include Osborne (1996a) for the period 1200–479, and Hornblower (1983) for the period 479–323.
3 See Douglas Adams (1979). *The Hitchhiker's Guide to the Galaxy*. New York, Pocket Books 1981.
4 The Mycenaeans had replaced the Minoan civilisation as the major power in the Aegean. The Minoans were based in Crete, and many tourists will have seen the palaces in Knossos and other places. Whether they realise that the palace in Knossos arguably owns as much of its present appearance to the imagination of the excavator Sir Arthur Evans as to the Minoans is another matter. Even so and for the record, I am in favour of the occasional 3D full-scale restoration, to give a vivid image of what life could have been in days long gone.
5 This way of giving a date does not mean that our data is imprecise. The Athenians used another calendar than we do, straddling our turn to a new year. They furthermore used the convention of dating something by stating the name of the chief magistrate (the archon *eponymous*). It is like dating something to 2012 by saying that it happened in the fourth year of Obama's presidency.
6 Cf. e.g. Robinson (1997) for non-Athenian examples.
7 For example, Ambrakia in the early sixth century, Chalkis in the late sixth century. Cf. Robinson (1997, Chapter 3).
8 For example, Megara and Heraclea Pontica in middle of the sixth century. Cf. Robinson (1997, Chapter 3).
9 Note that this is not the Athenian by that name (Chapters 4–5), it is his grandfather on his mother's side. (Who said this should be easy?)
10 They arrived too late to take part in the battle at Marathon and 300 Spartans made a brave stand at Thermopylai in 480.
11 The Spartans' motive for this action is obscure. They had enjoyed guest-friendship with the Peisistratids. Possibly the Spartans hoped to incorporate Athens among their network of allies (Ober, 1996, p. 36; Osborne, 1996a, p. 294); or possibly the Spartans were afraid of an Athens friendly with the Persians, since Hippias had made overtures to the tyrant of Lampsacus who had Persian connections (Lewis, 1988).
12 Cf. Pébarthe (2000) on the economic background to the conflict.
13 The Spartans had refused to raze Athens to the ground as, for example, the Thebans had suggested.
14 For example, Sparta maltreated her ally Elis, and revealed imperialistic ambitions by sending a military force to take on the Persians in Asia Minor.

3 The emergence of the *polis* and its institutions

1 On the *polis* in general, see Hansen and Nielsen (2004).
2 The description here draws mainly on Donlan (1989, 1997), Donlan and Thomas (1993), Hansen (1993), Morris (2006), Murray (1993), Osborne (1996a), Raaflaub (1993, 1997), Thomas (1993), Thomas and Conant (1999).
3 Sallares (2007, p. 19), Morris (2006).
4 On population growth in this period, cf. Scheidel (2003), who also offers a rebuttal of the theory of *explosive* population growth.

5 The traditional translation "king" is misleading for the position of these *basileis* in the sense that it was much less formalised and powerful than that title suggests.

6 Note, however, that the famous passage in the *Iliad* (Book 2) when the ugly and crippled warrior Thersites at a meeting with the army speaks up against Agamemnon (the paramount *basileus* among the Greek) can be interpreted in two ways. Either that Agamemnon could not be certain that the army would follow his command or that of other leaders. Or, since Odysseus abuses Thersites and shuts him down, it could be taken to imply that the gathering was only expected to ratify elite decisions.

7 In fact if extraction is sufficiently severe it appears that even subsistence production will suffer, as seems to have happened in Hellenistic Egypt, see, for example Hedlund, Lundahl and Lyttkens (1989).

8 Georges (1993) suggests that the hoplite equipment may have been less expensive than commonly assumed and perhaps partly possible to manufacture within the household.

9 Cf. Morris (2006). Not everybody is convinced that a deep fall occurred in Greece, as there was, for example, early flourishing in Lefkandi and Athens (Thomas and Conant, 1999, Chapters 3–4). Cf. also Morris (2006) on gradualist models.

10 The argumentation here is not affected by "grey zones" of no-man's land which probably existed between communities, especially in mountainous areas (Penttinen, 2001, p. 96). What is important is that large areas were defined as belonging to one *demos* or the other (living in the "grey zones" would have been insecure and less attractive).

11 See Morris (2007) and Scheidel (2003) on the demographic development in archaic Greece.

12 Cf. Donlan (1989, pp. 24–25), Donlan (1994), Donlan and Thomas (1993), Raaflaub (1993, p. 79).

13 Cf. North (1981, Chapter 5; 1990) on the importance of ideology in this kind of context.

14 Andreades (1979, pp. 21, 121, 138); Austin and Vidal-Naquet (1977, p. 55). On the archaic period, cf. also, for example, Davies (2001), who suggests that records found in the foundation of the Artemis (Kroisos) Temple at Ephesos indicate that some sort of turnover tax was being levied. Harbour dues existed already in the Late Bronze Age, cf., e.g. Heltzer (1978, p. 130).

15 Cf. Osborne (1996a, p. 102), Polignac (1994), Snodgrass (1980, pp. 55–65), Thomas (1993, p. 80), and Thomas and Conant (1999, 124). The use of temples to make a territorial claim suggests that territoriality was an issue at least by the first half of the eighth century, cf. Osborne (1996a, pp. 88–104).

16 Davies (1997, p. 25) argues that "regional trajectories of repopulation and development in the Dark Age and after clearly differed so sharply from each other in nature, scale and date that no one model for the 'rise of the *polis*' can possibly be valid".

17 Compare Snodgrass (1993, p. 38): "the rise in population, so often found in a newly-established and secure regime of sedentary agriculturalists". For agricultural production, the relative security of property rights is an issue of equal importance to new production techniques.

18 Cf. Forsdyke (2006) and van Wees (2006).

19 This may help explain why also some leaders from existing *poleis* found it attractive to take part in colonisation, as we know they did (Thomas and Conant, 1999, p. 133).

20 Murray (1993, Chapter 12), Ober (1989), Whitehead (1983).

21 Even though the development of mass fighting in tight formation made the ordinary farmers as a group more important, it is unlikely that it did much to protect the *individual* farmer from exploitation. "[It] is clear that the farmers who served in the hoplite army were not a conscious, unified class" (Raaflaub, 1997, p. 53).

22 Note that the surviving texts that display the "middling ideology" were all aimed at aristocratic audiences (Morris, 2000, p. 163); Foxhall (1997, pp. 119–120) argues that the "ethos of the community" may be only "the egalitarianism of the equally powerful".

23 In a similar vein, Barzel (2000) shows how the introduction of a collective action mechanism, which facilitates opposition, can be a credible commitment on the part of the ruler to restrain his own behaviour (no transgressing).

24 Raaflaub (1993, p. 51, 1997), Donlan and Thomas (1993). For example: Spartan expansion into Messenia; the annexation by Argos of the Asinaia region; the Lelantine war between Chalcis and Eretria, which may have led to the destruction of Lefkandi (Donlan and Thomas, 1993; Thomas and Conant, 1999, pp. 102, 123).

25 On borrowing ideas and institutions across polities, cf. generally Renfrew and Cherry (1986), and on ancient Greece see Snodgrass (1986, p. 53), who, as noted above, argues that several examples "suggest that the Greek *poleis* kept an alert eye on the constitutional progress of their peers, and were ready to learn from them".

26 Thomas and Conant (1999, pp. 120–125). Offices were reserved for members of a clan known as the Bacchiadae.

27 Again the case of Corinth comes to mind. As mentioned above, impersonal offices (and a collegial board where heads of Bacchiad families sat for life) were introduced soon after 750, and this roughly coincides with the time when the Corinthia region came under unified control.

28 Cf. also Ober (1994) and Hanson (1995, Chapter 6), on the emerging "rules of war", and Hanson (1991, Chapter 6, 1995, 1999), and Osborne (1987, Chapter 7), on the logic of hoplite warfare.

29 It is also possible that the Spartan example had something to do with it. The extent to which the Spartans had to reorganise their society in the late eighth and seventh centuries in order to retain control of their territorial possessions suggests – and perhaps suggested also to their contemporaries – that there was a limit to this process, a point beyond which significant decreasing returns to scale in the size of a *polis* could set in.

30 van Wees (1994) argues that mass fighting was already important in Homer, and furthermore that already the Homeric heroes wore the hoplite panoply, but that phalanx fighting did not appear until after 650. However, he also argues that heavy infantry gained in importance during the seventh century so his position seems compatible with the argumentation here.

31 Hypothetically, the formalisation of laws could also be interpreted as an attempt to enlist the common people – in particular the hoplites – to oppose would-be tyrants, by emphasising the unlawfulness and unconstitutional nature of their rule. In aristocratic poetry, rule by one man is presented as an outrage against the whole community (Osborne, 1996a, p. 192), whereas in reality the outrage may have been felt almost exclusively among the elite. Several tyrants seem to have introduced measures that benefited the common people. Cf., e.g. Raaflaub (1993, pp. 72–73).

32 Cf., for example, van Wees (2006).

33 Murray (1993, pp. 220ff.); Ober (1989, p. 58), Starr (1977, pp. 21–54, 123–128).

34 To continue with the Corinth example, it became necessary to define who belonged to the Bacchiadae.

4 The road to democracy part one: a structural approach

1 This chapter extends the analysis in Lyttkens (2010a).

2 As mentioned in Chapter 1, there are different views as to when the Athenians established a "democracy". If I was to take a stand in that debate, I would follow Raaflaub (2007a) in arguing that it was after the reforms mid-fifth century that we should call Athens a (male) democracy. Not until then did the common people have equal opportunities to take part in public decision making, which entails their participation as jurors, in the council and as magistrates, and of course in the Assembly. For other views on the timing of democracy (Solon, Kleisthenes etc.), cf. Raaflaub, Ober, and Wallace (2007).

3 We must also ask ourselves whether the aristocracy in archaic Greece could envisage

that a shift of political power away from themselves and to the population at large would induce the individual farmer to make productive investments, and that the subsequent increase in the value of agricultural production would trickle back to benefit the aristocracy through taxation and the production of public goods. Note that the benefits to the aristocracy in this case would occur considerably later in time than the loss of political power. The main example of a productive investment in Fleck and Hanssen (2006) is the planting of olive trees, trees that bear full fruit only *c*.15–20 years after plantation (*Encyclopaedia Britannica*, 2006). Fleck and Hanssen assume that both the aristocrats and the ordinary farmers are fully informed about the parameters of the model. With respect to the discounting of benefits, it is worth noting that the decision makers in archaic Athens probably were at least over 30 years of age (30 being the age limit for both the ephors in Sparta and for jurors and councillors in classical Athens; members of the Spartan *gerousia* were above 60), and so on average would probably have been dead 20 years later (Sallares, 1991, pp. 107–129). They would, however, have been concerned not just for themselves but also for the future of their aristocratic families.

4 Cf. also Aristotle *The Athenian Constitution* 3.6.

5 That Kylon should have done this without hoping for some internal support seems to me to be unlikely.

6 The homicide law remained in force right down until the age of Demosthenes, whereas the rest of his laws were revised by Solon.

7 In this work, it is taken as a given that Solon is a historical character who did at least some of the things attributed to him in our ancient sources. Note however, that by 2012 scholars question not only his laws and constitutional measures but also his poetry. The latter, for example, has been argued to be of the Homeric kind – a compilation of oral tradition, which suggests that perhaps Solons is a fictitious character (Lardinois, 2000).

8 Athens suffered military defeats in the late seventh century against Megara, Mytilene and perhaps Aegina (Morris, 2002).

9 This is a structural account, remember, and we ignore details.

10 No definite conclusion will ever be reached regarding the precise nature of Solon's reforms (Blok and Lardinois, 2006a; Hansen, 1999; Manville, 1997; Morris, 2002; Osborne, 1996a). Wallace (2007) sees the birth of Athenian democracy in Solon's reforms but both Foxhall (1997) and Davies (2003) warn against attributing, with hindsight, democratic visions to Solon. Cf. Chapter 5 for an extended discussion of Solon's reforms and motives.

11 The four classes were the pentakosiomedimnoi (those owning property that produced 500 measures), the hippeis (production of 300–500 measures), the zeugitai (200–300 measures) and the *thetes*. It is usually presumed that the bulk of the hoplites belonged to the zeugitai. As noted in section 1.6, even these facts are not uncontested. For example, Rhodes (2006) leans towards the suggestion that what Solon did was to "filter out" the highest class from three already existing classes.

12 This is far from certain, however, cf. Chapter 5, n. 6.

13 We may see a reflection of the short-term nature of the solution in the fact that troubles emerged in the 580s over the appointment of archons (Aristotle *The Athenian Constitution* 13.1–2).

14 A city in the north-west of Asia Minor, on the trading route to the Black Sea.

15 A similar effect would follow from any increase in tax revenues.

16 Hansen (1999, p. 148), notes that in order to break up old groupings it would have sufficed to use lottery, as Aristotle reports to have been the case (*The Athenian Constitution* 21.4).

17 Hansen (1999, p. 48); Osborne (1996a, pp. 300–303).

18 Ostwald (1988, p. 306), assumes that he appealed to the Assembly, as does Ober (1996, p. 38). Kleisthenes had been archon in 525/4, which would have made him a

lifelong member of the Areopagos. It is possible that this entitled him to address the people in the Assembly. We do not know if/how he bypassed the compulsory pre-treatment in the Council.

19 On the absence of political parties, cf. Hansen (1999) and Tridimas (2011).

20 Testimonies, presentation of facts, etc., were often made orally and without documentary support. A decision was taken on the spot, guided by the preliminary decree of the council (sometimes just a decision to present an issue for open debate) and by the debate in the Assembly. When forced to choose which side to support, the individual voter must largely have based his judgement on the individual politician's reputation, and on the voter's own previous experience and memories.

21 Cf. also Ps-Xenophon *The Athenian Constitution*, and Finley (1983, Chapter 5).

22 Strauss (1986, p. 91), has suggested that it was possible to make drastic changes in one's political programme, but the evidence does not seem strong.

23 Note however that in a direct democracy one votes directly for an issue rather than for a political party. An indication that the common people usually constituted a majority in the Assembly is the fact that the decision to replace democracy with an oligarchic regime in 411 was taken under circumstances that prevented many of the poor from participating (Hansen, 1987, p. 11). Additionally, it is often argued that the Athenian citizens placed a high value on political participation as such. See, e.g. Rahe (1984). North (1990) has argued that people will express their ideological preferences when the cost for doing so is low, as it is in a democracy.

24 This coincides in time with the reform that allowed the third property class, presumably the bulk of the hoplites, to become archons (Aristotle, *The Athenian Constitution*, 26.2). This reform may have been the cause of the attempt or the reason it failed or both.

25 More aptly labelled The Greater Athenian State (Morris, 2009).

26 Note that rowers in the fleet comprised not only citizens but also metics and slaves, Cf. Gabrielsen (1994, Chapter 5).

27 Some scholars argue, however, that traditional accounts exaggerate the changes between the fifth and fourth centuries, e.g. Millet (2000a) and Ober (1989, pp. 95ff.).

28 The initiative in legislation remained with the Assembly.

29 Hansen (1999, p. 290). An anonymous referee however informs me that this is based on a decree that will be shown to be a forgery.

30 Morris (1996), p. 37, also suggests that there was "a broad trend toward granting political powers to the demos between 525 and 490", based upon the fact that Herodotos mentions several experiments with popular rule at the time of Kleisthenes' reform.

31 Robinson (1997, p. 80, n. 59). As noted in section 1.6, the often informative writings of the fourth century are coloured by the political debate of that century.

32 Pitsoulis (2011) suggests that the growing importance of the hoplites explains the introduction of majority rule; the hoplites wanted a constitutional form that would give them a bigger chance of enforcing their claims.

33 Cf. Raaflaub, Ober, and Wallace (2007) for critical views on this interpretation.

34 One could argue (with some historians) that the Athenians were disappointed with the way democracy worked, but this does not imply that they would be willing to shift power to the rich elite. They could have made other changes. The use of the *graphe paranomon* from 415 and onwards looks like such a measure, designed to make democracy work differently and with fewer mistaken decisions, cf. section 7.4.

35 Herodotos 6.14, 7.18.1, 8.46, 8.90, Gabrielsen (1994, pp. 37–39).

36 Cf. Chapter 6 on possible earlier uses of this tax in Athens.

37 Much remains obscure regarding the symmory system(s) and lists of those liable to perform trierarchies and other liturgies (Gabrielsen, 1994, Chapter 8).

38 Kaiser (2007) shows that the mechanisms involved in taxation lend support to the rational-actor model of Athenian taxpayers.

5 The road to democracy part 2: institutional change as individually rational action

1 Those who want to dig deeper into these issues will find Blok and Lardinois (2006b), Raaflaub *et al.* (2007) and Osborne (1996a) to be useful starting points; other useful secondary sources include, for example Ober (1989, 1996), and obviously the accounts in the *Cambridge ancient history* (volumes III part 3, IV, V), as well as the brief summary in Hansen (1999).

2 Andrewes (1982a), Hansen (1999, pp. 31, 50, 164), Osborne (1996a, pp. 217–220), Blok and Lardinois (2006a, b).

3 "All traditions of whatever kind picture Solon as a lawgiver. However, exactly which Solonian laws should be attributed to him and which ones are later additions or forgeries, is a matter of debate. It is precisely the power exerted by the political debate in the fourth century [...] which accounts both for the preservation of many of Solon's laws and for the fictional laws attributed to him" (Blok and Lardinois, 2006a, p. 10).

4 Solon (fr. 32–34) explicitly prided himself for not having attempted to become a tyrant.

5 Chattel slavery is so called because men and women are bought and sold in the marketplace, cf., e.g. Migeotte (2009).

6 Hansen (1999, p. 31), argues that we do not know if Solon created such a council and points to the fact that its oldest indisputable attestation comes in 411. Rhodes (2006) prefers to state the same situation in opposite terms – there is no good reason to disbelieve in it. Wallace (2007) is also sceptical.

7 According to Aristotle (*The Athenian Constitution* 8.2), the Areopagos elected the archons before Solon changed the procedure, but this discussion in Aristotle is problematic, cf. Hansen (1999, pp. 49ff.).

8 For a contrary view, cf., e.g. Harris (2006) or Wallace (2007). My assumption implies that Solon was trying to give away as little as possible from the traditional elite in terms of economic and political concessions, but to do what was needed to stop the revolution. Since we do not know how much he really would have had to give away of elite privileges (nor did *he* know, presumably) to achieve continued elite rule, we cannot formally differentiate between the assumption of self-interest and an assumption that Solon for other reasons was interested in finding a reasonable balance between the parties.

9 When Solon lists what he promised to the people in revolt, he does not mention political power (Wallace, 2007, p. 69).

10 Adkins (1972, p. 23), Starr (1977, pp. 150–151).

11 This should not be taken to imply that the rich non-aristocrats had no land at all. Rather we may assume that they would often have started as middling farmers. Cf. Starr (1977, pp. 124–126). For a possibly contrary view on the land holdings of the newly enriched families, cf. Snodgrass (1980, p. 101).

12 This is a statement that Hansen (1999, p. 189) sees as an anachronism.

13 Manville (1997, p. 132), Ober (1989, pp. 62–63). Manville (1997, p. 132) also notes that a formalisation of citizenship is implied by the rules that regulated immigration, if Plutarch is to be believed (*Solon* 24.2). He attributes to Solon a law that restricted citizenship to those who were permanently exiled from their country or who moved to Athens with their families to practice a trade (though even Plutarch himself seems not entirely inclined to believe in it).

14 Hence I do not agree with the statement that those of impure descent together with the impoverished nobility "offer no clue to the nature of the main body of Pisistratus' supporters" (Andrewes, 1982b, p. 396). In my view, these groups might have been relatively numerous and – most importantly – they had much at stake.

15 Aristotle (*The Athenian Constitution* 20.1) reports that some of Solon's laws fell into disuse under the tyranny and Manville (1997, p. 178), notes that the regulations

concerning immigration (cf. above) may have been among those laws that were conveniently forgotten.

16 On Solon against tyranny, cf. Solon, fr. 9–11 and 32–34, and Aristotle *The Athenian Constitution* 14.2.

17 Solon had perhaps taken a course in economics? The importance of stability in the rules of the game – e.g. with respect to the behaviour of the central bank vis-à-vis inflation – has been a belief on level with the Immaculate Conception for some of my colleagues.

18 An alternative interpretation would be that Solon foresaw everything that would happen, but saw no other way out of the revolutionary situation.

19 This section largely follows Lyttkens (1997).

20 Cf. Chapter 6 for more information on Athenian taxation and the liturgy system.

21 Herodotos 6.14, 7.18.1, 8.46, 8.90, Gabrielsen (1994, pp. 37–39).

22 It does not matter if it was realised at the time that people were spending in order to prove their eligibility. Only those whose wealth exceeded a certain limit could afford to undertake such expenditure, just as education is used on the job market to signal a high level of innate ability (Spence, 1973). Hence liturgical spending could also be seen as a correctly designed incentive mechanism to reveal which persons pass the property qualification.

23 To the extent that land was the only kind of wealth that counted, an inspection of one's property would be a bad idea for those outside of the traditional aristocracy who had made their fortunes in other ways.

24 Davies (1981, pp. 98, 167; 1971, p. 371). The contestant belonged to the Alkmaionid family, with a certified need to establish their political position because they had been exiled from Athens for having taken part in the killing of the followers of Kylon. This curse was invoked when Isagoras and the Spartans tried to force the Alkmaionids and 700 other families into exile after Kleisthenes' appeal to the people.

25 Pritchard (forthcoming) estimates that the running expenses for the whole festival programme in Athens on average came to about 100 talents per year in the period 430–350.

26 The only specific source of public financing that we know of in Athens at this time are the so-called naukraric funds (cf. below).

27 Wycherley (1978, p. 248). The source however is late (Plutarch *Solon* 23.5).

28 The predecessor of the trireme – the pentekonter – was less expensive, could have other uses, and was often privately owned.

29 An individual showed up with his own ship as late as in the battle of Salamis in 480. This was probably a trireme, but it is clear from Herodotos' (8.17) account that it was exceptional (Haas, 1985, p. 40).

30 Gabrielsen (1994, Chapter 1), Herodotos (5.82–88, 5.94–95), Andrewes (1982a, pp. 372–374), who also argues that the Athenians probably already had a fleet in the mid-eighth century.

31 For a contrary view on Athenian ships, cf. Haas (1985).

32 The existence of a sixth-century predecessor to the trierarchial system is an old idea, but Lyttkens (1997) was probably the first to connect it specifically to Solon's political reforms. Much of earlier discussion focused on the apparently insolvable issue surrounding the so-called *naukrariai*. By the time of Solon, the population of Attica was organised into 48 *naukrariai* (Aristotle *The Athenian Constitution* 8.3). It has often been assumed that this served as the basis for an institution similar to the trierarchy, e.g. Thomsen (1964). However, as shown by Gabrielsen (1985, 1994), we do not know whether the *naukrariai* were connected with the fleet at all. Hence we only know that the *naukraroi* were probably officials who sometimes handled public funds, and that these funds may occasionally have been used for naval purposes.

33 It may be worth noting that, according to tradition, Solon tried to regulate against *private* ostentatious expenditures at burials (Plutarch *Solon* 21.4–5).

34 Some accounts suggest that one should credit Peisistratos with ambitions to "suppress the ruinous competition for power among the aristocrats" (Andrewes, 1982b, p. 398). This seems to me somewhat far-fetched when personal power and glory were so clearly at stake.

35 After spending some time on the Acropolis – a nice spot for a picnic but somewhat hard as a mattress.

36 Ober (1996, p. 41). For example, Ostwald (1988, p. 322), suggests that the positive goal of Kleisthenes was to "eliminate from the public life of Athens the dynastic rivalries which he saw as the cause of disunity harmful to the political life of Athens", while Snodgrass (1980, p. 198), concludes that there "is much to be said for the modern view that Kleisthenes [...] was a skilled manipulator [...] who unwittingly stumbled on a democratic solution".

37 Cf. Osborne (1996a, p. 300), on Aristotle (idealist view) vs. Herodotos (aristocratic rivalry). It is not surprising that the source closer to Kleisthenes in time (i.e. Herodotos) endorses what I see as the more realistic picture of Kleisthenes.

38 "There is no reason to suppose that Cleisthenes was a 'protodemocrat' in the era before 508/7" (Ober, 2007, p. 86).

39 The *diapsephismos* is sometimes discussed without it being seen as the main factor behind the uprising and subsequent events, for example, Salmon (2003), Ober (2007 p. 86), and Wallace (2007).

40 Or possibly the phratries (Ostwald, 1988, p. 310), which were some sort of kinship groups.

41 Manville (1997, p. 179), Ostwald (1988, p. 304). That Kleisthenes sought the support of former Peisistratid adherents may seem surprising, given the role of the Alkmaionids in the overthrow of the Peisistratids. However, it would certainly not be the only time in history that a new ruler endeavours to take over the power base of his opponent.

42 As mentioned above, Plutarch (*Solon* 24.2) reports that Solon instituted a law that restricted immigration to certain groups.

43 I could add that the expulsion of 700 families on the arrival of Kleomenes could plausibly have been a step in the *diapsephismos*.

44 Cf., e.g. Ostwald (1988, pp. 334–346), for some different interpretations of ostracism.

45 Nor could anyone have foreseen that the Persian threat would soon change the course of Athenian politics to the extent that it did. To argue that Kleisthenes had reason to believe that "the kind of popular support that had helped him carry his reforms could not be counted on to last" (Ostwald, 1988, p. 336) seems to me like a projection of late-fifth and fourth-century politics.

46 Solon had begun the process, since the fact that he admitted new groups into the ruling elite would have served to reduce the traditional hold of the elite over the population (Ober, 1996, p. 38).

47 On the English case, cf. also North and Weingast (1989) and Weingast (1995).

48 Hence I follow Rhodes (1993), and Badian (1971) in disbelieving the figure of 500 preelected candidates indicated in *The Athenian Constitution* (22.5). This is unlikely to be correct, given that the total number of eligible persons cannot have been many more than 500 altogether in any one year. *Contra*, e.g. Develin and Kilmer (1997).

49 Cf., e.g. Badian, (1971) on the moot question of when the second class became eligible. In 458/7, the third class was admitted.

50 Hansen (1999, p. 50 and *passim*); Aristoteles (*Politics* 1294b6–9, 1273a17), Herodotos 3.80.6.

51 Hansen (1999, p. 236); Sinclair (1988, p. 18).

52 Rihll (1995), however, does not believe that lottery implied any downgrading of the post as archon.

53 This appears as something like an inverse of the Groucho Marx principle – "I don't want to be a member of a club that would accept me as a member".

54 Yes, as indicated above, this is the guy with the "wooden wall", the expansion of the Athenian fleet, the architect behind the victory at Salamis, etc.

55 Conceivably, this was prompted by a (false) sense that the Persian threat had levelled off. That Persia had definite plans against central Greece did not become a certainty until work on the canal through the Athos peninsula began in 483 (Hammond, 1988, p. 525).

56 The notion that the introduction of the lottery system is connected to the intra-elite conflicts of the 480s is not new, e.g. Badian (1971), Osborne (1996a); Forsdyke (2000), though Lyttkens (2008) may be the first who makes a point of the very significant precise timing, immediately after the first ostracism. What previous studies fail to take full account of, however, is the position of the Areopagos.

57 Incidentally, the introduction of the lottery system could therefore help explain the statement of Aristotle (*The Athenian Constitution* 23) that the Areopagos became powerful after the Persian Wars (though he gives other reasons). This is a statement that modern authorities have noted without much enthusiasm and some scepticism. Rihll (1995) argues that it may have reflected the power of the Areopagos to disqualify elected magistrates at the before-office scrutiny. He believes that the Areopagos was stripped of its powers because the council blocked the appointment of many officials who had been elected by popular vote.

58 Compare Sherlock Holmes pointing out to Inspector Gregory "the curious incident of the dog in the night-time", the curious incident being, as you might remember, that the dog did *nothing* in the night-time (Sir Arthur Conan Doyle, 1892, *The adventure of silver blaze*).

59 Rhodes (1993, p. 148), Andrewes (1982a, p. 386).

60 A nice solution would be if evidence existed to the effect that the polemarchos was elected while the other archons were selected by lottery. However there is no such evidence. An early date for the introduction of the system has also been connected to a potential religious origin (Zeus has been mentioned, though Tyche, the goddess of chance, seems more appropriate). Hansen (1999, pp. 50–51), however, is sceptical: "Seeking the advice of the gods by means of the lot is, indeed, an age-old device in every country all over the world [...]. Priests were often selected by lot: priests are the servants of the god, let him choose [...] [however] there is not a single good source that straightforwardly testifies to the selection of magistrates by lot as having a religious character or origin." Analogies such as the choice in the Iliad as to who should meet an adversary in individual combat seem to me largely irrelevant. The social context is somewhat different – to put it mildly – from that of choosing a magistrate to govern the city for one year.

61 Cf. Badian (1971) for a critical review of this argument.

62 One can see how he could have benefited from the reform, given that the rule that you could only be archon once was already operational. Themistokles had already been archon in 493/2 and so could not be archon in the future. We do not know when the rule of only serving once in a lifetime was introduced (Rhodes, 1993, p. 244; Forrest and Stockton, 1987). In practice, everybody assumes that the rule had already applied by Kleisthenes' time, as one would otherwise have expected Kleisthenes to hold the position a second time after his success against Isagoras in 508/7.

63 Badian (1971, p. 27). Conceivably, the fact that the lottery reform of 487 is inconspicuous in the ancient sources could be due to its failure to achieve its intended goal, rather than due to it being a "minor change", as Badian argues.

64 This is argued by Badian (1971) in opposition to those who believe that devaluation of the archons (in favour of the generals) was the object of introducing the lottery system. Ste. Croix (2004) agrees with Badian on the non-democratic nature of the measure, but favours the view that a promotion of the generals was the intention.

65 E.g. Cawkwell (1988), Rhodes (1993). For the 50 years after 508/7 we know the names of more than 40 eponymous archons, but that is still only about 10 per cent of

all the archons (which is particularly significant if the designation of the eponymous archon was determined by lot).

66 Cf., e.g. Aristotle *The Athenian Constitution* 9.1., 22.1.

6 Taxation – a ubiquitous phenomenon if there is one

1 As shown, for example, by Lieberman (2003) in his comparative study of Brazil and South Africa, two countries with considerable differences in how the population view public authorities.

2 I am not alone in these feelings about taxation. A public-finance colleague was happy to use this quote as a chapter heading when I made her aware of it.

3 Tax collectors tend to have a bad reputation in most societies, it seems. Personally I had a falling out with one tax official who displayed an intelligence somewhat below that of my armchair (according to my unbiased opinion).

4 Rumour does not tell whether it was stashed under the mattress, the traditional hiding place in Swedish lore.

5 Cf. Lysias 25.8, Ps. Xenophon *The Athenian Constitution*, and Finley (1983, Chapter 5).

6 Cf. Levi (1988, pp. 17–23). One should note that state revenue may be increased in other ways than through taxation. For example, if the ruler controls some vital resource, state revenue may be maximised by enforcing a favourable price structure, as the Hellenistic rulers of Egypt appear to have discovered (Hedlund, Lundahl, and Lyttkens, 1989).

7 The analysis of the structure of taxation in Athens draws partly on Lyttkens (1994). For a recent overview of taxation in Athens and Greece generally, cf. Gabrielsen (forthcoming), who also notes the surprising paucity of studies on this important topic. See also Andreades (1979) for a somewhat outdated but still very useful overview of public finance in Athens. For shorter accounts, see Austin and Vidal-Naquet (1977), Bergh and Lyttkens (2011), Hansen (1999) and Jones (1957, Chapter 4). On military expenditure, cf., e.g. Migeotte (2000) and Pritchard (forthcoming). On metics cf. also Whitehead (1977, pp. 16–17 and 75–78).

8 In modern discussions of this subject a distinction is often made between indirect and direct taxes. However, as Gabrielsen (forthcoming) points out, such a distinction would have been meaningless to the ancient Greeks. Furthermore it seems a bit old-fashioned in economics (and the burden of some taxes traditionally labelled "direct" can be shifted to others than those who formally pay the tax).

9 Bresson (2008, p. 104).

10 Today we may see this as a regressive tax, but it seems doubtful whether at that time it would have occurred to anyone to see this tax as a heavy burden for the poor (the theory of tax incidence had not been invented).

11 Jones (1957, pp. 101–104), Hansen (1999, pp. 218–224). For example, the officials who received the revenues from the tax farmers were carefully audited.

12 Levi (1988, Chapter 4), has found that tax farming in republican Rome is consistent with these arguments – it entailed lower transaction costs than the available alternatives.

13 Solon reputedly carried a reform whereby any citizen had the right to bring a case on behalf of an injured party, but this rule was followed only if the injured party was for some reason unable to bring justice himself (Hansen, 1999, p. 192).

14 Harrison (1971, pp. 211ff.), MacDowell (1978, p. 62). Hansen (1999, pp. 193–194) states that the accuser received one-third of the withheld property.

15 If the prosecutor failed to secure one-fifth of the votes at the trial, or abandoned the prosecution, he was fined 1,000 drachmas.

16 Permanent tax officials might easily become powerful as history showed when the Athenians started electing and re-electing some financial magistrates in the fourth century, cf. Hansen (1987, pp. 120–21).

17 Kron (forthcoming, cited in Ober 2010) has estimated that the late fourth-century wealth distribution in Athens yields a Gini-coeffiicient of 0.71, only a slightly more unequal wealth distribution than Canada in 1998 (0.69). Morris (1998) points out that the estimates of land holdings by Osborne (1992) and Foxhall (1992, 2002) suggest a Gini-coefficient of somewhere around 0.38 (strikingly low compared to other ancient and medieval societies). Cf. Ober (2010).

18 Herodotos 6.14, 7.18.1, 8.46, 8.90, Davies (1992, p. 29), Gabrielsen (1994, pp. 37–39).

19 This is the most accepted view (e.g. Möller, 2007) Gabrielsen (1994, Chapter 2), however argues that even this interval should not be taken as a too precise estimate, for example, because properties worth less than three talents could fall into the liturgical category. Some scholars, e.g. Brun (1983), argue that the wealth of liturgists must have been substantially greater, because otherwise the return on the capital would not have sufficed to cover the expenditure, but this, as Gabrielsen (1994, p. 52), notes, ignores the fact that individuals frequently had to borrow in order to finance a liturgy.

20 Gabrielsen (forthcoming) argues that in the second half of the fourth century, the number of liturgists must have been around 4,400 because 1,200 trierarchs would be needed each year and there was the two-year exemption rule. For the purpose of my analysis it does not matter much if the liturgists were 300 or 1,000, nor if their number increased to 4,000 late in the fourth century. If there was such an increase it probably simply reflected a reduction in the possibilities among rich Athenians to sustain these expenditures. The earlier view that Demosthenes in 340 restricted the number of trierarchs to just 300 has been refuted by Gabrielsen (1989). However, it is possible that Demosthenes shifted the burden for trierarchies towards the richest group.

21 Davies (1971), Gabrielsen (1994, part 3) on the trierarchy. Pritchard (forthcoming) estimates an average cost per trierarchy of 4,436 drachmas.

22 Cf. Pritchard (forthcoming).

23 Gabrielsen (1994, pp. 85ff.). There is doubt as to whether some of the figures mentioned in speeches refer to half or full trierarchies (Jones, 1957, p. 146 n. 78).

24 Cf. Davies (1971, pp. xxi–xxii).

25 In Athens, daily wages in the Erechtheion accounts of 408/7–407/6 were 1–1.5 drachmas per day; nearby in the Eleusinian accounts of 329/8 and 327/6 daily wages were 1.5–2.5 drachmas per day.

26 It is often suggested that a normal return on landed property was 8 per cent, that is, 480 drachmas per talent (Jones, 1957, pp. 24 and 30; Ste. Croix, 1953, p. 39; Ober 2010). If that was so, and your wealth amounted for example to five talents, then a syntrierarchy (3,000 drachmas) could take more than your total yearly return on that wealth ($0.08 \times 6,000 \times 5 = 2,400$ drachmas).

27 As mentioned above, even for landed property, there was no register of who owned what (Finley, 1952, 14–15). There was however documentation in some cases for other reasons, for example, regarding the mining leases.

28 Cf. Gabrielsen (1987a), and Harrison (1971, pp. 236–238).

29 Gabrielsen (1994, p. 44): "the trierarchy was primarily viewed and treated as a fiscal entity".

30 The wording of Thukydides (3.19.1) is ambiguous (Möller 2007) and Gabrielsen argues that at Athens the *eisphora* is first attested in 434/3 (Gabrielsen (forthcoming). Several authors argue that the *eisphora* may well have existed earlier in the fifth century (Brun, 1983, pp. 22–23; Thomsen, 1964; Davies, 1981, p. 147). In the description of the *eisphora* in the fourth century, I follow mainly Ste. Croix (1953), Hansen (1991), Jones (1957, Chapter 2, 1974, Chapter 8), Davies (1971, 1984), and Rhodes (1982), rather than the analyses of Brun (1983), Thomsen (1964) or Ruschenbusch (1985).

31 However, the Athenians and the citizens of other *poleis* sometimes persuaded the temples to lend them money from the wealth that had been deposited with them. The

Athenians it seems did this in order to finance their wars – surely the most expensive public undertaking there was (Pritchard, forthcoming; Migeotte, 2000).

32 Möller (2007). This is a contentious issue. Jones (1957, pp. 28–29), suggests an exemption limit of 2,500 drachmas, calculating that as many as 6,000 citizens were liable. Rhodes (1982) argues for a much smaller number. Both Davies (1981, p. 149), and Hansen (1999, pp. 112–115), argue for an even smaller number of taxpayers (Hansen for the period after 357). On the other hand, both Brun (1983), pp. 19–22, and Thomsen (1964), p. 202, argue for *more* than 6,000 persons liable for the *eisphora*, but such a high figure can be hard to reconcile with the total taxable wealth.

33 As mentioned above (fn. 20 this chapter), the suggestion that Demosthenes in 340 limited the number of trierarchs to 300 has been refuted by Gabrielsen (1989). Nevertheless, much remains obscure regarding the symmory system(s) and lists of those liable to perform trierarchies and other liturgies (Gabrielsen, 1994, Ch. 8). It is also possible that a list of around 1,000 persons liable for liturgies was drawn up already in the 390s or 380s (Rhodes, 1982), but Davies (1981) argues that the documents in question concerned an earlier list of *eisphora* payers rather than a list of liturgy payers, while Gabrielsen (1987b) argues that documents concerned a large-scale effort to recover public debts (tax arrears).

34 Whitehead (1977), p. 75, notes that it would have been easy to ignore the registration requirement, but does not explicitly connect this with the severity of the punishment.

35 It is also possible that individual citizens who informed the authorities about offenders were awarded part of the revenue. This was the practice with some other taxes.

36 Cf. Bergh and Lyttkens (2011). They assume 40,000 metics, of which half were tax-paying males and half were female, of which one quarter worked and paid the tax.

37 Jones (1974, Chapter 8) however suggests that the yield of the *metoikion* was unpredictable, that it would have been difficult to keep an up-to-date census, and hence that it would not have been possible to audit the official. Note that the Athenian tax farmers never appear as the kind of organised pressure group that their Roman counterparts developed into.

38 On the basis of the figures collected by (Loomis, 1998), one gets the impression that a normal price for the service was 3–6 obols, which would suggest a daily income somewhere between, for example 1–12 drachmas. The total male population in Attica (including slaves) could be around 150,000. If 20 per cent (50 per cent) of these men visit a prostitute 6 (12) times a year for a price of 0.5 (1.0) drachma, then the total yearly income from prostitution in Attica comes to 15 (150) talents. Subtracting some income for subsistence still leaves considerable scope for tax revenue.

39 Traditionally it has been argued that the Athenians quickly gave up the attempt and revived the tribute probably in 410, cf. Andrewes (1992, p. 58 with n. 44). However, Vincent Gabrielsen has pointed out to me that there is no evidence that the tribute was reintroduced (personal communication).

40 Pritchard (forthcoming), Aristotle *The Athenian Constitution* 60.2, Lysias 7.2.

41 The Peisistratids needed revenue to foster public cults and build temples, to improve the water supply, to make public loans to farmers, and to finance warfare (Andrewes, 1982b).

42 Amit (1965, p. 103), Gabrielsen (1994, p. 26).

43 If it was a tax revolt, it would fit the bill primarily if the tax was a relatively new phenomenon. A new interpretation along such lines would be that the tax was introduced as a reaction to the worsened financial situation of the Peisistratids that followed with the Persian expansion. While such an interpretation certainly makes sense, it requires that Aristotle is wrong (which is perfectly possible but not uncontroversial) since he connects the tax also with Peisistratos himself (he died in 527). Of course Aristotle's statement could be a reflection of the later tradition that associated direct taxation with tyrants.

44 Auriol (2008). Cf. also Rosenthal, Bates, and Levi (1994) on the use of honour systems to procure revenue. We may also note that the development of new sources

of public finance rather than trying to cut expenditure is consistent with revenue-maximising rule. The victorious *choregoi* also received tripods, famously placed on monuments in "the tripod street". A still surviving example is the monument of Lysikrates in Athens.

45 Gabrielsen (1994, Chapter 3), Jordan (1975, pp. 61–70), Hansen (1999, p. 111).

46 Gabrielsen (1994, Chapter 1), argues that institutional developments leading to the establishment of the trierarchy ran parallel to an expansion of the Athenian fleet in the 480s.

47 Aristotle *The Athenian Constitution* 22.2, Hansen (1999, p. 52). Of course, the reason that Aristotle states that the generals were elected from this year and onwards could be that he assumes that it must have happened the same year as the formalisation of the *choregia*.

48 Cf., e.g. Capps (1943), Finley, (1983, 36, n. 27), Gabrielsen (1994, 35).

49 Or *ex machina* as the Romans would say.

50 Cf. Gabrielsen (1986) and Lyttkens (1992) for a more detailed analysis of this behaviour. The earliest clear indication seems to be Lysias 20.23 which is dated around 410. Other examples are Aischines 1.101, Demosthenes 42.22–23 and 45.66, Isaios 7.38–41 and 11.47, and Isokrates 7.35 and 18.48, 60.

51 Cf. Davies' (1981, pp. 68–69 and Chapter 6) analysis on the declining importance of wealth and public spending as a political power base. Already the Solonian reforms (594) and the later reforms of Peisistratos and Kleisthenes had curtailed the power of the old, landed aristocratic families. Ober (1989) notes that "by the third quarter of the [fifth] century [...] the established road to a political career [was] more problematic" because "the Athenians became increasingly suspicious of the old symbols of aristocratic [...] power" (p. 86).

52 Cf. Veyne (1976, Chapter 2), on the importance of voluntary spending by the wealthy in classical and Hellenistic Greece.

53 There is an extensive discussion in the literature of what the reforms meant in terms of the change in the number of liable persons and the tax burden for a member of the list. However, the question *why* the *proeisphora* system was chosen to collect the tax is in fact seldom asked. There are obvious alternatives to the organisation that actually was chosen. The *eisphora* could have been farmed out. Or it could have been collected by officials. A commonly observed advantage of the *proeisphora* is that the tax revenue was available immediately, before the tax had been collected from the individual taxpayers. However, it seems to me that perhaps too much may have been made of this. Not all of the revenue of the *eisphora* would always be needed immediately – a large part of it would probably be devoted to the running costs of the military forces and could be financed by instalments. Anyway, a plausible assumption is that the *proeisphora* entailed a quicker collection of the tax only if the *proeispherontes* were cooperative.

54 It might seem that the rich Athenians also gained by the fact that the *proeisphora* was defined as a liturgy (Davies, 1981, p. 149) so that the exemption rules (no liturgical service in consecutive years) ensured that the wealthy *proeispherontes* would be relieved of other liturgies. This, however, is something of a chimera. If the total liturgical expenditure is seen as exogenously given, and if the group of liturgists is also given, then the effect would mainly be to reallocate liturgies in time – the expected expenditure per liturgists could be more or less unaffected (a part of the burden may, however, be reallocated from the most wealthy members of society to the not quite so wealthy liturgists).

55 Thus contrary to what Aristotle says (*Politics* 1272a15–16), imposing "political" taxes on the rich but recompensing them with political influence is not just a feature of oligarchies.

56 The argument is akin to Levi's analysis of the introduction of the income tax in eighteenth century Britain: "Citizens allowed the income tax only [...] when they felt some

confidence that their political influence was adequate to limit its application" (Levi, 1988, p. 140). Levi suggests that implicit bargains of this kind presuppose some forum for repeated co-operation, such as the one represented by the Athenian assembly, council and courts. Cf. also Davies (1981, pp. 88–89), where he argues that the property of the rich gave them a sort of "quasi-veto": if they consistently tried to avoid all obligations (i.e. no longer quasi-complied), they could seriously impair the execution of public policy. Cf. also Ober (1989, pp. 215ff.).

57 Under the usual assumptions of decreasing marginal utility of income (consumption) and leisure, cf. any textbook in economics, e.g. Frank (2006).

58 If it is instead a tax on labour income then there is a countervailing effect, because it now pays less to work. Because your income from work is being taxed, you want to reduce your working time and increase your leisure. This is called a substitution effect. In the present case it will tend to decrease labour supply (and GDP). Whether the income effect or substitution effect dominates is an empirical matter.

59 Public revenue fell to 130 talents in the social war (357–355) and had by the late 340s recovered to 400 talents per year. It was also 400 talents at the beginning of the Peloponnesian War. Note that the 522 talents calculated by Pritchard includes private expenditure, e.g. by the trierarchs.

7 Institutions and markets

1 Acemoglu and others (2005), Acemoglu and Robinson (2006), Greif (2005), North (1990, 2005), Paldam and Gundlach (2008).

2 Compare the parallel analysis by Olson (1982) of encompassing organisations, that is, organisations that have become so large that they "have some incentive to make the society in which they operate more prosperous, and an incentive to redistribute income to their members with as little excess burden as possible" (p. 53).

3 Though it is noted by, for example, North (1990, p. 48).

4 Ober (2008, pp. 43ff.). Athens however did not have the largest territory, both Syracuse and Sparta were bigger.

5 Snodgrass (1986).

6 Lyttkens (2010b) argues that the reason why this interpretation seems to be missing from the literature is probably to be found in the intellectual influence of Finley's path-breaking book *The ancient economy* (1973). As mentioned in Chapter 1, Finley argued that economic analysis was not applicable to the ancient societies, that economics factors played no independent role (being embedded), and that the ancient economies were technically stagnant slave societies. Today however Finley's position is increasingly challenged (see Chapter 1) but his view of the ancient economies has shaped the belief system of many still active scholars.

7 Cf. Loomis (1998, Chapters 14–15), in particular p. 241, on the nominal wage levels. The older figure refers to the Erechtheion building accounts, the second to accounts from Eleusis.

8 On the proceeds from the silver mines, cf., e.g. Isager and Hansen (1975). The state revenue from the silver mines increased from 350 and onward, was still increasing in 330, but fell thereafter (op. cit., p. 44).

9 Note that the relevant supply of silver would refer to the international market for silver of which ancient Athens formed but a part. The grain market was regulated in various ways, see section 7.3.

10 To be precise, if working and participating in the assembly meeting were equally pleasant, and very much *ceteris paribus*, then the implication is that 6,000 adult citizens earned less than the assembly pay and the rest (30,000 minus 6,000) earned more. This assumes that everybody worked for a living. To the extent that some lived as rentiers, even fewer Athenians earned below the level of assembly pay.

11 This recapitulates and extends the presentation in section 1.4.

12 Salmon (2000), however, points out that it is difficult to draw far-reaching conclusions on the basis of the available evidence.

13 Some believe that the dependency on imported grain began later than commonly assumed, and also that it was demand for *better quality* wheat that drove the early grain imports, for example Möller (2007, p. 363). Hansen (2006) however shows that the population in ancient Greece greatly exceeded the carrying capacity of the land and hence that import of grain was important in many parts of Greece (cf. section 2.1).

14 Loomis (1998, p. 254): "economic forces of supply and demand are a [...] likely explanation for differences in wage rates across occupations and over time in Athens in the fifth and fourth centuries".

15 Several authors argue that the fourth century marked a change in Athens. For example, Cohen (1992, p. 4) summarises: "Fourth-century Athens was very different. The Athenians functioned through a market process in which unrelated individuals [...] sought monetary profit through commercial exchange." Burke (1992) similarly places the onset of "commercialism" after *c.*340. Ober (2008, p. 40) notes that the preference for institutional innovation is especially evident in the prosperous late classical era of 354–322 BC.

16 This is the usual argumentation about the 401/0 figure. It is commonly assumed that trade must have been exceptionally low in 401/0 compared to "normal" times. However, note that for the same reason there ought to have been an accumulated shortage of many import goods in Attica. Furthermore, it is arguable whether peace was the normal condition in Athens: "From the end of the fifth century to the middle of the fourth, Athens was a society at war, relieved by occasional short periods of peace" (Hansen, 1999, p. 116). And the second half of the fourth century witnessed the conflict with Philip of Macedon.

17 Hansen (1999) suggests 195 ordinary working days while Isager and Hansen (1975) base their calculation on a yearly income of 300–350 drachmas.

18 Coinage has attracted a vast literature, dealing with many themes that I will not discuss here: the various reasons for city-states to issue coins, the symbolic meanings of coinage, coinage as a reflection of or instigator of social conflicts, etc. Cf., for example, the overviews in von Reden (2002) and Bresson (2008). The popularity of the subject is understandable. Coins have a tendency to be found: they were valuable so people buried them in the ground, and they were small, so people dropped them. And contrary to ceramics they normally come to us intact (and we can collect them). However, to draw conclusions from the finds of coins and their distribution is a precarious undertaking (Picard, 2007).

19 Bresson (2009) argues that there may even have been a monetary union between cities issuing electrum coins.

20 Bresson (2008, p. 22). Aristotle *The Athenian Constitution* 51.3–4.

21 Bresson (2008, p. 104).

22 Please note that I use the word "foreigner" in a non-technical sense, i.e. I do not distinguish here between *xenoi* and metics.

23 The importance of private property rights is evidenced by the survival of an old rule that stated that magistrates could execute on the spot some types of offenders if the offenders confessed, mainly thieves and robbers (Aristotle *The Athenian Constitution* 52.1). This hard stance against those who abuse propety owners is common in primitive societies (presumably because it originally would jeopardise the survival of the person robbed of his belongings).

24 The preliminary steps had been taken by the introduction of lottery for archonships in 487, implying that the Areopagos was not such a prominent group of individuals after all, see section 5.4.

25 The composition of the courts is a contested issue, i.e. whether it is mainly the more affluent citizens who volunteer for these assignments. Cf. Hansen (1999, pp. 183ff.).

26 One realises that there is something of a lacuna in our information about the status of the judicial system in Athens between 510 and 462. It is tempting to hypothesise that Kleisthenes and others did not abolish the travelling judges, and did not restore the full judicial powers of the elite. At least this would make the change of the status of the Areopagos in 462 less dramatic and more easily explicable (see section 5.4 for my interpretation of the events leading up to the change in 462).

27 Cf. Hornblower (1983, p. 172).

28 Bresson (2008, p. 37). Sometimes though similar goods from neighbouring *poleis* could be sold under the same label without being considered to be counterfeit, cf. Brun (1997).

29 The Economic Freedom of the World Index by Gwartney, Lawson, and Norton (2008) consists of five dimensions representing various aspects of economic freedom: (1) Size of government. Expenditures, taxes, and enterprise, (2) Legal structure and security of property rights, (3) Access to sound money, (4) Freedom to trade internationally, (5) Regulation of credit, labour and business.

30 The logical reaction from farmers in Attica would be to switch to other crops, thus increasing the reliance on imported grain.

31 That is, writing a contract so that for every possible situation or contingency, it specifies what each party should do, how you ascertain that they have done it, what will happen if they have not done it, how you ensure that relevant punishment is meted out if they have failed to do it, etc., etc.

32 With all these "parties" this is beginning to feel like a conversation between Groucho and Chico (A day at the opera?), two of the famous Marx Brothers (no relatives of Karl).

33 Henrich *et al.* (2001), Henrich *et al.* (2005), Henrich *et al.* (2010).

34 The last known ostracism took place in 415, followed shortly afterwards by our first certainly datable example of the use of the *graphe paranomon*, cf. Hansen (1999, p. 205). In addition, the Athenians had procedures for political crimes and maladministration, cf. Hansen (1999), pp. 212ff.

35 The *graphe paranomon* and similar measures will be the object of an upcoming analysis.

36 Indeed, individualism is seen as a heritage of ancient Greece (Greif, 2005, p. 769). The upper class was characterised by a highly competitive individualistic ethos, at least from Homeric times (Murray, 1993, Chapter 12).

37 This reasoning is inspired by the habitus theory, cf. Bourdieu (1986, 1990), which ultimately accounts for the logic and reason of everyday practices. People learn by their everyday actions to recognise the limits of their potentialities. Through the mechanism of habitus, objective conditions are (subconsciously) converted into subjective aims and motivations in accordance with the principle "to make a virtue of necessity".

38 With the latter notion, Levi (1988) suggests that individuals may choose to pay taxes even in situations where in principle it is individually rational to evade the burden (e.g. because the probability of detection is low), but only if it is believed that others also pay their taxes and that the revenue is used in a way they find beneficial. When these two conditions cease to be fulfilled, tax evasion follows.

8 Economic analysis of institutional change in ancient Athens – the past meets the present

1 Another type of institutional change is when a new policy is launched in order to show that those in power are doing something about a problem. Reforms undertaken with this motivation are unlikely to have major impact, though the principle of unintended consequences applies to these as well. Health care is an area where this seems to be going on extensively. In recent years, policy changes in Sweden include the family

doctor reform, DRG-systems, provider–purchaser split within public health care, out-sourcing of hotel services, intraprenad, a voucher system, lean production and free choice of GP. Arguably, few of these have had a major impact on the fundamental structure of Swedish health care.

2 Another institutional change that most probably improved the working of Athenian democracy was when the *graphe paranomon* replaced ostracism (section 7.4).

3 It remains to be seen whether the system will prove to be politician-safe. It is not obvious that politicians will accept, e.g. that pensions may have to fall temporarily in certain scenarios. Recently such a situation immediately led to a political desire to fiddle round with the parameters in the system Kruse (2009).

Bibliography

Acemoglu, Daron and Robinson, James A. 2006. *Economic origins of dictatorship and democracy*. New York: Cambridge University Press.

Acemoglu, Daron, Johnson, S., Robinson, J. A. and Yared, P. 2005. "Income and democracy", *CEPR Discussion Paper Series*.

Adams, Douglas. 1979. *The hitchhiker's guide to the galaxy*. New York: Pocket Books 1981.

Adkins, A. W. H. 1972. *Moral values and political behaviour in ancient Greece*. London: Chatto & Windus.

Amemiya, Takeshi. 2007. *Economy and economics of ancient Greece*. Abingdon: Routledge.

Amit, M. 1965. *Athens and the sea*. Bruxelles-Berchem: Latomus Revue d'Études Latines.

Andreades, A. M. 1979. *A history of Greek public finance*. New York: Arno Press. First published in 1933.

Andreau, Jean and Descat, Raymond. 2011. *The slave in Greece and Rome*. London: The University of Wisconsin Press. First published in French in 2006.

Andrewes, A. 1982a. "The growth of the Athenian state", pp. 360–391 in *The Cambridge ancient history*, vol. III.3. Cambridge: Cambridge University Press.

Andrewes, A. 1982b. "The tyranny of Pisistratus", pp. 392–416 in *The Cambridge ancient history*, vol. III.3. Cambridge: Cambridge University Press.

Andrewes, A. 1992. "The peace of Nikias and the Sicilian expedition", pp. 433–463 in *The Cambridge ancient history*, vol. V. Cambridge: Cambridge University Press.

Aoki, Masahiko. 2001. *Toward a comparative institutional analysis*. Cambridge, MA: The MIT Press.

Arrow, Kenneth. 1972. "Gifts and exchanges", *Philosophy and Public Affairs* 1:343–362.

Auriol, Emmanuelle. 2008. "Status and incentives", *RAND Journal of Economics* 39:305–326.

Austin, M. M. and Vidal-Naquet, P. 1977. *Economic and social history of ancient Greece*. London: Batsford Academic and Educational Ltd.

Badian, E. 1971. "Archons and Strategoi", *Antichton* 5:1–34.

Bang, Peter Fibiger. 2008. *The Roman bazaar. A comparative study of trade and markets in a tributary empire*. Cambridge: Cambridge University Press.

Bang, Peter Fibiger. 2009. "Review article: The ancient economy and new institutional economics", *Journal of Roman Studies* 99:194–206.

Barzel, Yoram. 1989. *Economic analysis of property rights*. Cambridge: Cambridge University Press.

Barzel, Yoram. 2000. "Property rights and the evolution of the state", *Economics of Governance* 1:25–51.

Bergh, A. and Erlingsson, G. Ó. 2008. "Liberalization without retrenchment: understanding the consensus on Swedish welfare state reforms", *Scandinavian Political Studies* 32:71–93.

Bergh, Andreas and Lyttkens, Carl Hampus. 2011. "Measuring institutional quality in ancient Greece", *Working Paper Series, Department of Economics, Lund University*, No. 11.

Bitros, G. C. and Karayiannis, A. D. 2008. "Values and institutions as determinants of entrepreneurship in ancient Athens", *Journal of Institutional Economics* 4:205–230.

Blamire, Alec. 2001. "Athenian finance, 454–404 BC", *Hesperia* 70:99–126.

Blok, Josine H. and Lardinois, André P. M. H. 2006a. "Introduction", pp. 1–12 in *Solon of Athens. New historical and philological approaches*, edited by J. H. Blok and A. P. M. H. Lardinois. Leiden: Brill.

Blok, Josine. H. and Lardinois, André P. M. H. 2006b. *Solon of Athens. New historical and philological approaches*. Leiden: Brill.

Borg, P. 2009. *Den långsiktiga finansieringen – välfärdspolitikens klimatfråga*. Rapport till expertgruppen för studier i offentlig ekonomi no. 1. Stockholm: Finansdepartmentet.

Boudon, R. 1982. *The unintended consequences of social action*. New York: St Martin's Press.

Bourdieu, P. 1986. *Social distinction – a social critique of the judgement of taste*. London: Routledge.

Bourdieu, P. 1990. *The logic of practice*. Cambridge: Polity Press.

Bresson, Alain. 2003. "Merchants and politics in ancient Greece: social and economic aspects", *Mercanti e politica nel mondo antico* 21:139–163.

Bresson, Alain. 2007. *L'économie de la Grèce des cités. I. Les structures et la production*. Paris: Armand Collin.

Bresson, Alain. 2008. *L'économie de la Grèce des cités. II. Les espaces de l'échange*. Paris: Armand Colin.

Bresson, Alain. 2009. "Electrum coins, currency exchange and transaction costs in archaic and classical greece", *Revue Belge de Numismatique et de Sigillographie* 155:71–80.

Brun, P. 1983. *Eisphora – syntaxis – stratiotika. Recherches sur les finances militaires d'Athènes au IV siécle av. J.-C.* Paris: Annales Littéraires de l'Université de Besançon 284.

Brun, Patrice. 1997. "Du fromage de Kythnos au marbre de Paros: la question des appellations 'contrôlées' dans l'antiquité grecque", *Revue des études anciennes* 99:401–409.

Burke, E. M. 1985. "Lycurgan finances", *Greek, Roman and Byzantine Studies* 26:251–264.

Burke, E. M. 1992. "The economy of Athens in the Classical era: some adjustments to the primitivist model", *Transactions of the American Philological Association* 122:199–226.

Capps, E. 1943. "Greek inscriptions: a new fragment of the list of victors at the City Dionysia", *Hesperia* 12:1–11.

Cawkwell, G. L. 1988. "ΝΟΜΟΦΥΛΑΚΙΑ and the Areopagus', *Journal of Hellenic Studies* 108:1–12.

Chankowski, Véronique. 2005. "Techniques financiéres, influences, performances dans les activités bancaires des sanctuaires grecs", *Topoi* 12–13:69–93.

Chankowski, Véronique. 2007. "Les places financières dans le monde grec classique et hellénstique des cités", *Pallas* 74:93–112.

Christesen, Paul. 2003. "Economic rationalism in fourth century BCE Athens", *Greece & Rome* 50:31–56.

Coase, R. H. 1937. "The nature of the firm", *Economica* 4:386–405.

Coase, R. H. 1960. "The problem of social cost", *Journal of Law and Economics* 3:1–44.

Cohen, Edward E. 1992. *Athenian economy and society. A banking perspective.* Princeton, NJ: Princeton University Press.

Davies, J. K. 1967. "Demosthenes on liturgies: a note", *Journal of Hellenic Studies* 87:33–40.

Davies, J. K. 1971. *Athenian propertied families 60–300 BC.* Salem, NH: The Ayer Company.

Davies, J. K. 1981. *Wealth and the power of wealth in classical Athens.* Salem, NH: The Ayer Company.

Davies, J. K. 1988. "Religion and the state", pp. 368–388 in *The Cambridge Ancient History*, vol. IV. Cambridge: Cambridge University Press.

Davies, J. K. 1992. "Greece after the persian wars", pp. 15–33 in *The Cambridge ancient history*, vol. V. Cambridge: Cambridge University Press.

Davies, J. K. 1994. "Accounts and accountability in classical Athens", pp. 201–212 in *Ritual, finance, politics*, edited by R. Osborne and S. Hornblower. Oxford: Clarendon Press.

Davies, J. K. 1997. "The origins of the Greek *polis*", pp. 24–38 in *The development of the polis in archaic Greece*, edited by L. G. Mitchell and P. J. Rhodes. London: Routledge.

Davies, J. K. 2003. "Democracy without theory", pp. 319–335 in *Herodotus and his world*, edited by P. Derow and R. Parker. Oxford: Oxford University Press.

Davies, J. K. 2007. "Classical Greece: production", in *The Cambridge economic history of the Greco-Roman world*, edited by W. Scheidel, I. Morris and R. Saller. Cambridge: Cambridge University Press.

Demsetz, H. 1967. "Toward a theory of property rights", *American Economic Review* 57:347–359.

Develin, Bob and Kilmer, M. 1997. "What Kleisthenes did", *Historia* 46:3–18.

Donlan, Walter. 1989. "The pre-state community in Greece", *Symbolae Osloenses* 64:5–29.

Donlan, Walter. 1994. "Chiefs and followers in pre-state Greece", pp. 34–51 in *From political economy to anthropology. Situating economic life in past societies, vol. 3. Critical perspectives on historic issues*, edited by C. A. M. Duncan and D. W. Tandy. Montréal: Blackrose Books.

Donlan, Walter. 1997. "The relations of power in the pre-state and early state polities", pp. 39–48 in *The development of the polis in archaic Greece*, edited by L. G. Mitchell and P. J. Rhodes. London: Routledge.

Donlan, Walter and Thomas, Carol. 1993. "The village community of ancient Greece: Neolithic, Bronze and Dark Ages", *Studi Micenei ed Egeo-Anatolici* 31:611–671.

Eliasson, Marcus and Ohlsson, Henry 2011. "The timing of death and the repeal of the Swedish inheritance tax", *Working Paper Series, Department of Economics, Uppsala University*.

Encyclopaedia Britannica. Olive. Retrieved 2006-12-06 from http://search.eb.com.

Engen, Darel Tai. 2005. "'Ancient greenbacks': Athenian owls, the law of Nikophon, and the Greek economy", *Historia* 54:359–381.

Evans, Jonathan St. B. T. 1989. *Biases in human reasoning. Causes and consequences.* Hove: Lawrence Erlbaum Associates.

Fehr, E. and Hoff, K. 2011. "Introduction: tastes, castes and culture: the influence of society on preferences", *The Economic Journal* 121:F396-F412.

Finley, Moses I. 1952. *Studies in land and credit in ancient Athens 500–200 B.C. The Horos inscriptions*. New Brunswick, NJ: Transaction Books.

Finley, Moses I. 1970. "Aristotle and economic analysis", *Past and Present* 47:3–25.

Finley, Moses I. 1973. *The ancient economy*. London: Chatto & Windus.

Finley, Moses I. 1981. *Economy and society in Ancient Greece*, Edited by B. D. Shaw and R. P. Saller. London: Chatto & Windus.

Finley, Moses I. 1983. *Politics in the ancient world*. Cambridge: Cambridge University Press.

Finley, Moses I. 1985. *Ancient history. Evidence and models*. London: Chatto & Windus.

Finley, Moses I. 1991. *The world of Odysseus*. London: Penguin Books. First published 1978.

Finley, Moses I. 1999. *The ancient economy. Updated with a foreword by Ian Morris*. Berkeley, CA: University of California Press.

Fleck, K. R. and Hanssen, F. A. 2006. "The origins of democracy: a model with application to ancient Greece", *Journal of Law and Economics* 49:115–145.

Forrest, W. G. and Stockton, D. L. 1987. "The Athenian archons: a note", *Historia* 36:235–240.

Forsdyke, S. 2000. "Exile, ostracism and the Athenian democracy", *Classical Antiquity* 19:232–263.

Forsdyke, S. 2006. "Land, labor and economy in Solonian Athens: breaking the impasse between archaeology and history", pp. 334–350 in *Solon of Athens*, edited by J. H. Blok and A. P. M. H. Lardinois. Leiden: Brill.

Foxhall, Lin. 1992. "The control of the Attic landscape", in *Agriculture in ancient Greece: Proceedings of the seventh international symposium at the Swedish Institute at Athens, 16–17 May, 1990*, edited by B. Wells. Stockholm: Svenska Institutet i Athen.

Foxhall, Lin. 1997. "A view from the top", pp. 113–136 in *The development of the polis in archaic Greece*, edited by L. G. Mitchell and P. J. Rhodes.

Foxhall, Lin. 2002. "Access to resources in ancient Greece: the egalitarianism of the polis in practice", pp. 209–220 in *Money, labour, and land: approaches to the economies of ancient Greece*, edited by P. Cartledge, E. E. Cohen and L. Foxhall. London: Routledge.

Frank, Robert H. 2006. *Microeconomics and behaviour*. New York: McGraw-Hill.

Friedman, Milton. 1953. "The methodology of positive economics", pp. 3–43 in Milton Friedman, *Essays on positive economics*. Chicago, IL: University of Chicago Press.

Gabrielsen, Vincent. 1985. "The naukrariai and the Athenian navy", *Classica et Mediaevalia* 36:21–51.

Gabrielsen, Vincent. 1986. "ΦΑΝΕΡΑ and ΑΦΑΝΗΣ ΟΥΣΙΑ in Classical Athens", *Classica et Mediaevalia* 37:99–114.

Gabrielsen, Vincent. 1987a. "The *Antidosis* procedure in classical Athens", *Classica et Mediaevalia* 38:7–38.

Gabrielsen, Vincent. 1987b. "The *diadikasia*-documents", *Classica et Mediaevalia* 38, 39–51.

Gabrielsen, Vincent. 1989. "The number of Athenian trierarchs after *c.*340 B.C.", *Classica et Mediaevalia* 40:143–159.

Gabrielsen, Vincent. 1994. *Financing the Athenian fleet*. Baltimore, MD: The Johns Hopkins University Press.

Gabrielsen, Vincent. forthcoming. "Finance and taxes", in *Blackwell's companion to ancient Greek government*, edited by H. Beck. Oxford: Blackwell.

Georges, Pericles. 1993. "Athenian democracy and Athenian Empire: review article", *International History Review* 15:84–105.

Greif, Avner. 1994. "Cultural beliefs and the organization of society: a historical and theoretical reflection on collectivist and individualist societies", *Journal of Political Economy* 102:912–950.

Greif, Avner. 1998. "Self-enforcing political systems and economic growth", pp. 23–63 in *Analytic narratives*, edited by R. H. Bates, A. Greif, M. Levi and J.-L. Rosenthal. Princeton, NJ: Princeton University Press.

Greif, Avner. 2005. "Commitment, coercion, and markets: the nature and dynamics of institutions supporting exchange", pp. 727–786 in *Handbook of new institutional economics*, edited by C. Ménard and M. M. Shirley. Dordrecht: Springer.

Greif, Avner. 2006. *Institutions and the path to the modern economy*. New York: Cambridge University Press.

Gwartney, J., Lawson, R. and Norton, S. 2008. *Economic freedom of the world: 2008 annual report*. The Fraser Institute, retrieved from www.freetheworld.com, January 2012.

Haas, C. J. 1985. "Athenian naval power before Themistokles", *Historia* 34:29–46.

Halkos, George E. and Kyriazis, Nickolas C. 2010. "The Athenian economy in the age of Demosthenes: path dependence and change", *European Journal of Law and Economics* 29:255–277.

Hammond, N. G. L. 1982. "The Peloponnese", pp. 321–359 in *The Cambridge ancient history*, vol. III.3. Cambridge: Cambridge University Press.

Hammond, N. G. L. 1988. "The expedition of Xerxes", pp. 518–591 in *The Cambridge ancient history*, vol. IV. Cambridge: Cambridge University Press.

Hansen, Mogens Herman. 1987. *The Athenian assembly*. Oxford: Basil Blackwell.

Hansen, Mogens Herman. 1991. *The Athenian democracy in the age of Demosthenes: structure, principles, and ideology*. Oxford: Blackwell.

Hansen, Mogens Herman. 1993. "Introduction. The *Polis* as a citizen-state", pp. 7–29 in *The Ancient Greek city-state*, edited by M. H. Hansen. Copenhagen: Munksgaard.

Hansen, Mogens Herman. 1997. "Polis as the generic term for state", pp. 29–37 in *Yet more studies in the ancient Greek polis*, edited by T. Heine Nielsen. Stuttgart: Franz Steiner Verlag.

Hansen, Mogens Herman. 1999. *The Athenian democracy in the age of Demosthenes: structure, principles, and ideology*. London: University of Oklahoma Press.

Hansen, Mogens Herman. 2004a. "The lifespan of the Hellenic *polis*", pp. 16–22 in *An inventory of archaic and classical poleis*, edited by M. H. Hansen and T. H. Nielsen. New York: Oxford University Press.

Hansen, Mogens Herman. 2004b. "Territory and size of territory", pp. 70–73 in *An inventory of archaic and classical poleis*, edited by M. H. Hansen and T. H. Nielsen. New York: Oxford University Press.

Hansen, Mogens Herman. 2004c. "A typology of dependent *poleis*", pp. 87–97 in *An inventory of archaic and classical poleis*, edited by M. H. Hansen and T. H. Nielsen. New York: Oxford University Press.

Hansen, Mogens Herman. 2006. *The shotgun method. The demography of the ancient Greek city-state culture*. Columbia, MO: University of Missouri Press.

Hansen, Mogens Herman and Thomas Heine Nielsen (eds). 2004. *An inventory of archaic and classical poleis*. New York: Oxford University Press.

Hanson, V. D. 1991. "The ideology of hoplite battle, ancient and modern", pp. 3–11 in *Hoplites. The classical Greek battle experience*, edited by V. D. Hanson. London: Routledge.

Hanson, V. D. 1995. *The other Greeks*. New York: The Free Press.

Hanson, V. D. 1999. *Wars of the ancient Greeks*. London: Smithsonian Books.

Harris, Edward M. 1997. "A new solution to the riddle of the *seisachtheia*", pp. 103–112 in *The development of the polis in archaic Greece*, edited by Lynette G. Michell and P. J. Rhodes. London: Routledge.

Harris, Edward M. 2002. "Workshop, marketplace and household: the nature of technical specialization in classical Athens and its influence on economy and society", pp. 67–99 in *Money, labour and land*, edited by P. Cartledge, E. E. Cohen and L. Foxhall. Abingdon: Routledge.

Harris, Edward M. 2006. "Solon and the spirit of the laws in archaic and classical Greece", in *Solon of Athens. New historical and philological approaches*, edited by J. H. Blok and A. P. M. H. Lardinois. Leiden: Brill.

Harrison, A. R. W. 1971. *The law of Athens: procedure*. London: Oxford University Press.

Hedlund, Stefan, Lundahl, Mats and Lyttkens, C. H. 1989. "The attraction of extraction: three cases of state versus peasantry", *Scandia* 55:45–71.

Heltzer, M. 1978. *Goods, prices and the organization of trade in Ugarit*. Wiesbaden: Dr. Ludwig Reichert Verlag.

Henrich, J., Boyd, R., Bowles, S., Gintis, H., Camerer, C., Fehr, E. and McElreath, R. 2001. "In search of *Homo economicus*: experiments in 15 small-scale societies", *American Economic Review* 91:73–78.

Henrich, J., Boyd, R., Bowles, S., Camerer, C., Fehr, E., Gintis, H. *et al.* 2005. "'Economic man' in cross-cultural perspective: Behavioral experiments in 15 small-scale societies", *Behavioral and Brain Sciences* 28:795–855.

Henrich, J., Ensminger, J., McElreath, R., Barr, A., Barrett, C., Bolyanatz, A. *et al.* 2010. "Markets, religion, community size, and the evolution of fairness and punishment", *Science* 327:1480–1484.

Hodgson, G. M. 1997. "The ubiquity of habits and rules", *Cambridge Journal of Economics* 21:663–684.

Hornblower, Simon. 1983. *The Greek world 479–323 BC*. New York: Methuen.

Isager, Signe and Mogens Herman Hansen. 1975. *Aspects of Athenian society in the fourth century B.C.* Odense: Odense University Press.

Jacoby, F. 1944. "ΓΕΝΕΣΙΑ. A forgotten festival of the dead", *The Classical Quarterly* 38:65–75.

Johnsen, D. B. 1986. "The formation and protection of property rights among the Southern Kwakiutl Indians", *Journal of Legal Studies* 15:41–67.

Jones, A. H. M. 1957. *Athenian democracy*. Oxford: Basil Blackwell.

Jones, A. H. M. 1974. *The Roman economy. Studies in ancient economic and administrative history*, edited by P. A. Brunt. Oxford: Basil Blackwell.

Jordan, B. 1975. *The Athenian navy in the classical period*. Berkeley, CA: University of California Press.

Kahneman, Daniel. 2011. *Thinking, fast and slow*. New York: Farrar, Strauss and Giroux.

Kahneman, Daniel and Tversky, Amos. 1979. "Prospect theory: an analysis of decisions under risk", *Econometrica* 47:263–292.

Kaiser, Brooks A. 2007. "The Athenian trierarchy: mechanism design for the private provision of public goods", *The Journal of Economic History* 67:445–480.

Kim, H. S. 2002. "Small change and the moneyed economy", pp. 44–51 in *Money, labour and land*, edited by P. Cartledge, E. E. Cohen, and L. Foxhall. Abingdon: Routledge.

Kiser, E. 1991. "Markets and hierarchies in early modern fiscal systems: a principal-agent analysis of the choice between tax farming and state bureaucracy". Paper presented at the annual meeting of the American Political Science Association, Washington DC.

Kruse, Agneta. 2009. "Rör inte min pension! Om värdet av stabila spelregler även i nedgång", *Ekonomisk debatt* 37:6–10.

Kruse, Agneta. 2010. "A stable pension system: the eighth wonder", pp. 47–64 in *Population ageing – a threat to the welfare state? The case of Sweden*, edited by T. Bengtsson. Heidelberg: Springer.

Kruse, Agneta and Ståhlberg, Ann-Charlotte. 1977. *Effekter av ATP – en samhällsekonomisk studie*. Lund: Department of Economics, Lund University.

Kyriazis, Nikolas and Metaxas, Theodore. 2010. "Bounded rationality and institutional change", *Evolutionary Institutional Economics Review* 7:1–19.

L'Homme-Wery, Louise-Marie. 2004. "La législation de Solon: une solution à la crise agraire d'Athènes?", *Pallas* 64:145–155.

Lardinois, André. P. M. H. 2000. "Have we Solon's verses?", pp. 15–35 in *Solon of Athens. New historical and philological approaches*, edited by J. H. Blok and A. P. M. H. Lardinois. Leiden: Brill.

Levi, Margaret. 1988. *Of rule and revenue*. London: University of California Press.

Lewis, D. M. 1988. "The tyranny of the Pisistratidae", pp. 287–302 in *The Cambridge ancient history*, vol. IV. Cambridge: Cambridge University Press.

Lichtenstein, Sarah and Slovic, Paul. 2006. *The construction of preference*. Cambridge: Cambridge University Press.

Lieberman, E. S. 2003. *Race and regionalism in the politics of taxation in Brazil and South Africa*. New York: Cambridge University Press.

Lindbladh, Eva and Lyttkens, Carl Hampus. 2002. "Habit versus choice: the process of decision-making in health-related behaviour", *Social Science and Medicine* 55:451–465.

Loomis, William T. 1998. *Wages, welfare costs and inflation in Classical Athens*. Ann Arbor, MI: University of Michigan Press.

Lundahl, Mats. 1983. "Insuring against risk in primitive societies", pp. 35–51 in *Social Insurance*, edited by L. Söderström. Amsterdam: North-Holland.

Lyttkens, Carl Hampus. 1992. "Effects of the taxation of wealth in Athens in the fourth century B.C.", *Scandinavian Economic History Review* 40:3–20.

Lyttkens, Carl Hampus. 1994. "A predatory democracy? An essay on taxation in Classical Athens", *Explorations in Economic History* 31:62–90.

Lyttkens, Carl Hampus. 1997. "A rational-actor perspective on the origin of liturgies in ancient Greece", *Journal of Institutional and Theoretical Economics* 153:462–484.

Lyttkens, Carl Hampus. 2004. "Athens – an incidental democracy. A case study of unintended consequences of institutional change", *Working Paper Series, Department of Economics, Lund University*, No. 19.

Lyttkens, Carl Hampus. 2006. "Reflections on the origins of the *polis*", *Constitutional Political Economy* 17: 31–48.

Lyttkens, Carl Hampus. 2008. "Appointment by lottery in Athens. A mistake with important consequences", pp. 426–434 in *Förbistringar och förklaringar. Festskrift till Anders Pilz*, edited by Per Beskow, Stephan Borgehammar and Arne Jönsson. Ängelholm: Skåneförlaget & Torgny HB.

Lyttkens, Carl Hampus. 2009. "Why the econometrician is in good spirits – a workshop through the looking glass", *European Journal of Health Economics* 10:239–242.

Lyttkens, Carl Hampus. 2010a. "Institutions, taxation, and market relationships in ancient Athens", *Journal of Institutional Economics* 6:505–527.

Lyttkens, Carl Hampus. 2010b. "Tankemönster som inspirationskälla", pp. 133–136 in *Tankemönster. En festskrift till Eva Rystedt*, edited by F. Faegersten, J. Wallensten and I. Östenberg. Lund.

Lyttkens, Carl Hampus. 2011. "Health, economics and ancient Greek medicine", *The Journal of Economic Assymetries* 8:165–192.

Lyttkens, Carl Hampus. 2012. "Surprising institutions." Paper presented at the Conference in Honour of Thráinn Eggertsson, Reykjavík, Iceland, 21 April 2012.

MacDowell, Douglas A. 1978. *The law in classical Athens*. Ithaca, NY: Cornell University Press.

Manville, P. B. 1997. *The origins of citizenship in ancient Athens*. Princeton, NJ: Princeton University Press. First published in 1990.

Mäki, Uskali. 1994. "Reorienting the assumptions issue", pp. 236–256 in *New directions in economic methodology*, edited by R. Backhouse. London: Routledge.

McCloskey, Donald. 1983. "The rhetoric of economics", *Journal of Economic Literature* 21:481–517.

McCloskey, Donald. 1985. "Economical writing", *Economic Inquiry* 23:187–222.

Merton, R. K. 1936. "The unanticipated consequences of purposive social action", *The American Sociological Review* 1:894–904.

Migeotte, Léopold. 2000. "Les dépenses militaires des cités grecques: essai de typologie", pp. 145–176 in *Èconomie antique. La guerre dans les économies antiques, Entretiens d'archéologie et d'histoire 5*, edited by J. Andreau, P. Briant and R. Descat. Saint-Bertand-de-Comminges.

Migeotte, Léopold. 2003. "Taxation directe en Grèce ancienne", pp. 297–313 in *Symposion 1999: Vorträge zur griechischen und hellenistischen Rechtsgeschichte*, edited by Gerhard Thür and Francisco Javier Fernández Nieto. Köln: Böhlau.

Migeotte, Léopold. 2009. *The economy of the Greek cities. From the archaic period to the early Roman Empire*. London: University of California Press.

Millet, Paul C. 2000a. "Mogens Hansen and the labelling of Athenian democracy", pp. 337–362 in *Polis and Politics. Studies in Ancient Greek History*, edited by P. Flensted-Jensen, T. Heine Nielsen and L. Rubinstein. Copenhagen: Museum Tusculanum Press

Millet, Paul. C. 2000b. "The economy", pp. 13–51 in *The short Oxford history of Europe. Classical Greece*, edited by R. Osborne. Oxford: Oxford University Press.

Möller, A. 2007. "Classical Greece: distribution", pp. 362–384 in *The Cambridge economic history of the Greco-Roman world*, edited by W. Scheidel, I. Morris and R. Saller. Cambridge: Cambridge University Press.

Morris, Ian. 1994. "The Athenian economy twenty years after *The Ancient Economy*", *Classical Philology* 89:351–366.

Morris, Ian. 1996. "The strong principle of equality and the archaic origins of democracy", pp. 19–48 in *Demokratia*, edited by J. Ober and C. Hedrick. Princeton, NJ: Princeton University Press.

Morris, Ian. 1998. "Archaeology as a kind of anthropology (a response to David Small)", pp. 229–239 in *Democracy 2500? Questions and challenges*, edited by I. Morris and K. A. Raaflaub. Dubuque, IA: Kendall/Hunt.

Morris, Ian. 2000. *Archaeology as cultural history*. Oxford: Blackwell.

Morris, Ian. 2002. "Hard surfaces", pp. 8–43 in *Money, labour and land*, edited by P. Cartledge, E. E. Cohen and L. Foxhall. Abingdon: Routledge.

Morris, Ian. 2004. "Economic growth in ancient Greece", *Journal of Institutional and Theoretical Economics* 160:709–742.

Morris, Ian. 2006. "The collapse and regeneration of complex society in Greece, 1500–500 BC", in pp. 72–84, *After collapse: the regeneration of complex societies*, edited by G. M. Schwartz and J. J. Nichols. Tucson, AZ: University of Arizona Press.

Morris, Ian. 2007. "Early iron age Greece", pp. 211–241 in *The Cambridge economic history of the Greco-Roman world*, edited by W. Scheidel, I. Morris and R. Saller. Cambridge: Cambridge University Press.

Morris, Ian. 2009. "The greater Athenian state", pp. 99–177 in *The dynamics of ancient empires*, edited by Ian Morris and Walter Scheidel. New York: Oxford University Press.

Morris, Ian and Manning, J. G. 2005. "Introduction", pp. 1–44 in *The ancient economy: evidence and models*, edited by J. G. Manning and I. Morris. Stanford, CA: Stanford University Press.

Morris, Ian and Weingast, Barry R. 2004. "Views and comments on institutions, economics and the ancient Mediterranean world: introduction", *Journal of Institutional and Theoretical Economics* 160:702–708.

Murray, Oswyn. 1990. "Cities of reason", pp. 1–25 in *The Greek city from Homer to Alexander*, edited by O. Murray and S. Price. Oxford: Clarendon Press.

Murray, Oswyn. 1993. *Early Greece*. Waukegan, IL: Fontana Press.

Murray, Oswyn. 1996. "Rationality and the Greek City: the evidence from Kamarina", pp. 493–504 in *The polis as an urban centre and as a political community*, edited by M. H. Hansen. Copenhagen: Munksgaard.

Neer, Richard. 2004. "The Athenian treasury at Delphi and the material of politics", *Classical Antiquity* 23:63–93.

North, Douglass C. 1981. *Structure and change in economic history*. New York: W. W. Norton & Company.

North, Douglass C. 1990. *Institutions, institutional change and economic performance*. New York: Cambridge University Press.

North, Douglass C. 2005. *Understanding the process of economic change*. Princeton, NJ: Princeton University Press.

North, Douglass C. and Weingast, Barry R. 1989. "Constitutions and commitment: the evolution of institutions governing public choice in seventeenth-century England", *The Journal of Economic History* 49:803–832.

Ober, Josiah. 1989. *Mass and elite in democratic Athens*. Princeton, NJ: Princeton University Press.

Ober, J. 1994. "The rules of war in classical Greece", pp. 53–71 in *The Athenian revolution. Essays on ancient Greek democracy and political theory*. Princeton, NJ: Princeton University Press.

Ober, Josiah. 1996. *The Athenian revolution*. Princeton, NJ: Princeton University Press.

Ober, Josiah. 2007. " 'I besieged that man': democracy's revolutionary start", pp. 83–104 in *Origins of democracy in ancient Greece*, edited by K. A. Raaflaub, J. Ober and R. W. Wallace. London: University of California Press.

Ober, Josiah. 2008. *Democracy and knowledge*. Princeton, NJ: Princeton University Press.

Ober, Josiah. 2010. "Wealthy Hellas", *Transactions of the American Philological Association* 140:241–286.

Offer, A., Pechey, R. and Ulijaszek, S. 2010. "Obesity under affluence varies by welfare regime: the effect of fast food, insecurity and inequality", *Economics and Human Biology* 8:297–308.

Ohlsson, Henry. 2011. "The legacy of the Swedish gift and inheritance tax, 1884–2004", *European Review of Economic History* 15:539–569.

Olson, Mancur. 1971. *The logic of collective action*. Cambridge, MA: Harvard University Press

Olson, Mancur. 1982. *The rise and decline of nations*. New Haven, CT: Yale University Press.

Olson, Mancur. 2000. "Dictatorship, democracy, and development", pp. 119–137 in *A not-so-dismal science*, edited by M. Olson and S. Kähkönen. Oxford: Oxford University Press.

Osborne, Robin. 1987. *Classical landscape with figures*. Dobbs Ferry, NY: Sheridan House.

Osborne, Robin. 1991. "Pride and prejudice, sense and subsistence: exchange and society in the Greek city", pp. 119–145 in *City and country in the ancient world*, edited by J. Rich and A. Wallace-Hadrill. London: Routledge.

Osborne, Robin. 1992. "Is it a farm? The definition of agricultural sites and settlements in ancient Greece", pp. 22–27 in *Agriculture in ancient Greece: proceedings of the seventh international symposium at the Swedish Institute at Athens, 16–17 May, 1990*, edited by B. Wells. Stockholm: Svenska Institutet i Athen.

Osborne, Robin. 1996a. *Greece in the making 1200–479 BC*. London: Routledge.

Osborne, Robin. 1996b. "Pots, trade and the archaic Greek economy", *Antiquity* 70:31–44.

Ostwald, Martin. 1988. "The reform of the Athenian state by Cleisthenes", pp. 303–346 in *The Cambridge ancient history*, vol. IV. Cambridge: Cambridge University Press.

Owens, Ron. 2009. *Solon of Athens. Poet, philosopher, solider, statesman*. Eastbourne: Sussex Academic Press.

Oxford Classical Dictionary, The, 3rd edn., edited by Simon Hornblower and Anthony Spawforth. Oxford: Oxford University Press.

Paldam, M. and Gundlach, E. 2008. "Two views on institutions and development: the grand transition vs the primacy of institutions", *Kyklos* 61:65–100.

Pébarthe, Christophe. 2000. "Fiscalité, empire athénien et écriture: retour sur les causes de la guerre du Péloponnèse", *Zeitschrift für Papyrologie und Epigraphik* 129:47–76.

Penttinen, A. 2001. *Berbati between Argos and Corinth*. Stockholm: Department of Classical Archaeology and Ancient History, University of Stockholm.

Picard, Olivier. 2001. "La decouverte des gisements du Laurion et les débuts de la chouette", *Revue Belge de numismatique et de sigillographie* 147:1–10.

Picard, Olivier. 2007. "Monnaie et circulation monétaire à l'époque classique", *Pallas* 74:113–128.

Pitsoulis, Athanassios. 2011. "The egalitarian battlefield: reflections on the origin of majority rule in archaic Greece", *European Journal of Political Economy* 27:87–103.

Polignac, F. de. 1994. "Meditation, competition, and sovereignty: the evolution of rural sanctuaries in geometric Greece", pp. 3–18 in *Placing the Gods. Sanctuaries and scared space in ancient Greece*, edited by S. E. Alcock and R. Osborne. Oxford: Clarendon Press.

Pomeroy, Sarah B. 1995. *Goddesses, whores, wives, and slaves*. New York: Schocken Books.

Pritchard, David. forthcoming. "Costing festivals and war in democratic Athens: Athenian funding priorities between 430 and 350 BC", in *The business of state: public finance in ancient Athens*, edited by H. van Wees, P. J. Rhodes, P. Pritchard, P. Fawcett, and G. Oliver. Oxford: Oxford University Press.

Raaflaub, Kurt A. 1993. "Homer to Solon: the rise of the *polis*. The written sources", pp. 41–105 in *The ancient Greek city-state*, edited by M. H. Hansen. Copenhagen: Munksgaard.

Raaflaub, Kurt A. 1997. "Soldiers, citizens and the evolution of the early Greek *polis*", pp. 24–38 in *The development of the polis in archiac Greece*, edited by L. G. Mitchell and P. J. Rhodes. London: Routledge.

Raaflaub, Kurt A. 2007a. "The breakthrough of Demokratia in mid-fifth century Athens", pp. 105–154 in *Origins of democracy in ancient Greece*, edited by K. A. Raaflaub, J. Ober and R. W. Wallace. London: University of California Press.

Raaflaub, Kurt A. 2007b. "Introduction", pp. 1–21 in *Origins of democracy in ancient Greece*, edited by K. A. Raaflaub, J. Ober and R. W. Wallace. London: University of California Press.

Raaflaub, Kurt A., Ober, Josiah and Wallace, Robert W. 2007. *Origins of democracy in ancient Greece*. London: University of California Press.

Raaflaub, Kurt A. and Wallace, Robert W. 2007. " 'Peoples' power and egalitarian trends in archaic Greece", pp. 22–48 in *Origins of democracy in ancient Greece* edited by K. A. Raaflaub, J. Ober and R. W. Wallace. London: University of California Press.

Rahe, Paul. 1984. "The primacy of politics in classical Greece", *American Historical Review* 89:265–293.

Reed, C. M. 2003. *Maritime traders in the ancient Greek world*. Cambridge: Cambridge University Press.

Renfrew, C. and Cherry, J. F. 1986. *Peer polity interaction and socio-political change*. Cambridge: Cambridge University Press.

Rhodes, P. J. 1993. *A commentary on the Aristotelian Athenaion Politeia*. Oxford: Clarendon Press. First published 1981.

Rhodes, P. J. 1982. "Problems in Athenian *Eisophora* and liturgies", *American Journal of Ancient History* 7:1–19.

Rhodes, P. J. 2006. "The reforms and laws of Solon: an optimistic view", pp. 248–260 in *Solon of Athens*, edited by J. H. Blok and A. P. M. H. Lardinois. Leiden: Brill.

Rihll, T. E. 1995. "Democracy denied: why Ephialtes attacked the Areiopagus", *The Journal of Hellenic Studies* 115:87–98.

Robinson, Charles Alexander Jr. 1967. *Ancient history. From prehistoric times to the death of Justinian*. London: The MacMillan Company.

Robinson, Eric W. 1997. *The first democracies*. Stuttgart: Franz Steiner Verlag.

Rodrik, D. 1999. "Where did all the growth go? External shocks, social conflict, and growth collapse", *Journal of Economic Growth* 4:385–412.

Rodrik, D. 2000. "Institutions for high-quality growth: what they are and how to acquire them", *NBER Working Paper* No. 7540.

Rosen, Harvey S. 2005. *Public finance*. New York: McGraw-Hill.

Rosenthal, Jean-Laurent, Bates, R. H. and Levi, Margaret. 1994. "An essay on giving and honor: markets, states, and the private provision of public goods", *Manuscript prepared for the Workshop on Benevolence, Research School of Social Sciences, Australian National University, Canberra, August 1994.*

Ruschenbusch, E. 1985. "Ein Beitrag zur Leiturgie und zur *Eisphora*", *Zeitschrift für Papyrologie und Epigraphik* 59:237–240.

Sallares, Robert. 1991. *The ecology of the ancient Greek world*. London: Duckworth.

Sallares, Robert. 2007. "Ecology", pp. 15–37 in *The Cambridge economic history of the Greco-Roman world*, edited by W. Scheidel, I. Morris and R. Sallares. Cambridge: Cambridge University Press.

Salmon, John. 2000. "Pots and profits", pp. 245–252 in *Periplous. Papers on classical art and arhaeology presented to Sir John Boardman*, edited by G. R. Tsetskhladze, A. J. N. W. Prag and A. M. Snodgrass. London: Thames and Hudson.

Salmon, John. 2003. "Cleisthenes (of Athens) and Korinth", pp. 219–234 in *Herodotus and his world*, edited by P. Derow and R. Parker. Oxford: Oxford University Press.

Scheidel, Walter. 2003. "The Greek demographic expansion: models and comparisons", *Journal of Hellenic Studies* 123:120–140.

Scheidel, Walter. 2010. "Real wages in early economies: evidence for living standards from 1800 BCE to 1300 CE", *Journal of the Economic and Social History of the Orient* 53:245–462.

Scheidel, Walter, Morris, Ian and Saller, Richard. 2007. *The Cambridge economic history of the Greco-Roman world*. Cambridge: Cambridge University Press.

Schlaifer, R. 1940. "Notes on Athenian public cults", *Harvard Studies in Classical Philology* 51:233–260.

Schoemaker, Paul J. H. 1982. "The expected utility model: its variants, purposes, evidence and limitations", *Journal of Economic Literature* 20:529–563.

Seidl, Christian. 2002. "Preference reversal", *Journal of Economic Surveys* 16:621–655.

Sellar, W. C. and Yeatman, R. J. 1975. *1066 and all that*. London: Methuen Paperbacks. First published 1930.

Selten, Reinhard. 2001. "What is bounded rationality?" pp. 13–36 in *Bounded rationality. The adaptive toolbox*, edited by G. Gigerenzer and R. Selten. Cambridge, MA: MIT Press.

Simon, Herbert. 1955. "A behavioural model of rational choice", *Quarterly Journal of Economics* 69:99–118.

Simon, Herbert. 1956. "Rational choice and the structure of the environment", *Psychological Review* 63:129–138.

Sinclair, R. K. 1988. *Democracy and participation in Athens*. Cambridge: Cambridge University Press.

Slater, W. 2009. "Véronique Chankowski, Athènes et Délos à l'époque classique. Recherches sur l'administration du sanctuaire d'Apollon délien", *Bryn Mawr Classical Review* 04:44.

Smith, Adam. 1776. "An inquiry into the nature and causes of the wealth of nations", edited by R. H. Cambell and A. S. Skinner. Indianapolis: Liberty Classics.

Snodgrass, Anthony. 1980. *Archaic Greece*. London: J. M. Dent and Sons.

Snodgrass, A. 1986. "Interaction by design: the Greek city-state", pp. 47–58 in *Peer polity interaction and socio-political change*, edited by C. Renfrew and J. F. Cherry. Cambridge: Cambridge University Press.

Snodgrass, Anthony. 1993. "The rise of the *polis*", pp. 30–40 in *The ancient Greek city-state*, edited by M. H. Hansen. Copenhagen: Munksgaard.

Spence, M. 1973. "Job market signaling", *Quarterly Journal of Economics* 87:355–374.

Starr, Chester G. 1977. *The economic and social growth of early Greece 800–550 B.C.* New York: Oxford University Press.

Starr, Chester G. 1986. *Individual and community. The rise of the polis 800–500 B.C.* New York: Oxford University Press.

Ste. Croix, G. E. M. de. 1953. "Demosthenes' *Timema* and the Athenian eisphora in the fourth century B.C.", *Classica et Mediaevalia* 14, 30–70.

Ste. Croix, G. E. M. de. 2004. *Athenian democratic origins*. New York: Oxford University Press.

Stehle, E. 2006. "Solon's self-reflexive political persona and its audience", pp. 79–113 in *Solon of Athens*, edited by J. H. Blok and A. P. M. H. Lardinois. Leiden: Brill.

Strauss, Barry S. 1986. *Athens after the Peloponnesian War*. New York: Cornell University Press.

Sugden, R. 2000. "Credible worlds: the status of theoretical models in economics", *Journal of Economic Methodology* 7:1–31.

Tangian, Adranik. 2008. "A mathematical model of Athenian democracy", *Social Choice and Welfare* 31:537–572.

Thomas, C. G. 1993. *Myth becomes history: pre-classical Greece*. Claremont, CA: Regina Books.

Thomas, C. G. and Conant, C. 1999. *Citadel to city-state*. Bloomington, IN: Indiana University Press.

Thomsen, R. 1964. *Eisphora: a study of direct taxation in Ancient Athens*. Copenhagen: Gyldendalske boghandel.

Tridimas, Geroge. 2011. "A political economy perspective of direct democracy in ancient Athens", *Constitutional Political Economy* 22:58–82.

van Wees, H. 2006. "Mass and elite in Solon's Athens: the property classes revisited", pp. 351–389 in *Solon of Athens*, edited by J. H. Blok and A. P. M. H. Lardinois. Leiden: Brill.

van Wees, Hans. 1994. "The Homeric way of war: the Iliad and the hoplite phalanx (II)", *Greece & Rome* 41:131–155.

Veyne, P. 1976. *Bread and circuses*. London: Penguin.

von Reden, Sitta. 2002. "Money in the ancient economy: a survey of recent research", *Klio* 84:141–174.

Wallace, Robert W. 2007. "Revolutions and a new order in Solonian Athens and archaic Greece", pp. 49–82 in *Origins of democracy in ancient Greece*, edited by K. A. Raaflaub, J. Ober and R. W. Wallace. London: University of California Press.

Weesie, J. and Wippler, R. 1986. "Cumulative effects of sequential decisions in organizations", pp. 257–279 in *Paradoxical effects of social behaviour. Essays in honor of Anatol Rapoport*, edited by A. Diekmann and P. Mitter. Heidelberg: Physica-Verlag.

Weingast, Barry R. 1995. "The economic role of political institutions: market-preserving federalism and economic development", *Journal of Law, Economics and Organization* 7:1–31.

Whitehead, D. 1977. "The ideology of the Athenian metic", *The Cambridge Philological Society* Supplementary Vol. 4.

Whitehead, D. 1983. "Competitive outlay and community profit: Φιλοτιμία in democratic Athens", *Classica et Mediaevalia* 34:55–74.

Williamson, Oliver E. 1985. *The economic institutions of capitalism*. New York: The Free Press.

Williamson, Oliver E. 2000. "The new institutional economics: taking stock, looking ahead", *Journal of Economic Literature* 38:595–613.

Wycherley, R. E. 1978. *The stones of Athens*. Princeton, NJ: Princeton University Press.

Index of passages cited

Note: all quotes from the ancient literature are from the *Loeb Classical Library*.

Note: Not all of the texts traditionally listed under a specific author are thought to be the genuine work of his hand. This is usually indicated by either putting the name in square brackets or by adding a "ps" (for "pseudo") before the name.

Index

Printed in Great Britain
by Amazon

57185125R00120